Edmund Seddon has enjoyed a long association with Liverpool Poly-technic, latterly as Senior Lecturer in economics. He has over thirty years' experience of teaching and examining the subject.

Edmund Seddon has written textbooks on applied economics, public finance and modern economic history.

Pan Study Aids for A level include:

Advanced Biology

Advanced Chemistry

Advanced Computing Science

Advanced Economics

Advanced Mathematics

Advanced Physics

Advanced Sociology

PAN STUDY AIDS

ADVANCED ECONOMICS

Edmund Seddon

Pan Books London and Sydney

First published in 1987 by Pan Books Ltd,
Cavaye Place, London SW10 9PG

9 8 7 6 5 4 3 2 1

© Edmund Seddon 1987

ISBN 0 330 29553 5

Text design by Peter Ward
Text illustrated by ML Design
Photoset by Parker Typesetting Service, Leicester
Printed in Spain by Mateu Cromo, S. A. Madrid

CONTENTS

8 Contents

SUGGESTED FURTHER READING

GENERAL

Lipsey, R. G., *An Introduction to Positive Economics* (Weidenfeld & Nicolson)
Livesey, F., *A Textbook of Economics* (Polytech Publishers Ltd.)
Samuelson, P., *Economics* (McGraw-Hill)
Stanlake, G. F., *Macro-economics, an Introduction* (Longmans)

APPLIED

Griffiths, A. and Wall, S. (editors), *Applied Economics, an Introductory Course* (Longmans)
Morris, D. (editor), *The Economic System in the UK* (OUP)
Prest, A. R. and Coppock, D. J. (editors), *The UK Economy, a Manual of Applied Economics* (Weidenfeld & Nicolson)

MICROECONOMICS

Breit, W. and Hochman, H. M. (editors), *Readings in Microeconomics* (Holt, Rinehart & Winston)
Lancaster, K., *Introduction to Modern Microeconomics* (Rand McNally College Publishing Company)

MACROECONOMICS

Gordon, R. J., *Macroeconomics* (Little, Brown & Company)
Greenaway, D. and Shaw, G. K., *Macroeconomics, Theory and Policy in the UK* (Martin Robertson – Oxford)
Parkin, M. and Bade, R., *Modern Macroeconomics* (Philip Allan)

PREFACE

This book has been written specifically for students preparing for the Advanced Level Examination in Economics. While it covers the principal features of the syllabuses of all the examination boards, particular attention has been given to:

Joint Matriculation Board (JMB)

The Associated Examining Board (AEB)

University of London School Examinations Board (London)

Oxford & Cambridge Schools Examination Board (O & C SEB)

These boards have given their permission for the reproduction of past examination questions, for which the author is most grateful.

The book is not intended as a last-minute crammer, but rather as a revision aid to be used throughout the course. For this reason, it has been structured to follow the traditional teaching sequence of the syllabus, hence the study of some chapters depends upon an understanding of earlier material. The student who is confident of this can be selective in his reading since, for the most part, chapter or section headings correspond to topics which frequently occur in examination papers. This is reflected in the examination questions which appear at the end of each chapter.

As a compressed textbook of the subject, the book is in some measure 'freestanding' and may therefore be of interest to professional and undergraduate students of economics at this level.

The contents of the book are entirely the responsibility of the author, as are any suggested approaches to examination questions.

THE EXAMINATION BOARDS

The addresses below are those from which copies of syllabuses and past examination papers may be ordered. The abbreviations (AEB etc) are those used in the text to identify actual questions.

Associated Examining
Board (AEB),
Stag Hill House, Guildford,
Surrey GU2 5XJ

University of Cambridge Local
Examinations Syndicate (CAM),
Syndicate Buildings,
1 Hills Road,
Cambridge CB1 2EU

Joint Matriculation Board (JMB),
Manchester MI5 6EU

University of London School
Examinations Department
(LOND),
52 Gordon Square,
London WC1H 0PJ

Northern Ireland Schools
Examinations Council (NI),
Examinations Office,
Beechill House, Beechill Road,
Belfast BT8 4RS

Oxford Delegacy of Local
Examinations (OX),
Ewert Place, Summertown,
Oxford OX2 7BZ

Oxford and Cambridge Schools
Examination Board (O & C),
10 Trumpington Street,
Cambridge CB2 1QB

Welsh Joint Education
Committee (WEL),
245 Western Avenue,
Cardiff CF5 2YX

INTRODUCTION TO THE ADVANCED LEVEL EXAMINATION

Recent years have witnessed continuing change in both the teaching and examining of most subjects. The traditional approach placed emphasis on rote learning and factual recall, whereas today there is increasing recognition of the need to develop other skills and new techniques for examining them. The trend is expressed in the new courses leading to the GCSE examinations, which set out to assess a wide range of abilities beyond the power to memorize, describe and narrate.

In examining economics at Advanced Level, all the Boards have already moved in this direction. In particular, Section B of the JMB syllabus sets out specific examination objectives which provide useful general direction for all candidates, regardless of Board. It makes clear that the examination paper is not constructed to test single skills in isolation and in sequence. Nesessarily, particular questions may require demonstrations of more than one skill.

KNOWLEDGE AND ABILITIES TO BE TESTED

KNOWLEDGE

(i)   Knowledge of the terminology of economics.

(ii)   Knowledge of specific facts relating to economics and economic institutions.

(iii)   Knowledge of general and specific methods of inquiry and of the main sources of information about economic matters and ways of presenting economic information.

(iv)   Knowledge of the main concepts, principles and generalizations employed within the field of economics and of the major economic theories held.

COMPREHENSION	(i)　　The ability to understand and interpret economic information presented in verbal, numerical or graphical form and to translate such information from one form to another. (ii)　　The ability to explain familiar phenomena in terms of the relevant principles. (iii)　　The ability to apply known laws and principles to problems of a routine type. (iv)　　The ability to make generalizations about economic knowledge or about given data.
APPLICATION	The ability to select and apply known laws and principles to problems which are unfamiliar or presented in a novel manner.
ANALYSIS AND SYNTHESIS	(i)　　The ability to recognize unstated assumptions. (ii)　　The ability to distinguish between statements of fact, statements of value and hypothetical statements. (iii)　　The ability to make valid inferences from material presented. (iv)　　The ability to examine the implications of a hypothesis. (v)　　The ability to organize ideas into a new unity and to present them in an appropriate manner. (vi)　　The ability to make valid generalizations.
EVALUATION	(i)　　The ability to evaluate the reliability of material. (ii)　　The ability to detect logical fallacies in arguments. (iii)　　The ability to check that conclusions drawn are consistent with given information and to discriminate between alternative explanations. (iv)　　The ability to appreciate the role of the main concepts and models in the analysis of economic problems.
EXPRESSION	The ability to organize and present economic ideas and statements in a clear, logical and appropriate form.

WEIGHTING OF ABILITIES

The marks allocated in the examination will be divided (as far as possible) as follows:

　Knowledge 30%; Comprehension 25%; Application 15%; Analysis and synthesis 15%; Evaluation 15%.

The Board then re-emphasizes that questions may frequently over-lap these broad objectives. *Expression* has no specific weighting since, inevitably, badly presented answers will be penalized throughout.

INDICATIVE CONTENT OF SYLLABUSES

To the extent that the different Boards seek to test the skills and abilities listed above, they do so necessarily within the confines of the sub-stance of their syllabuses. This is broadly the same for every Board and is reflected in the content and sequence of this book.

EXAMINATION STRUCTURE

There are differences in detail between Boards, some of which are listed below.

AEB Economics: Syllabus 618. Three Papers. *Paper 1* – 1¼ hours; fifty compulsory multiple choice questions, *30%*. *Paper 2* – 1½ hours, one or more compulsory data response questions, *20%*. *Paper 3* – 3 hours, five from twelve essays, *50%*.

JMB Economics: Two Papers. *Paper 1* – Part 1, 1½ hours; approxi-mately fifty compulsory multiple choice questions, *35%*. Part 2, 1 hour; one compulsory data response question, *15%*. *Paper 2* – 3 hours; four essays from twelve, *50%*.

Oxford & Cambridge

Economics, Syllabus 9633. Three Papers. *Paper 1* is compulsory, Papers 2 and 3 are options. *Paper 1* – Part 1, 1¾ hours; fifty compulsory multiple choice questions. Part 2, 1½ hours; two from six essays. *Paper 2* – Applied Economics, 3 hours. There are four sections: The British Economy; Documents and Commentaries; Economic Numeracy; Com-parative Economics. Four questions must be answered from at least three sections. *Paper 3* – 3 hours, British Social & Economic History since 1780.

Economic & Political Studies, Syllabus 9635. Four Papers. *Paper 1* is compulsory – Principles of Economics, 3 hours, four essays from twelve. *Papers 2, 3 & 4* are options: 3-hour essay papers – Political Thought; Representative Government; British Constitutional History since 1830.

London

Economics, Syllabus 120. 3 Papers. *Paper 1*, 3 hours; five essays from ten or twelve, at least two from each section, *40%*. *Paper 2*, 1¼ hours; fifty compulsory multiple choice questions, *30%*. *Paper 3*, 1¾ hours; three data response questions from 5, *30%*.

MULTIPLE CHOICE QUESTIONS

Multiple choice papers enable the examiner to test the candidate's knowledge of the full range of the syllabus. He is also able to test certain numerical, analytical and reasoning skills which cannot easily be assessed in an essay.

The structure of these papers differs between Boards and changes in detail occur as examiners introduce new techniques. *Cambridge Local Examinations Syndicate, Northern Ireland Schools Examinations Council, Oxford Delegacy of Local Examinations, Oxford and Cambridge Schools Examination Board and the Welsh Joint Education Committee share a common multiple choice paper.* It is of the *single completion* type: five possible answers being offered, only one of which is correct.

AEB The paper falls into two sections. Section 1 (34 questions) requires single completion, with one correct answer from four. Section 2 (16 questions) is of the *multiple completion* type, with four possible answers offered, of which one or more are correct.

JMB This paper divides into four sections. Section 1 (25 questions), requires single completion, with one correct answer from four. Section 2 (8 questions), is of the *matching pairs* variety. Groups of questions provide two lists of information containing statements which must be matched. Section 3 (12 questions) is for multiple completion, with one or more correct answers from five. Section 4 (5 questions), is of the *assertion/reason* type. An assertion is accompanied by a reason. The candidate must then decide whether each, considered separately, is a true statement. If both are considered true, it must then be decided whether the reason is a valid explanation of the assertion. There are five possible outcomes to this more complex type of question.

Advice for the Multiple Choice Paper

Since you will not be penalized for incorrect answers, it is important that you answer all questions. You have a very limited time for each question, so build up your confidence on a first run-through the paper by answering the simple questions about which you are certain. You now have more time on a second run to deal with the more complex questions. Finally, if some questions appear to have defeated you, make your best guess.

DATA RESPONSE QUESTIONS

Most Boards, if they do not have a separate data response paper, include questions of this type elsewhere in their examinations. The purpose is to test the candidate's ability to relate economic theory to topical statistical and documentary material. In so doing, he demonstrates the higher order of skills – analysis, synthesis, evaluation and application.

AEB The paper comprises two or three compulsory questions, each based upon a document, table of figures, graph or diagram. Each question has three parts, of progressive difficulty. The first requires a simple explanation or description of the material. The other two move to the higher order of skills.

JMB There is one compulsory question in three parts, based upon a document coupled with some statistical information. As with the AEB, the parts of the question are of a progressive order of difficulty.

London A choice of three from five, with at least one based upon statistical data.

Oxford and Cambridge The Applied Economics paper contains questions which are similar in character to data response questions. Section A, The British Economy, requires an understanding of current economic issues. Section B, Documents and Commentaries, is based upon set books which have been notified in advance. Section C, Economic Numeracy, calls for the interpretation and amplification of statistical information. Section D, Comparative Economics, is based upon topical international issues.

Advice for the Data Response Paper

As for all examinations, read the instructions to candidates very carefully. Accept the advice to study the questions before beginning to write. Where the parts of the question are of progressive difficulty (as with AEB and JMB), do not write at excessive length on the simpler descriptive parts. Pay attention to the allocation of marks to these question sections where they are shown, e.g. AEB. In the more complex parts which require interpretations and conclusions, do not content yourself with further simple description – this will score no marks.

When interpreting data and drawing conclusions, demonstrate your grasp of basic economic theory to establish your assumptions. Where competing theories suggest different assumptions, make clear how these will affect your conclusions. Do not hesitate to introduce *relevant* empirical material where this will reinforce these conclusions.

In analysing real as distinct from fictional data, beware of the dangers inherent in certain quantitative techniques. For a full account of these, refer to Chapter 3.

ESSAY PAPERS

Those Boards which have already introduced separate data response papers have one essay paper which seeks to test the whole range of skills. In the case of JMB, four must be answered from twelve questions which have a bias to applied aspects. This is rather less marked with AEB – with five questions to be answered from twelve – and still less marked with London. The London paper divides into two sections, approximating roughly to micro and macro; five questions have to be answered from ten or twelve, with at least two from each section. Those Boards without data response papers mostly retain two essay papers, usually splitting between micro and macro-economics. In the case of Oxford and Cambridge, the division is between Principles and Applied.

Advice for the Essay Paper

It is vitally important to allocate your time so that you are able to attempt all questions; they all have equal marks. Remember that the first quarter of the mark for each question is relatively easy to score, the second quarter more difficult, the third quarter very difficult while the last quarter may be beyond reach.

Read the whole paper carefully, selecting the questions which you are certain to attempt and, if in doubt, postpone a final decision on others. Take the easiest question first and make time. Before beginning to write, be perfectly certain that you fully understand every aspect of the question; some will fall naturally into different parts, which call for different skills. Avoid devoting the whole essay to simple description, remembering that an instruction to analyse, evaluate or assess requires the display of the higher order skills. *Make sure that every aspect of the question is covered*, periodically referring back to the paper.

If you believe that the question is open to more than one interpretation, make this clear to the examiner in your introduction, indicating the path that you are going to follow. Then follow it in a systematic, logical, structured development which leads you to a natural conclusion. This is half the battle.

Make sure that everything you write is relevant to the question. There are no marks for a well-written answer to a question you have set yourself.

If you are pressed for time, remember that breadth is preferable to depth. Marking schemes are prepared to cover a range of central points. It is easier for the examiner to find marks for you if you make reference to them all rather than belabouring just one.

Illustrate with diagrams where appropriate, but make sure that you construct them accurately. If they are wrong, the examiner knows that you have not grasped the principles. Remember, too, that you are using them to illustrate what you are writing; don't leave them in limbo, surrounded by unrelated text.

Understand the purpose of the examination, which is in *economics*. When selecting your questions, identify the relevant piece of theory and apply it. Do not make the mistake of believing that the question can be answered by 'general knowledge' or 'common sense'.

Finally, a tidy well-presented script is of great importance. Economize, but not unnecessarily, in paper.

LIST OF TABLES

BASIC CONCEPTS AND TECHNIQUES

THE ECONOMIC PROBLEM

CONTENTS

1. PERSPECTIVE ON ECONOMIC THOUGHT

1.1 ORIGINS

The growth of economics as a distinct field of study is to be associated with the development of capitalism. Indeed it may be argued that prior to this development there was no economic problem as perceived by the modern economist. During the Middle Ages there was a fairly substantial volume of trade, but the spiritual discipline exercised by the Church and the organizational disciplines applied to commerce and manufacturing under the guild system did not permit individualistic, entrepreneurial activity. Between the fifteenth and eighteenth centuries these disciplines gradually relaxed in the face of a resurgent spirit of individual free enterprise. By the eighteenth century a capitalistic system of organization was firmly established in manufacturing, trade and increasingly in agriculture, which is to say that the functions of providing land, labour and capital to the productive process had been gradually separated. These 'factors of production' were now brought together to satisfy the demands of markets distant in time and place, by entrepreneurs motivated by the quest for profit. The new system of organization allowed, indeed demanded, an 'industrial revolution' rooted in the specialization of labour, the provision of capital on a large scale and mass production for mass markets. Inevitably this implied an infinitely greater complexity in organizational relationships and a much greater degree of uncertainty in society's everyday business of earning a living. The problems which were now brought to the surface were to become the substance of the new discipline of economics.

1.2 MERCANTILISM

Mercantilism represents one of the first attempts to examine systematically the behaviour of the economy. Mercantilist thinking predominated during the sixteenth and seventeenth centuries in a period in which 'nation states' were gradually evolving throughout Europe, often in conflict with each other and, as previously noted, at a time when the authority of the Church and the guilds was being weakened. In such chaotic and often dangerous times mercantilists advocated strong, centralized state authority which could provide a regulatory framework for the emerging, undisciplined market economy and resist the attentions of aggressive neighbours through economic self-sufficiency. This latter aim implied firstly the acquisition of colonies to provide those materials which could not be produced at home and secondly, the maintenance at all times – if necessary through protectionism – of a 'favourable balance of trade' which would ensure a continuing influx of gold, considered by Sir Thomas Mun to be 'the sinews of war'. Addiction to protectionism persisted into the nineteenth century with a generation which, having whole-heartedly accepted the philosophy of 'laissez-faire', still resisted the parallel doctrine of 'laissez-passer'.

1.3 THE PHYSIOCRATS

A more comprehensive approach to the new subject was made by a French school of philosophers, the Physiocrats, who were to have an important formative influence upon the work of Adam Smith. The most complete expression of their thinking is to be found in the *Tableau Economique* (Francois Quesnay, 1694–1774). Quesnay and his associates were the first to point to the interdependencies within the economy, but writing before the industrial revolution had gathered momentum, they prescribed the dominant role in the economy to agriculture rather than industry. However, their most important contribution to subsequent thinking sprang from their overall philosophy. Physiocracy means 'rule of nature' and its followers set out to recognize these rules. Human law was at best always imperfect, and should therefore be kept to a minimum. To the extent that it was socially necessary, it should seek only to reflect the laws of a universe which was naturally harmonious. In relation to their study of economic phenomena, the concept of economic harmony was to prove of lasting significance. Almost every economist of note since the Physiocrats has made the assumption that there are natural rules which govern the working of the economy and that it is the task of the economist to discover them.

1.4 ADAM SMITH (1723–1790)

At one time Professor of Moral Philosophy at Glasgow University, Smith is often considered to be the father of modern economics. His book, *The Wealth of Nations*, was the first systematic attempt to explore every aspect of a political economy. As tutor to the son of the Duke of Buccleuch, he had travelled widely in France and been much influenced by the Physiocrats. His concept of an 'invisible hand' which guides the working of the economy derives from this influence. However, there was nothing mystical in his analysis of a worldly economy. In contrast to the Mercantilists he considered that governments, remote from the world of business affairs, had no economic role other than the provision of external defence, internal law and order and a small number of services which would not otherwise be provided by private enterprise. That an unregulated 'laissez-faire' market economy would produce the most harmonious and prosperous results was for Smith assured by the 'enlightened self-interest' of the individual in a competitive society. The rationale for this belief rests upon a number of propositions. First, the solution to the economic problem lies in the optimal allocation of scarce resources between competing alternatives. Second, it can only be the individual – and not government – who is competent to rank the priorities of these alternatives. Third, a free market will guarantee that resources are allocated in response to this scale of priorities. A high price signifies a high priority, thereby attracting more resources. A low price indicates a low priority, with resources now being deflected to other uses. The fourth proposition was subsequently to prove contentious: if it is assumed that there is no impediment to the free operation of the market mechanism, then there will always be some price – however low – at which the market is cleared. It followed that there existed no possibility of long-term involuntary unemployment of resources. This view was supported by Say's Law of Markets (see below).

Smith's work set the philosophical seal on a capitalist system which by his time was well advanced. His influence cannot be over-estimated, his views having attracted both ardent supporters and – as we shall see – virulent critics right down to the present time.

1.5 SAY'S LAW OF MARKETS

The optimism of Smith and his followers was buttressed by the theories of the French economist, Jean-Baptiste Say (1767–1832). He reasoned that the sole motivation for production is the desire to acquire the produce of others. If an individual increases his own output, then he generates for himself sufficient income to take from the market goods equivalent to those which he himself has produced. The assumption is, of course, that all income will be spent upon either consumer goods or capital goods at a rate sufficient to guarantee the continuing full employment of all productive resources. In other words, supply would create its own demand. If on occasion some income was saved and not spent, Say argued that in the long run the result would be the same. The accumulation of savings would produce a fall in interest rates; this in turn would encourage an increase in investment in capital goods, while discouraging saving. The system was therefore self-regulatory and a full employment equilibrium would be maintained.

While some economists were not entirely happy with this line of reasoning, the effect of savings on the level of spending was not to be dealt with satisfactorily until John Maynard Keynes analysed the relationship in the twentieth century.

Smith's sanguine view of a prosperous, harmonious and expanding economy was not shared by all of his successors – perhaps most notably, Malthus.

(a) Thomas Robert Malthus

A professor of political economy at the East India Company's college at Haileybury, Malthus (1766–1834) was arguably the first professional economist. He is mostly remembered for his entirely pessimistic *Essay on Population* in which he argued that while population grew *geometrically* (2,4,6,8) food production increased *arithmetically* (1,2,3,4). Man would inevitably breed at a rate which ensured that he could never rise above a subsistence standard of living. The only checks to population growth were 'moral restraint, vice and misery'. Since he placed little confidence in man's moral capacity and since birth control was viewed as a vice, the only effective check was 'misery' in the shape of 'war, pestilence and famine'. Such views led to economics being described as 'the dismal science' and gave rise to much debate amongst his contemporaries. While later generations were to witness a revolution in agricultural productivity and a levelling off of population in advanced countries, it may be thought that Malthus's views still hold much relevance for the underdeveloped world.

Less well-known than his work on population was his attempt to explain the problem of general economic depression or 'gluts', when more was produced than consumed and unemployment ensued. In contrast to J. B. Say, Malthus pointed to the possibility of money being taken out of circulation through excessive saving, thus diminishing the demand for goods. A century was to elapse before Keynes fully explored the connection.

(b) David Ricardo (1772–1823)

Like his friend Malthus, Ricardo took a pessimistic view particularly in respect of population growth, which he related to his theory of rent for which he is best remembered. As population expands, so more land will be taken into cultivation. Since the quantity of good land is limited, the additional land will be of inferior quality. A differential therefore arises between the output of land of the first quality and that of the second. Since the output of both must sell at the same market price, there is now a tendency both for profit margins to be squeezed and for prices to rise. As this occurs, the capitalist must now pay his labour force higher wages to cover their subsistence. Economic growth would therefore only profit the rentier class, who would demand higher rents for their land to the impoverishment of the hard-working capitalist. By an 'iron law' the population would always expand at a rate which ensured that wages would only ever be at a level sufficient for the bare survival of the labouring classes.

While Ricardo's theory of economic rent has been adapted to explain certain economic phenomena, his predictions – like those of

Malthus – were not realized. Population growth levelled off and agricultural productivity expanded.

1.7 THE SCIENTIFIC SOCIALISTS

While Malthus and Ricardo did not share Smith's optimistic view of the future of capitalism, they had many basic assumptions in common. With others they are often referred to as the English Classical School. However, by the mid-nineteenth-century these assumptions were under challenge. It was certainly the case that the advent of capitalism and the industrial revolution had wrought changes which were imposing severe strains upon England's social and political institutions. It has sometimes been said that while the industrial revolution did much to solve the problems of production, it only intensified those of distribution. Inequality grew and poverty flourished in the midst of abundance.

In this context the reaction came on the one hand from 'Utopian Socialists' such as Robert Owen, who promoted ill-fated schemes for model communities. These were straws in the wind and a more solid response to the apparent deficiencies of the capitalist system came in the work of Karl Marx (1818–1883).

Marx was much influenced by the ideas of the German philosopher Hegel, who believed that human history was determined in a realm of ideas which were subject to continuing change. The process of change was very precise. The moment that an idea was generated, it gave rise to its opposite. From the conflict of the two emerged a synthesis, a new idea which in turn produced its opposite. This process Hegel described as *'dialectical'*.

Marx adapted this concept to fit his own view of economic development. For him history was determined not by the conflict of abstract ideas but by the economic circumstances of a particular time. A society's political institutions, laws, morals, religion, art, literature and cultural mores were all determined by the system through which it achieved economic adjustment. The continuing 'class struggle' between conflicting economic groups was the driving force behind historical change. Having substituted a materialist basis for Hegel's world of ideas, Marx described his approach as 'dialectical materialism', or alternatively it may be called 'economic determinism'.

In the *Communist Manifesto* which Marx published in conjunction with Engels in 1848, he explains why the capitalist system – according to the dialectic – contains the seeds of its own destruction and why a communist state must necessarily emerge. For Marx there was no 'invisible hand' producing a harmony of interest throughout society. Capitalism itself had transformed a class of landless peasants into an urban proletariat with a growing class consciousness. When this class became fully aware of the injustice which it suffered, it would unify and rise up against its bourgeois oppressors.

While Marx wrote a great deal on this theme he made little reference to the state of society which would exist once the downfall of capitalism had been accomplished. Nor did he attempt to explain why the dialectical process of history should apparently cease once the communist state had been established. It was left to Lenin to amplify and apply Marx's insights. After the revolution in Russia there would be a 'dictatorship of the proletariat' which would last until a true communist society emerged with the withering away of the state.

In 1917 the USSR became the first major power to adopt the principles of Marx with his insistence that a market system, a society without central economic control, could produce only chaos and injustice.

That Marx's predictions have not been fulfilled in the Western world may be attributed to the flexibility and adaptability of the capitalist system and to the growth of a labour movement which sought improvement in its economic circumstances through negotiation rather than revolution. Moreover, during the past century governments have increasingly intervened in social and economic affairs to modify a system which today Smith would not recognize as capitalist.

1.8 THE NINETEENTH-CENTURY NEO-CLASSICISTS

While some economists rejected from moral conviction the premises upon which classical economics were based, others were employing equally rigorous analysis in an attempt to explain the way in which the 'invisible hand' of a laissez-faire, free market economy worked in practice. Central to this analysis was the examination of a problem which had perplexed earlier writers, the 'paradox of value'. How is value determined? Why is it that water which is essential to life has little value, while diamonds which are of trival use have great value? Smith, like Marx after him, found the explanation in a *labour theory of value*. The high value of diamonds was explained by the great amount of labour involved in their discovery, extraction, cutting and so on, whereas water was easily acquired. This line of thinking was developed by John Stuart Mill into a *cost of production theory*. For him the labour theory was incomplete. The value which labour contributed to the end product was attributable to its *scarcity*, the fact that its use for one purpose denied its use to another. Once this was recognized it had to be agreed that land and capital were equally in scarce supply and had a cost. A natural value therefore resulted from the cost of the various inputs.

This theory also had its shortcomings and later economists re-examined the problem. The solution which emerged was based in the concept of *utility*, an idea developed by economists such as Heinrich Gossen (1810–1858), Carl Menger (1840–1921), Stanley Jevons (1835–1882) and Alfred Marshall (1842–1924). Utility may be defined as 'the ability to satisfy a human want' and is therefore entirely subjective to the individual at a given point in time, and amoral. A casino may offer greater utility than a hospital. The further concept of *marginal utility* means the additional utility derived from one more unit of consumption of any good. The marginal utility theorists then made three important observations. Total utility expands with further consumption. However, the utility yielded by every extra unit consumed – i.e. marginal utility – *diminished* with further consumption. Third, the rational buyer will attempt to pursue each line of purchases to the point where the utility yielded by the marginal or least important unit equates with the price which he pays. Since all units are interchangeable, the price of all is determined by the least important. The paradox of value was thus resolved. Water is consumed in vast quantities and its *total* utility is immense. However, it is cheap because its *marginal* utility is low. Conversely, diamonds are in short supply with a low total utility but a high marginal utility; they are therefore expensive.

Marginal analysis not only cleared up the paradox of value but was subsequently applied to a variety of other economic problems. It may be considered one of the major contributions of the economists of this period.

(a) Alfred Marshall and partial equilibrium analysis

Marginal analysis was a major step forward, but much work remained to be done in the examination of the intricate processes and the many variables involved in price and output decision-making. Marshall put forward the famous 'scissors' analogy to explain how demand and supply interact to achieve market equilibrium. One blade of the scissors is demand and the other is supply. It is neither possible nor necessary to determine which blade does the cutting; they are interdependent. This analogy provides the foundation for Marshall's partial equilibrium analysis, a useful technique which – still in use today – examines the determinants of price in one market while assuming all other factors to be constant.

(b) Leon Walras (1834–1910) and general equilibrium

Walras was perhaps the nineteenth-century's greatest builder of abstract economic systems and the first to make extensive use of mathematical analysis. Smith had asserted that market prices always tend towards their equilibrium levels. While this seems a reasonable assumption for individual markets, it appears less certain for the economy as a whole. Why should prices not diverge permanently from their 'natural' levels?

The solution which Walras produced lay in an abstract model of the whole economy made up of two markets: a product market selling to households and a factor market with households selling productive resources to businesses. In each case buyers and sellers wish to maximize their own utility; they interact in a way which produces a *general equilibrium,* a state which can be recognized by the fulfilment of two conditions. First, each individual's consumption of goods and services is balanced in a way which makes it impossible further to increase utility. Second, the quantity of goods and services which the economy produces is exactly equal to the quantity demanded.

1.9 EARLY TWENTIETH-CENTURY MAINSTREAM ECONOMISTS

By the 1920s and 1930s theorists were beginning to make modifications to traditional thinking. Among them were Edward Chamberlin in the USA (*The Theory of Monopolistic Competition*, 1933) and Joan Robinson in England (*The Economics of Imperfect Competition*, 1933), who applied marginal analysis to firms which did not have the characteristics of Smith's model. Implicit in the traditional view of the market as the optimal allocator of resources was the concept of 'perfect competition'. If the price mechanism were permitted freely to signal society's changing priorities, and productive resources were transferred in response from one use to another, then the economy would remain flexible and capable of maximizing utility. However, in the nineteenth century no attempt had been made to prescribe the conditions in which perfect competition might exist. Once these conditions had been outlined, it became obvious that in the twentieth century there was a growing monopoly influence not only in markets in end products, but also in the supply of the factors of production: land, labour and capital. If it were possible to use this power artificially to restrict supply in order to raise price and secure a monopoly profit, then the market was distorted; it was no longer able to allocate resources with optimal efficiency. There no longer existed a natural harmony between the interests of buyers and sellers. The observation that in the real world economic activity took place in a variety of market conditions ranging from the hypothetical extreme of perfect competition to that of perfect monopoly led to the modification of the classical model in terms of imperfect competition by Joan Robinson and monopolistic competition by Edward Chamberlin.

1.10 THE KEYNESIAN REVOLUTION

As previously noted, Say's Law of Markets pre-empted the possibility of any long run economic depression. Malthus had questioned Say's assumptions, suggesting the possible implications for demand of the accumulation of unused savings, but his ideas remained undeveloped. The period between the wars, however, saw a situation which could not be explained by classical economic analysis. This analysis could explain only economic equilibrium at full employment of all productive resources. From 1920 to 1939 it was apparent that equilibrium was being sustained at very high levels of unemployment. In this context the attention of economists shifted from the principles governing the *direction* of resources between competing alternatives (*microeconomics*) to the factors influencing the *level* of resource use (*macroeconomics*).

Observing that despite falls in wages there was no inevitable tendency to full employment equilibrium, the new macroeconomics

addressed itself to examining the relationship between certain variables expressed as aggregates such as the level of national income,
the volume of saving, the rate of consumption and investment expenditure.

Pre-eminent among the new economists was John Maynard
Keynes, whose work was in due course to exercise an influence upon
economic thought comparable with that of Smith and Marx. The new
approach is most comprehensively expressed in Keynes's *General
Theory of Employment Interest and Money* (1936). It is a general theory in
that Keynes seeks to explain how equilibrium may be established at
any level of employment, not simply the *particular* case of *full* employment. He focuses upon national income as the key variable which
indicates the level of economic activity. National income is itself
determined by the level of effective demand which comprises both
consumption and investment expenditure, i.e. in the Keynesian
sense, expenditure upon capital goods. If demand were to fall due to
an autonomous increase in saving, then in the short term there would
be over-production and some people would consequently be thrown
out of work as stocks accumulated. To begin with they would look for
work at comparable wages but meanwhile their purchasing power
would decline, reducing effective demand still further. In due course
they might accept employment at lower wages, but by this time the
continuing fall in demand would have generated a situation in which
the new wage was insufficiently low to guarantee employment for
everybody. Wage rates might continue to decline, but not sufficiently
rapidly to avoid a downward spiral into depression.

The policy implications of the Keynesian analysis were far-
reaching. If depression was the consequence of a deficiency of
demand in the private sector, then government had a compensatory
role to play by increasing expenditure in the public sector. In the
post-war period this view became the foundation for the economic
policies of British governments of both parties. The early results
seemed entirely favourable, with unemployment held to very low
levels, but by the 1960s inflation was beginning to accelerate at the
same time as unemployment was beginning to increase. This observation ran counter to the predictions of those economists who had
developed and applied Keynesian thinking – that there was an
inverse relationship between rates of inflation and unemployment. It
was in this context that greater attention was given to a school of
economists who revived and refined classical thinking and who have
been described as '*monetarists*'.

1.11 THE COUNTER-REVOLUTION IN MONETARY THEORY

'Monetarism' is usually associated with Professor Milton Friedman
and the University of Chicago. Friedman himself has protested that
the word 'monetarism' – if it means anything – signifies only a
reassertion of the quantity theory of money which attempted to
explain the phenomenon of inflation. However, the popular connot-

ation has come to imply a general restatement of pre-Keynesian positions. In the short term in the market place, it is demand which is flexible and the dominant factor; it is equally susceptible to manipulation to produce quick responses. Conversely supply is inflexible, being constrained by the availability and adaptability of productive resources. Only in the long run can these be developed and even then with less certainty by governments. Post-war Keynesians concerned themselves with the short term. ('In the long term,' said Keynes, 'we are all dead.') A stimulus to demand would manifest itself in increased income, employment and output and scarcely at all in prices. Monetarists, however, have concentrated on the view that in the long term demand works mainly upon prices and only indirectly upon output and employment. What is important is that price variations determine the quantity of productive resources taken into employment. If in the long term monetary demand continues to expand at an excessive rate, the primary effect is upon prices and not upon output. Inflation accelerates and the factors of production are priced out of the market. The phenomenon of inflation accompanied by rising unemployment is thus explained; there is no trade-off between the two.

The acceptance of these propositions has major significance for government policy. Any attempt to spend a way out of recession can only be self-defeating, since the overall impact will be an increase in the rate of inflation which in turn raises unemployment to still higher levels. It follows that governments in democracies can do nothing other than attempt to create an environment in which the market can function more effectively. From a macroeconomic point of view, this means the pursuit of monetary policies which pre-empt the possibility of inflation. While monetarists assert the presence of a consistent relationship between the rate of growth of the money supply and the general price level, they maintain that so little is known about the precise way in which this relationship works that governments should make no attempt to 'fine tune' the economy. The best that can be done is to establish and adhere to a fixed rate of monetary growth sufficient to accommodate any *real* economic growth, then allow the market to adjust itself accordingly.

1.12 THE CAMBRIDGE ECONOMIC POLICY GROUP (CEPG)

While arriving at policy conclusions very different from those of the monetarists, the CEPG is interesting in that it agrees that the economy is inherently stable and that Keynesian 'fine tuning' is inappropriate and itself a destablizing agent. While monetarists recommend a monetary growth rule, the CEPG advocates a tax rule.

Emphasis is still placed upon aggregate demand in the determination of output and employment, but the orthodox Keynesian approach is criticized for a number of reasons. Timelags between the introduction of a new policy and its final impact on the economy were so lengthy that the outcome was wholly unpredictable. Similarly the impact of the 'multiplier' was repeatedly underestimated, while short-term forecasting models have in general proved unreliable.

Prices and incomes policies are also rejected as a means of continuing the inflationary pressures which may be induced by an expansion of demand. In periods of rising economic activity, the growth of real incomes will be high relative to workers' expectations, therefore there is less likelihood of excessive wage demands which trigger a wage/price spiral. It is thought that incomes policies may even be positively damaging to the extent that they thwart workers' expectations and lead to increased wage demands.

Experience, it is recognized, demonstrates that an increase in demand leads to balance of payments difficulties as imports increase and exports are diverted to the home market. This problem is not to be resolved by devaluation, which would only serve to raise import costs, wage demands and inflation. The solution lies in import controls. In response to the criticism that these would lead to the kind of retaliation which was witnessed in the 1930s, the CEPG argues that these controls would seek not to reduce the existing level of imports but only to prevent that level from rising. No other country would be worse off. Indeed, as UK exports increased during the economic up-turn, scope would be created for the expansion of imports.

As previously noted, the CEPG believes that the economy is relatively stable – at least in the medium term – and while eschewing 'fine tuning' believes in a medium-term strategy based upon a 'fiscal rule'. This rule has the form of a composite tax rate ('the par tax rate'), set at a level which will achieve the desired targets for income, output, employment and the balance of payments. Once established, 'the rule' should be adhered to and only altered if the targets themselves are altered.

1.13 CONCLUSION

From this introductory outline of the development of economic thought, some insights should have been gained into the nature of the subject. What is immediately apparent is that economics is no precise science in which there is general agreement even on basic premises. Theories continue to evolve in an attempt to explain the phenomena of a rapidly changing world. When they fail to do so, they must necessarily be modified or discarded. That economists are frequently reluctant to comply is simply, as Keynes observed, a reflection of instinctive human conservatism. It follows, as he also noted, that the economist should retain a flexible mind since the subject is concerned with a system of thinking rather than a set of dogma. The nature and scope of this system will be examined in the next section.

2. DEFINITION AND SCOPE

2.1 SCARCITY AND CHOICE IN A SOCIAL CONTEXT

The economic problem is rooted in the scarcity of goods and services relative to the demand for them. It is an observable feature of human psychology that however rapid the increase in productive capacity, it is always outstripped by the increase in human wants. Scarcity – like the poor – remains with us. It follows that some wants must remain unsatisfied and we are confronted with the problem of establishing a scale of priorities. What principles will govern our decision to select some items at the expense of others, and in what quantities will we produce those items which we do select? 'A study of scarcity and the mechanisms by which we make choices' takes us so far in our definition of economics, but one vital ingredient is missing. Essays have been written on the desert island economics of Robinson Crusoe, who was certainly faced with the physical constraints of scarcity and the problem of choosing how to deploy his labour and materials in some activities rather than others. If he had had a 'hot line' to the outside world, there are many experts from the agricultural scientist to the engineer whom he might have consulted, who would have advised him on how to extract the most from his limited productive resources. The one expert who would have had nothing to tell him would have been the economist. The latter emerges only when the problems of scarcity and choice are placed in a social context. As previously noted (1.1) such was the case in eighteenth-century England with the emergence of capitalism as a complex social process of production. Crusoe's choices were not confined by political or legal systems or by social or moral aspirations. Economics operates within such confines as they presently exist, remembering that the way in which the economic problem is resolved is a major factor in determining these self-same constraints.

2.2 ECONOMICS, PSYCHOLOGY AND 'ECONOMIC MAN'

Economics has frequently been criticized for its assumption of '*economic man*' who continuously makes rational choices on purely materialistic grounds. The US economist Thorstein Veblen accused his more orthodox colleagues of reducing the individual to 'a lightning calculator of pleasures, and pains, who oscillates like a homogeneous globule of desire of happiness under the impulse of stimuli that shift him about the area but leave him intact' ('Why Is Economics Not an Evolutionary Science?', *Journal of Political Economy*, 1897). Such criticism calls for comment if the scope and direction of economic inquiry is to be fully understood. If economics appears unduly preoccupied with materialistic matters, this does not imply any particular assumptions about the psychology of human motivation. Human wants may well originate in a wide diversity of factors relating to culture and upbringing, leading to an equally wide diversity in the possible means of gratifying those wants. Rather than being moved by the simple economic desire for more, men may want self-esteem or the esteem of others, social acceptability or power over others or a host of other objectives. The economist is not concerned with any of this. Where psychology finishes, economics begins. The economist is concerned with why – subject to certain incomes, prices and so on – men will purchase a particular selection of goods and services in particular quantities *regardless of their motivation*. The fact that their choice is at least in part governed by material economic considerations is sufficient reason for his inquiry.

It may further be argued in support of the economic approach that it provides insights which are useful in the investigations of other social sciences from which it is not sharply separated. It can for example assist the political scientist to understand the power structures of democratic societies, and the sociologist to understand many interactions within society. Indeed, it is the case that the economist's approach can provide an added dimension wherever people are the focal point of study.

Finally, it may be observed that in relation to other disciplines, the economist is the servant of, for example, the politician and the legislator. While he may indicate the likely economic consequences of certain courses of action, it is not his function to determine ends or goals. Rather is he concerned with analysing the means by which those goals may be achieved. It is in this sense therefore that economics may be adjudged to be materialistic and amoral.

2.3 MICROECONOMICS AND MACROECONOMICS

Classical economics concerned itself mainly with the subject matter of what today would be described as microeconomics. It was preoccupied with the direction of resource use, with the principles governing the allocation of scarce resources between competing alternatives. It is certainly true that some attention was given to macroeconomic matters, but it was only in the 1930s – with the growing absorbtion of Keynes and his contemporaries with the principles governing the *level* of resource use – that the distinction between microeconomics and macroeconomics came to be made. It should then be stressed that this twofold division does not imply that one part of the subject can be studied to the exclusion of the other; they are interdependent. However, this conventional distinction is useful for the purpose of study and it is the approach adopted in this book. We should now therefore elaborate some of the detail.

(a) Microeconomics

The term derives from the Greek word *micro*, meaning small. Microeconomics, therefore, examines the decision-making process of small units, households, firms and to some extent units of government in the market-place. The household is taken to be the family unit which makes joint economic decisons. The market is assumed to begin at the front door. When the household enters the market, it has two roles.

First, it is a consumer of goods and services. Second, it provides the economy with the *factors of production* necessary for the productive process. *Land* includes all natural resources such as agricultural or building land, forests and minerals. *Capital* comprises all those man-made items such as tools and equipment, structures and amenities which contribute to further production. *Labour* is the productive effort of workers by hand and by brain. In return for the productive resources which they sell, households receive incomes which they spend as consumers.

The firm is the second basic microeconomic unit. It purchases the factors of production from households and directs them into the productive process which satisfies the demand of households for consumer goods. Like households, firms deal through markets and internally are usually organized on non-market principles. Owners normally appoint managers, who in turn direct employees.

Units of government include those regulatory agencies or aspects of government microeconomic policy which impinge upon matters such as pricing, licencing or subsidies and which therefore have an impact on the behaviour of firms and households in the market. The way in which the market serves to co-ordinate this behaviour will be considered in the next section.

(b) Macroeconomics

This term derives from the Greek word *'macro'* meaning large. Macro-economics is therefore concerned with the study of large-scale economic phenomena, in particular income and employment, inflation and growth. To the extent that governments are disposed to intervene in the economy, these are the major policy targets. As we shall see at a later stage, these aggregates are interactive; any attempt to influence one will have implications for the rest.

Having defined the nature of the economic problem and the function of economic science in analysing it, we turn next to an examination of alternative solutions.

3. ECONOMIC SYSTEMS

3.1 THE FREE MARKET ECONOMY

As previously noted, the free market solution to the economic problem has had its advocates from Smith to the present day, and indeed mainstream economic theory has been largely concerned with analysing the way in which markets work.

(a) The functions of the market

Modern economies are based upon intensive specialization, with each individual making a tiny contribution to the end product. In return they receive a portion of that product. Markets are the mechanism through which is determined what is produced and in what quantities, for whom and how it is produced, and the size of the reward which goes to those who have contributed the factors of production. In resolving this complex problem of co-ordination, markets have three functions.

(i) Signalling information In the simplest situation 'the market' is the conjunction of one buyer and one seller who bargain with each other until agreement is reached and the transaction is completed. Each has become aware of the terms upon which the other will do business. In a more sophisticated situation such information is more widely propagated through the price system. The system disseminates knowledge about the relative scarcity of goods and services. A rise in the price of one good relative to the rest signals an increasing relative scarcity, while a fall in price indicates a relative abundance. In response to these signals, the owners of the factors of production will redirect resources to areas of relative scarcity from those of relative abundance. In short, the price structure provides freely available information about society's economic problem.

(ii) Incentives While knowledge of the way in which resources may be most effectively deployed is vital, the people who control those resources must have some incentive to put them to these uses. As Adam Smith observed: 'It is not from the benevolence of the butcher, the brewer, or the baker that we expect our dinner, but from their regard to their own interest . . .' (*The Wealth of Nations*, Book 1, Ch.2). Incentives are provided through the market in a variety of ways. The consumer benefits from his knowledge of relative prices since he is able to allocate his limited income in directions which maximize his satisfaction. Similarly the producer, if he is alert to the most productive ways in which he can utilize his resources, enjoys the best possible income. Profit plays a most important part in this process. The entrepreneur requires an incentive if he is to undertake the trouble and risk of co-ordinating the resources provided by others. Without his willingness to do so, production does not take place. He therefore looks for a margin above the cost of the inputs which he employs. If he miscalculates, his 'profit' is negative and he soon goes out of business. The resources which he commanded are then taken up by an entrepreneur who is able to interpret the signals emitted by the market more accurately.

(iii) Distribution of income The market divides the end product between those who have contributed to it in proportion to the value which it places upon their contribution, rather than rewarding the effort or sacrifice which they make. Talents, skills and other resources which are in scarce supply are best rewarded and a motivation is now provided for the relief of this scarcity.

(iv) The interaction of functions It should now be stressed that the three functions of the market are interdependent. If an impediment to one function arises, then all are affected and the market ceases to operate effectively, e.g. a subsidy to one product at the expense of a tax on another produces a false signal to producers and consumers alike. Resources are transferred from one use to another with a corresponding distortion of incentives and rewards.

(b) Advantages of the market

Supporters of the market solution argue that, whatever its imperfections, it provides the most accurate and sensitive means of resolving the economic problem. To advocates of 'planning', they respond that what is at issue is *who* does the planning. In the market economy the process is entirely decentralized, but planning does indeed take place. It is the individual consumer and producer who determines the uses to which resources are put, rather than the politician and bureaucrat. A willingness to pay a particular price for a good is seen as the equivalent of a vote in favour of its production. Moreover, the process is continuous and all (at least those with an income) are enfranchized. This approach has clear political implications, since a free market is considered to be an indispensable aspect of liberal democracy.

(c) Criticisms of the market

Critics point to the deficiencies of the market, firstly as an efficient allocator of resources. The growth of monopoly power in the twentieth century not only in product markets but also in factor markets enables suppliers artificially to restrict supply in order to secure higher prices and a monopoly profit. The resulting distortion of relative prices leads to a sub-optimal allocation of resources. The market signals are no longer accurate. A second alleged deficiency is that as a democratic economic voting device the power of an individual's vote depends upon the size of his income. Left to itself, it is then argued, the market produces an unacceptable inequality in the distribution of incomes. Third, as social objectives have changed there are thought to be certain *'collective goods'* such as health and education which are considered the right of all regardless of their power in the market. They should therefore be provided collectively rather than by the market.

These arguments provide an economic justification for state intervention in the workings of a market economy.

3.2 THE COMMAND ECONOMY

The chief characteristics of this solution to the economic problem are that central government makes the basic decisions in respect of resource allocation, production targets, income distribution and growth rates, and does so in accordance with its collective preferences rather than in response to the preferences of the individual. In short, such a society is collectivist and centralized in contrast to the individualism and decentralization of the free market. In practice, such are the complexities of a modern economy that it would be impossible for any group of planners, however sophisticated, to plan every detail. Certain classes of economic decision may consequently be delegated to lower government echelons or to some artificially created market mechanism. Even with such modifications, problems arise.

(a) Efficient resource use

Without the test of the market and the criterion of profit which lead to the switching of resources, what principles will be employed to assess whether resources have been utilized in the most efficient way? In the USSR a partial response has been to set notional profit targets in different parts of an industry in order that some comparisons may be made.

(b) An extended chain of command

Central planning requires a complex, hierarchical and highly bureaucratic command structure. There are inevitably time-lags as decisions made at the centre are handed down to be translated into action on the shop floor. There will be an equally slow feedback to the centre. The weakness of such a monolithic structure is its inflexibility, its lack of sensitivity to changing circumstances.

(c) Co-ordination

A highly specialized modern economy comprises a vast number of interdependencies. The output of industry A will depend upon inputs from industries B and C. Targets for each cannot therefore be established independently, hence there emerges a major problem of co-ordination, which must be resolved if the right quantities are to arrive in the right place at the right time.

(d) Incentives

Is it possible to create incentives by invocation or command? If not, then there must be some system of material incentives if managers and work-force are to make their best efforts. This in turn implies some differentiation in rewards. When this is centrally planned, what criteria will be employed to establish differentials?

(e) Political implications

The economic objectives of the command economy will by definition be determined at the centre and will be contingent upon the political goals of the leadership. In practice this has implied the expansion of the industrial and military infrastructure at the expense of satisfying consumer preferences. Such centralization of both the political and economic decision-making process has proved inconsistent with notions of individual liberty and therefore unacceptable to Western democracies.

3.3 THE MIXED ECONOMY

In practice there has never existed either a perfectly free market economy or a pure command economy. Even in the heyday of 'laissez-faire', Smith recognized that there were certain economic goods such as defence and law and order which could not appropriately be provided by the market. In the centrally planned economy of the USSR, the price mechanism still has a limited function in allowing consumers to spend their planned incomes on goods which they choose from the planned supply. The dilution of the command principle in favour of the market may be observed today in a number of centrally planned economies around the world. However, over the past two hundred years the modification of the market principle in favour of a measure of central planning has been more striking. In the UK, no sooner had the philosophy of 'laissez-faire' been accepted than the pendulum began to swing the other way. Throughout the nineteenth century, on both humanitarian and pragmatic political grounds, governments increasingly intervened in ways which influenced market outcomes. For example, legislation affected the terms and conditions governing the employment of women and children, the operation of railways and safety provisions in the workplace. Gradually, responsibilities were also given to local authorities to ensure the provision of basic education and public health. By the turn of the century the pendulum had gathered momentum with society, through the medium of local rather than central government assuming greater responsibility for the provision of goods and services. The 1939–45 War may be seen as a watershed at which the free enterprise capitalist society which Adam Smith had known and advocated finally receded in favour of the *mixed economy*. The implication of a 'welfare state' was a guarantee to all of certain minimal living standards 'from the cradle to the grave'. If this obligation were to be met then the state would necessarily have a major role in economic decision-making. As previously noted (1.10), the new macroeconomics of John Maynard Keynes became the cornerstone upon which government economic policies were built. The market would continue to play a dominant role but only within the context of planned objectives, particularly in respect of employment. At the micro level, government would also intervene as necessary to influence the direction of resource use as well as the distribution of economic benefits. In order that government could effectively carry its new responsibilities, it was thought necessary that it should occupy the *'commanding heights'* of the economy and large areas of industry were consequently taken into public ownership. In this way was laid the economic foundation of 'Butskellism', the consensus, middle-of-the-road politics advocated by R. A. Butler and Hugh Gaitskill which was to survive into the mid-1970s. By this time the early successes of the new approach had been overtaken by an increasing array of problems and while the principle of the mixed economy was not challenged, the nature of the mix was now contested. Politics polarized together with suggested solutions to current economic problems. Since 1979, 'Thatcherism' has been associated with attempts to 'roll back the frontiers of the state', to dilute the mixture in favour of a freer operation of the market at the expense of less central government planning.

EXAMINATION PRACTICE 1

It is important for the student to have a very clear view of the nature and scope of his subject. This has been developed at length in Chapter 1 and a question in this area commonly occurs with all Boards, usually in the essay paper.

ESSAYS

Contrast the free enterprise and centrally planned approaches to solving the economic problem. Consider whether or not the growth of living standards in an economy might be significantly influenced by the type of economic system.   (*JMB, June 1984*)
Key References 3.1 and 3.2.

Describe briefly the main features of a command economy and assess its advantages and disadvantages.   (*AEB, November 1985*)
Key References 3.2.

How does the market economy determine what to produce, how to produce and for whom to produce?
                    (*O & C SEB, 9635/1, July 1984*)
Key References 3.1 but also, in more detail, Ch.8, 1 & 2.1–7.

Discuss the view that a mixed economy is an inevitable practical compromise between a free market and a command economy.
                    (*AEB, November 1983*)
Key References 3.3 but also having regard to 3.1 & 3.2.

METHODOLOGY

CONTENTS

1. THE ECONOMIC APPROACH

1.1 A SINGLE DISCIPLINE

We have previously observed that economics is concerned with a multiplicity of topics – scarcity and choice, markets and prices, inflation and unemployment for example. Despite the diversity of material which it examines, economics is nevertheless a single discipline; what unifies it is a common system of thinking about problems. Many modes of investigation are employed, borrowed from other fields of inquiry and adapted to the examination of economic phenomena. Usefulness rather than methodological purity, however, is the criterion upon which particular techniques are employed. Mathematical *deductive* reasoning is employed extensively in, for example, the analysis of prices and markets in order to make predictions. However, of equal importance is an historical *inductive* approach which enables first premises to be established and which tests the outcomes of predictions. John Maynard Keynes summarized the many facets of economic analysis as follows: 'The master-economist . . . must understand symbols and speak in words. He must contemplate the particular in terms of the general and touch abstract and concrete in the same flight of thought. He must study the present in the light of the past for the purposes of the future. No part of man's nature or his institutions must lie entirely outside his regard. He must be purposeful and disinterested in a simultaneous mood; as aloof and incorruptible as an artist, yet sometimes as near the earth as a politician.'

Reaching out as it does to so many other areas of study, economics will be seen to be more easily distinguished by the problems which it addresses rather than the investigative techniques which it employs. One characteristic is however of supreme importance: whatever the method of inquiry, the economic approach is always objective and dispassionate.

1.2 THE NATURE OF ECONOMIC ABSTRACTION

Students fresh to economics are often puzzled by the apparent absence of relationship between abstract economic theory and the world of their everyday experience. It is certainly true that economists frequently abstract from reality in order to simplify the infinite complexity of economic relationships. The task of the chemist in explaining the relationships of molecules in a chemical reaction is

immeasurably easier. Molecules are never motivated by social ambi-
tion, by altruism or greed or the lust for power. If the economist were
to attempt to allow for every aspect of the behaviour of every
individual, he would have no chance of understanding the way in
which the economy works. He therefore finds it necessary to
generalize, to abstract from what he considers to be unimportant
detail. At this juncture he finds himself in some difficulty. On what
criteria does he retain the 'important' and discard the 'unimportant'?
There is no 'right' answer. The appropriate degree of abstraction
depends upon the objective of the analysis. What for some purposes
would be a gross over-simplification would for others be excessively
complex. For example, the size of national income is determined by
many millions of decisions made by producers and consumers, far
too great a number for the economist to incorporate in his analysis.
As we shall see later, he simplifies by examining only a number of
important 'aggregates'. Whether or not his judgment proves correct
will ultimately be borne out by the reliability of his predictions.
(Friedrich von Hayek has criticized 'the lost generation' of post-war
Keynesian economists for their 'pseudo-science' – their disposition,
in his view, to abstract too much.) Economics is therefore as much art
as science.

**1.3 ECONOMIC THEORIES
AND MODELS**

The simple observation and description of phenomena has little value
in itself, which is why theory plays a crucial role in all scientific
inquiry. It is not, as in common parlance, an untested assertion of
alleged fact. Rather is it an attempt to simplify, thereby explaining the
relationship which exists between observed phenomena and how
that relationship works. It is a framework within which economic
data can be systematized and analysed, and as such provides the
foundation for practical policy. For example, in the 1960s theory
assumed an inverse relationship between inflation and unemployment and this seemed to be borne out by the historical record. It then
became a basis for public policy. When in the 1970s this relationship
broke down, existing theory was evaluated and developed and in due
course became the basis for a new direction in public policy. It should
then be recognized that unlike the physical sciences, theories in the
social sciences rarely acquire the certainty of 'laws'. They are useful
only for as long as they continue to explain current phenomena.
Nevertheless, since economic issues revolve around questions
of cause and effect, solutions depend upon a combination of data
analysis and theoretical reasoning. The compilation of data alone
provides nothing more than a sterile picture of things as they have
been.

   Having developed his abstract theories, the economist uses them
to build models of relationships which exist in parts of or the whole of
the economy. He is then able to experiment with his model to take
some view on what will be the result of a given change in a given

variable, e.g. what would be the effect upon prices and employment of a 2% fall in the rate of increase of the money supply? The model in its simplest form may be nothing more than a statement expressed in words, e.g. 'privately owned businesses are motivated by the desire to maximize profits'. This statement provides the foundation for a behavioural model of the economy. As will be the case in this book, the model frequently adopts the form of a graphical presentation or an algebraic equation. The most elaborate and sophisticated models with a multiplicity of variables are stored on computers, e.g. 'the Treasury model' which the government relies upon for its economic forecasts. There are an increasing number of such computer models at, for example, the London Business School, the Manchester Business School and a number of stockbrokers, each of which manifests a different theoretical viewpoint and therefore attaches differing significance to the variables which it incorporates. Models are necessarily modified in the light of experience.

1.4 POSITIVE AND NORMATIVE ECONOMICS

From what has been said in the previous section it is apparent that economists frequently disagree. The reason for this disagreement may be explained by looking at the positive and normative aspects of the subject.

(a) Positive economics

Positive statements about economics are of the sort which assert that if A occurs then B will follow, provided that C remains constant. It is in this area that the scientific aspect of economic investigation is most clearly visible. It is also an area in which there is frequently a wide measure of agreement amongst economists. That it appears not to be so to the lay public is in part attributable to the high profile of the social sciences. Everyone is in some sense an amateur economist and has something to say on matters such as inflation and unemployment. He then observes that professional economic opinions appear to be as diverse as his own and concludes that economics is largely 'hot air'. On the other hand, debate amongst physicists on the nature and origins of 'black holes' in the universe will be widely unnoticed and the public is unlikely to express any passionate concern. To the extent that genuine disagreement arises in positive economics, this may be compared with disagreement amongst mathematicians about the validity of some as yet unproved theorem. In each case disagreement will be resolved by the development of a carefully reasoned argument in support of one's own position and an attempt to detect flaws in the reasoning of others. Secondly, some disputes arise from different interpretations and statistical quantifications of past experience. For example, there may be disagreement about the effects of tax cuts upon the level of economic activity. The arguments will rely very heavily upon statistical data and upon the assumption that 'other things remain equal'. Since in the real world they rarely do, agreement will be that much harder to achieve but persistent statistical inquiry may serve to narrow the area of difference.

(b) Normative economics

A more self-evident reason for disagreement among economists lies in the area of normative economics. Normative statements will incorporate, explicitly or implicitly, the concept 'should' or 'ought'. The positive statement that if A occurs B will follow gives no indication of whether outcome B is thought to be desirable. If the economist asserts that B is either good or bad, then he is making a normative statement. A should or should not then be permitted to occur. When he makes such value judgments he wears at least part of the mantle of the political scientist, or more fundamentally the moral philosopher. This may on occasion prove necessary if his pronouncements – particularly on matters of public policy – are to carry weight. As previously observed, for example, the view that a market produces the best outcomes is deeply rooted in a philosophical view of the supreme importance of the individual in the universal scheme of things. This contrasts with the collectivist view in which the importance of society collectively transcends that of the sum total of the individuals who comprise it. Like others, therefore, economists will make different moral judgments not only on policy objectives but also on the means of achieving them.

2. SOME FUNDAMENTAL IDEAS

2.1 ECONOMIC TERMINOLOGY

Like other disciplines economics has its own jargon. Ideas are frequently expressed through words which are given a precise meaning which differs from their everyday usage. Some of the more important are examined below.

2.2 EFFICIENCY AND THE PRODUCTION POSSIBILITY FRONTIER

Economists are concerned with the efficient use of scarce resources. Few would quibble with the goal of having more for no extra cost or effort, whether it be more material goods or more leisure to follow cultural pursuits or engage in more social contacts. Since efficiency is such a central concept, economists examine it with a great deal of precision.

The problem of choosing how to allocate resources with maximum efficiency can be illustrated by means of a simple diagram which shows a *production possibility curve*. It is derived from a number of simple assumptions which are made in Table 1.

This society devotes all of its resources to the production of only two goods, food and coal. It may if it wishes concentrate exclusively upon food production, solely upon coal, or it may select a variety of combinations. These assumptions are expressed graphically in Figure 1.

Table 1. Production
possibility schedule

Food (in thousands of tonnes)	Coal (in thousands of tonnes)
0	525
100	515
200	495
300	465
400	420
500	360
600	295
700	205
800	95
850	0

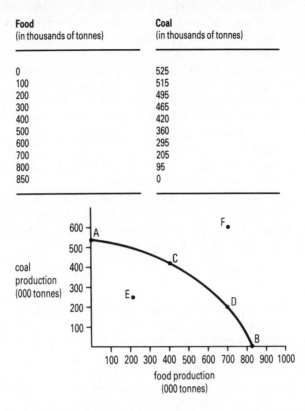

Figure 1. *Production possibility curve.* The curve indicates all the possible combinations of food which can be produced with all resources fully employed.

At point A on the curve nothing but coal is produced and at point B nothing but food. The intermediate points C and D represent possible combinations which may be selected. Combinations which lie inside the curve, such as E, are also a possibility. However, the curve itself marks a production possibility *frontier*, since it separates combinations which are possible from those which are impossible with the given resources and technology. Point F on the outer side of the curve is of this order.

It will be observed that the curve is convex to the origin and this is characteristic of production possibility curves.

The significance is that it becomes progressively more difficult to produce more units of one good in the sense that it becomes necessary to forego ever-increasing proportions of the other. The explanation for this is to be found in the observation that the factors of production – land, labour and capital – are not homogeneous. In the illustration, food production at first expands on good farmland at the expense of the loss of relatively little coal. In due course, however, it becomes necessary to farm less fertile land in the coalfields while rich coal seams are lost to production.

Finally, we are now in a position to relate the concept of efficiency to that of the production possibility frontier. Interior points to the left of the curve such as E indicate an inefficient and wasteful use of resources, since it would be possible to have more food or coal or combinations of both without any extra sacrifice. There are two possible explanations for this inefficiency. First, there may be a poor organization of the division of labour. In the illustration, it may be the case that as food production is expanded at the expense of coal, it is the most skilled miners who are the first to become farmers. The second explanation lies in the incomplete use of resources. The production possibility frontier assumes the full employment of all resources, but if this is not the case then the economy will lie within the production possibility frontier.

From this account it will be concluded that production is said to take place efficiently if it is impossible within the constraints of given resources and technology to increase the output of one good without simultaneously decreasing that of another.

2.3 OPPORTUNITY COST

For the economist the rather loose term *cost* has the more precise connotation of *opportunity cost*. This concept measures the value of doing something in terms of the lost opportunity to pursue the best alternative activity with the same time or resources. On many occasions opportunity cost may properly be measured in monetary terms. The opportunity cost of a pound spent on beer is the lost opportunity to spend the pound on fish and chips! In other instances activities which have no measurable monetary cost still have important opportunity costs when measured in time. An hour of study means the forfeiture of an hour on the sports field.

The nature of opportunity costs is revealed graphically in the production possibility curve. Figure 1 shows that extra resources being devoted to the production of more food, means the loss of opportunity for the coal which they might otherwise have produced. Geometrically the opportunity cost of food production is shown by the slope of the curve. The fact that this curve is convex tells us that the opportunity cost of more food increases as more resources are devoted to this use and does so more than proportionately.

2.4 THE MARGIN

The introduction of marginal analysis into economic thinking has already been referred to (1.8). Defined in general terms, the margin or the adjective 'marginal' indicates the effects of a unit increase or decrease in some economic activity. It is a most important instrument for examining economic phenomena and has a number of applications. Some of the more important are explained below. Others will be discovered later.

(a) Marginal Cost

Precisely, this is the addition to total cost resulting from one more unit of output. In the practical world errors have frequently been made in consequence of producers insisting upon prices which in every instance cover *average* costs. The benefits of *marginal* cost pricing can be explained by reference to the fare structure of British Rail. It is possible to charge substantially lower fares for off-peak travel, since it is clearly preferable to have trains full rather than half-empty, *provided that* the price charged covers the marginal cost of the service, i.e. the extra labour, electricity, tickets etc. No return is necessary to the fixed capital investment in permanent way, rolling stock and premises, since those costs remain whether or not the trains run.

(b) Marginal productivity of labour/capital

This concept may be defined as the increase in total output which results from the employment of one more unit of labour/capital. Economic theory uses this idea in attempting to explain the basic principles governing the reward which goes to each of these factors of production in return for its services.

(c) Marginal revenue

This is the addition to total revenue resulting from one more sale, and as we shall see later is a concept of great importance to the pricing policy of the supplier, who exercises a degree of monopoly power.

2.5 THE ENTREPRENEURIAL FUNCTION

Examination of the three preceding concepts leads us to conclude that many economic decisions have certain factors in common. They can be summarized as objectives, choice between alternative activities and constraints which apply to both objectives and choice.

Objectives are commonly concerned with the maximization or the minimization of something. Firms may seek to maximize revenue and minimize costs. Consumers will wish to maximize utility. Moreover, wherever there is economic choice there must exist at least two alternative activities through which the objective can be accomplished. The firm may increase revenue by diversifying its product range, or it may reduce costs by reorganization or the introduction of new techniques. The consumer has the choice of different goods; the worker of different employments. Whatever the choice, the decision-maker must determine the best means of achieving his objective.

All decisions are subject to the ultimate constraint of scarcity. The consumer is limited by his income, the producer by the availability of resources and current technology.

Entrepreneurial activity is the business of attempting to reduce constraints, of exploring new activities through which objectives can be achieved and of experimenting with new objectives. In this sense, therefore, all economic decisions involve some degree of entrepreneurship and the accompanying risk that the wrong decision may be made. The consumer will vary his consumption pattern, the worker his lifestyle in respect of jobs and leisure; but most significantly, the business organizer without whom production will not take place seeks to innovate, to improve the activities by which objectives can be attained. He will simultaneously vary his own objectives and attempt to influence those of others. That such activity is a distinctive form of labour involving risk is the economic justification of profit which is its reward. It is in this last sense that the term 'entrepreneur' is normally used.

EXAMINATION PRACTICE 2

The review of the nature of economic study is completed in Chapter 2, with the focus upon some particularly important concepts. Full questions based exclusively upon these concepts are unlikely; more probably they will appear in application to other material. Nevertheless, some examples are given.

MULTIPLE CHOICE

An economy with fixed amounts of capital and labour produces only two goods X and Y. Its production possibility frontier is given by the equation $Y = 200 - 15X$.

When the economy is at full employment, and the output of Y is less than 200, the opportunity cost of producing an additional unit of Y is

(a) $\frac{1}{200}$ of a unit of X
(b) $\frac{1}{15}$ of a unit of X
(c)   15 units of X
(d)   185 units of X
(e)   200 units of X.   (*O & C SEB shared paper, June 1984*)

Key References 2.2 and 2.3. *Answer* (b).

The production possibility schedule for cars and tanks is as follows:

Cars	Tanks
16	0
15	1
14	2
13	3
11	4
9	5
7	6
0	7

The opportunity cost of the second tank in terms of cars is

(a)   1
(b)   2
(c)   7
(d)   14

(*AEB, June 1985*)

Key References 2.2 and 2.3. *Answer* (a).

ESSAYS

Explain what is meant by:
(a)   micro-economics and macro-economics.
(b)   positive economics and normative economics.

Discuss the relevance of each concept to the problem of scarcity and choice.   *(AEB, June 1985)*
Key References (a) Ch.1, 2.3 and (b) Ch.2, 1.3 and 1.4.

What difficulties confront the scientific study of economic behaviour and how do economists try to overcome them? To what extent do you think that objectivity is possible or desirable in the study of economics?   *(JMB, June 1982)*
Key References 1.1–4.

QUANTITATIVE TECHNIQUES

CONTENTS

1. GRAPHS USED IN ECONOMIC ANALYSIS

1.1 TWO-VARIABLE DIAGRAMS

Much economic analysis requires attention to be paid simultaneously to two variables. For example, in examining the operation of markets it is necessary to watch the price of the good while observing the quantity bought and sold. It is therefore useful to display figures in a two-dimensional graph which demonstrates the behaviour of two economic variables. In this way a large quantity of data can be shown much more easily and clearly than would be possible with a long prose description or a lengthy table of figures. Data interpretation and analysis are thus facilitated.

The numerical value of one variable is measured along the bottom line of the graph, the *horizontal axis*, starting from the origin, labelled 'O'. The numerical value of the other variable is also measured from the origin along the *vertical axis*.

Figure 2 is a typical graph used in economic analysis. It shows a hypothetical demand curve (DD) for Brand X detergent. Reading off from point (a) we see that at a price of £1 per carton 5 million will be sold. At point (b), a reduction in price to 75 pence increases sales to 7 million. Note that information about price and quantity is all that the diagram tells us. We learn nothing, for example, about the quality of Brand X or the sort of people who buy it. It is important to remember

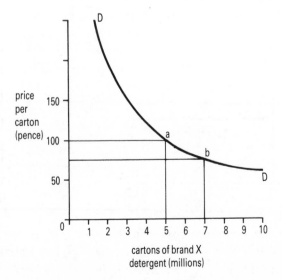

Figure 2. *Demand curve for detergent.* At a price of £1 per carton, 5 million are sold. At a price of 75p, sales increase to 7 million.

therefore that graphs do not tell the whole story. They focus upon two variables of primary interest, while ignoring many details which may be important.

1.2 DEFINITION AND MEASUREMENT OF SLOPE

Curves in graphs may rise or fall and will do so with varying rapidity. In Figure 2 the demand curve slopes down from left to right, telling us the rate at which detergent sales increase as price falls. In such cases the curve is said to be *negatively sloped*, since one variable falls as the other one rises.

The four diagrams in Figure 3 show all the possible types of slope for a straight-line relationship between two variables, X and Y. Figure 3(a) shows a *negative* slope similar to the demand curve in Figure 2. Figure 3(b) shows that both variables increase together; it has a *positive* slope. Figure 3(c) has a *zero* slope, since the value of Y remains the same regardless of the value of X. Figure 3(d) shows an *infinite* slope, with the value of X unchanged regardless of the value of Y.

Figure 3. *Slopes in straight-line graphs.* The four diagrams show the labels given to different types of slope.

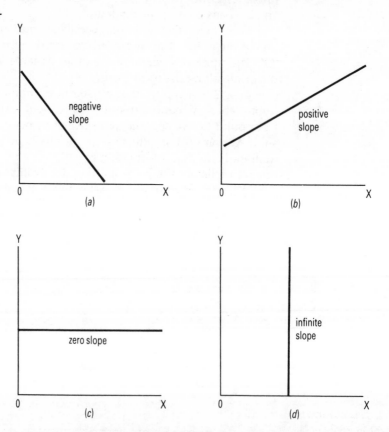

The slope of a curve can be measured in just the same way as the gradient of a hill in a road map. Figure 4 shows two straight lines, both positively sloped but at different rates. In Figure 4(a) a horizontal movement AB of 5 units corresponds to a vertical movement, BC of 1 unit. The slope is BC/AB=1/5. In Figure 4(b) the slope is steeper. The horizontal movement of 5 units corresponds to a vertical movement of 2 units The slope is BC/AB=2/5. Note that the slope of a straight line is the same wherever on that line it is measured. This will not be the case with lines that are curved.

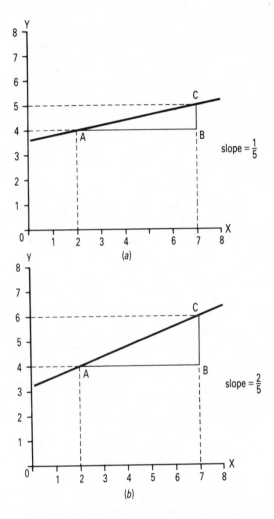

Figure 4. *Measurement of slope.* Slope shows the unit increase vertically relative to the unit increase horizontally, i.e. the ratio of the 'rise' to the 'run'.

Figure 5 illustrates some typical slopes of curved lines, 5(a) showing a curve which is negatively sloped throughout. In Figure 5(b) the curve is positively sloped throughout. Figure 5(c) illustrates a curve which is at first positively sloped and then negatively sloped, while Figure 5(d) shows the opposite.

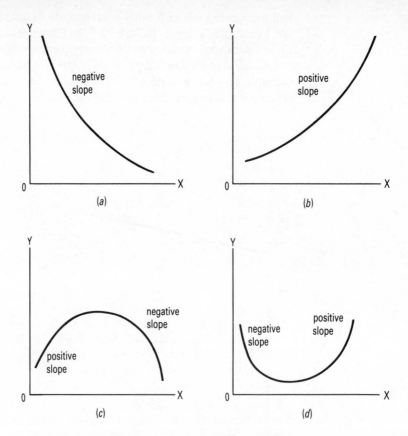

Figure 5. *Curved graph slopes*. Note that in 5(c) and 5(d) the slopes of curves are reversed, with movement to the right along the X axis.

It is possible to measure the slope of a curve at any particular point by constructing a tangent to the curve at that point. In Figure 6 the line TT is tangent to the curve at point C, where the slope of the curve is precisely the same as the slope of the tangent. It is measured in the same way as in Figure 4.

Slope of curve at C = slope of tangent TT = BC/AB=4/10 = 0.4

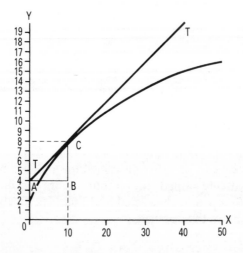

Figure 6. *Measuring slope at a point on a curve*. TT is tangental to the curve at C. The slope of TT is BC/AB or 4/10.

1.3 45° LINES

The point at which a straight line cuts the vertical axis is described as the Y *intercept*, e.g. in Figure 6 the Y intercept lies at 4 where the tangent TT meets the Y axis. When a line has a Y intercept at zero it is called a *ray through the origin*, or more simply a *ray*. Rays have several special uses, in particular those with a slope of 1. These are called 45° lines since they form an angle of 45° to both horizontal and vertical axes. Their usefulness rests upon the fact that they mark off points at which X and Y are equal so long as both are measured in the same units. In Figure 6, the vertical distance to any point on the ray always equals the horizontal distance to the same point, e.g. at point A, Y=4 and X=4.

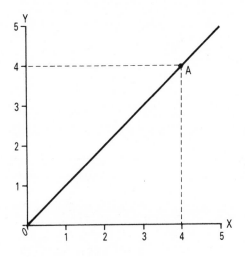

Figure 7. *The 45° line.* All vertical distances from the X axis to the ray equal the horizontal distance from the Y axis to the same point.

1.4 CONTOUR MAPS

The problem of accommodating three variables in a graph can be resolved through the use of 'contour maps'. A standard geographic map gives only two dimensions, latitude and longitude, but a contour map gives a third – altitude – and contour lines connect locations at the same height above sea level. Economic contour maps are similar in character.

Figure 8 illustrates the principle using the specific case of a production contour map. Each contour line shows different combinations of capital and labour which yield the same output, Z. For example, at point A, 80 units of capital in combination with 40 units of labour will yield 1500 units of output. However, another combination of labour and capital at point B will produce the same result and, other things being equal, the entrepreneur will be indifferent to which combination he adopts. Higher levels of output imply greater inputs of both labour and capital. Data presented in this way is described by economists as a *production indifference map*.

Figure 8. *Production indifference map*. Each contour shows different combinations of labour and capital, each of which yields the same output.

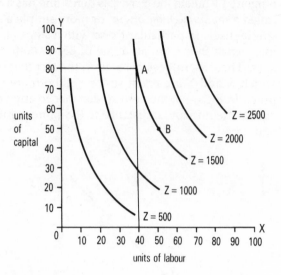

2. PROBLEMS OF INTERPRETATION

2.1 TIME SERIES AND GROWTH TRENDS

One of the most popular types of graph – frequently encountered in newspapers – is the time series which seeks to illustrate trends in, for example, share prices, unemployment or imports. The horizontal axis always represents the time scale divided into convenient units, while the vertical axis shows some variable of interest. These graphs can be very useful in giving an instant perspective of events, but they can also be dangerously misleading. For example, it would be simple to demonstrate that the cost of imports has continued to increase enormously in the forty year period 1946–1986, and taken in isolation this might lead to erroneous conclusions. Correct interpretation requires three further observations:

(*a*)   The growth of population during the period.
(*b*)   Changes in the price level.
(*c*)   Growth of real national income.

What we should be concerned to know is the change in the volume of imports per head of population and as a proportion of real national income, i.e. having allowed for inflation.

2.2 CHOICE OF TIME SCALE

By accident or design the selection of time scale may affect the interpretation of the data, e.g. for cyclical and structural reasons there may be an underlying upward trend in unemployment. If the time series covers only the first half of the year, it may suggest a slowing in the rate of increase or even a positive decrease. This ignores seasonal factors as school-leavers enter the labour market, and the effect on employment of the winter months.

A graph covering the whole year gives a more reliable perspective.

2.3 OMISSION OF ORIGIN This is a common fault in daily newspapers. Some variables have considerable magnitudes, e.g. exports, GNP, money supply. Shown on the vertical axis, there is always a temptation to save space by omitting the origin and the lower figures, and showing only the range within which the graph moves. This has the effect of grossly exaggerating peaks and troughs. The illustration in Figure 9(a) omits the origin and gradations on the vertical axis, so the 10% drop in February gives the impression that the export trade collapsed. The trend is seen in a truer perspective in Figure 9(b).

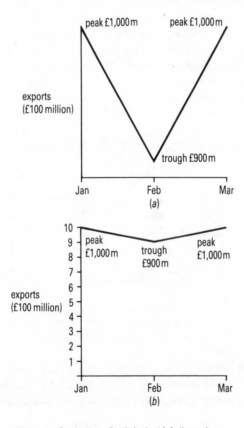

Figure 9. *Omission of origin*. In 9(a) distortion results from the absence of origin and vertical gradations. The trough is exaggerated; 9(b) gives a truer picture.

3. NATIONAL INCOME ACCOUNTING

3.1 THE CIRCULAR FLOW OF INCOME

National Income can be viewed in two ways – as a circular flow of real things or as a countervailing flow of money values. This concept is illustrated in Figure 10.

The economy is organized into private and public sectors; society provides both with the factors of production, land, labour and capital and – some economists will add – enterprise. The economy returns to society producer goods (i.e. capital) and consumer goods and services. This is illustrated by the inner circle. In the outer circle, the economy pays society wages, rent, interest and profits in return for the factors of production. For the volume of its production it receives a price calculated at market prices.

The first conclusion is that national income, national expenditure and volume of production are simply different aspects of the same thing. National income may be seen as the aggregate of incomes generated in the process of production; as the total volume of national expenditure which corresponds to it; or as the money value of all goods and services produced in both public and private sectors.

Second, national expenditure takes place at market prices which include expenditure taxes. When spent by government, these taxes will increase aggregate demand (national expenditure). To avoid double counting, they must be deducted if national income is to equate with national expenditure. Otherwise the same sum of money will have been spent twice but only distributed once in income.

These insights provide the basis for National Income accounting.

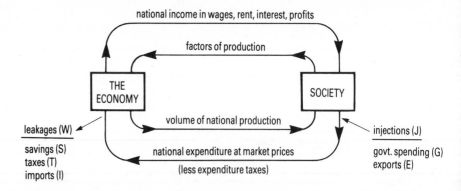

Figure 10. *The circular flow of income.* There are two countervailing flows. The inner circle is the 'real' economy of factors of production and goods and services. The outer circle is the 'monetary economy' which sets money values on economic activity.

3.2 AN INSTRUMENT OF ECONOMIC PLANNING

It was only after 1945 that government made itself responsible for national economic planning. Prior to the Second World War 'laissez-faire' prevailed, with no role for government in business affairs.

Consequently there was no call for official national income statistics and the only research was by academics such as the statistician, Sir Arthur Bowley.

The first official estimates were produced in 1941 by the Central Statistical Office and the Economic Section of the Cabinet Office, two new government agencies established for the purpose of wartime planning. The techniques which were developed at this time were continued and elaborated in peacetime, and since 1941 government has published an annual White Paper, *National Income and Expenditure*, in the spring. These estimates are refined and published in greater detail during the autumn in a 'Blue Book'.

These figures provide the statistical basis for government economic planning. They are to be seen as a set of accounts for the economy as a whole, comparable with annual company accounts, and in a similar way provide a view of performance during the preceding year and a practical foundation for developing new policies.

3.3 PROBLEMS OF CALCULATION

From different sources of data attempts are made to calculate national income, using both the income and expenditure approaches. Several problems are encountered.

(a) Allowing for inflation

In a period of sustained inflation it means little to be told that national income has doubled in ten years if allowance is not made for changes in the value of money. The longer the period over which comparisons are made, the more unreliable the comparisons. In a number of tables in the Blue Book, this difficulty is resolved by using index numbers and by reducing all figures to constant prices. A base year is selected – changed on current practice every five years – and allowance is then made for changes in the purchasing power of money. Index numbers, however, have their own difficulties (see Section 4). It should also be noted that just as there are problems in comparing levels of national income in different years, so there are similar problems in comparing the national incomes of two countries with different price levels.

(b) Capital depreciation

In the course of generating the national income, capital will of course have been consumed. If we wish to calculate *net* national income, then an allowance must be made for capital depreciation. To do this for the whole economy is extremely difficult if there is to be any degree of accuracy. Consequently, there is a preference for the concepts of Gross National Product (GNP), i.e. national income before capital depreciation, or similarly Gross Domestic Product (GDP) which focuses on income generated internally.

(c) Stock appreciation

This appears as a negative item in the accounts. At the beginning and the end of the year, valuations are made of physical stocks and work in progress. Since any increase in value is likely at least in part to result from inflation, an appropriate deduction is made.

(d) Incomplete or inaccurate data

The accuracy of calculations made by the income approach depends upon the reliability of returns made to the Inland Revenue. There is generally recognized to be a substantial 'black economy', unofficially estimated to amount to as much as £30 billion annually. High marginal rates of income tax perhaps encourage undeclared second jobs, as does the system of social security benefits. There is also evidence of a good deal of business being conducted on a 'cash only' basis and of legitimate tax avoidance being practised on a wide scale. All of this will lead to an underestimate of the true national income.

(e) Notional rents

A house provides the same income or service whether it is occupied by a tenant or the owner. The rent paid by the tenant will appear in the national income accounts. It would therefore seem logical to attribute some notional income to the owner-occupier. However, there are formidable difficulties in accurately assessing the rent which a house would fetch *if* it were put on the open market.

(f) Unpaid services

In a similar way, there are many services which are performed without payment and which are therefore unrecorded. A great deal of real income is generated without valuation through the services of the housewife and the do-it-yourself man. Payments made to the professional gardener will be recorded, but the same job carried out by the amateur in his own garden will remain unrecorded. (*Note:* This difficulty will be particularly acute in estimating the national incomes of underdeveloped countries with a heavy dependence on labour of this sort.)

(g) Double counting

There is always a danger of including the same items twice or more, e.g. care must be taken to avoid adding the values of the raw material, the semi-finished and the end product.

4. INDEX NUMBERS AND INFLATION

4.1 MEASUREMENT OF CHANGES IN THE VALUE OF MONEY

This is done with index numbers. A number of these are compiled for a variety of purposes, but the one most commonly referred to is the Retail Price Index which is constructed by pricing a typical 'basket' of goods in the base year and giving it the value of 100. Thus, if the RPI in 1980 were 235, starting from a base of 100 in 1975 this tells us the basket of goods which cost £100 in 1975 subsequently cost £235. In fact the price of a basket of, say, 250 items is unlikely to have been precisely £100, it may have been £500. Nevertheless the index number 100 is ascribed to it. Changes relative to this base are then calculated on the following formula.

$$\text{RPI in given year} = \frac{\text{Cost of market basket in given year}}{\text{Cost of market basket in base year}} \times 100$$

4.2 INDEX NUMBER PROBLEMS

In compiling index numbers several problems must be faced.

(a) Weighting

The first difficulty is to determine which goods and services to include and then to decide how much of each to select. This is the problem of weighting which can be illustrated in Table 2. Suppose there are only three commodities – A, B and C – and there is equal weighting, the index number for the base year is constructed as follows.

Table 2. Equally weighted index numbers

Base Year

Commodity	Price	Weight	Index
A	£5	1	100
B	£4	1	100
C	.50p	1	100
		3	300

Index for all items=100

During the year the following changes occur:

Base year +1

Commodity	Price	Weight	Index
A	£4	1	80
B	£6	1	150
C	.55p	1	110
		3	340

Index for all items=113.3

The index number in the second year is 113.3, which shows an increase in the price level of 13.3%.

If in accordance with some principle the goods are weighted differently, then clearly the results will be different, as shown in Table 3.

Table 3. Differentially weighted index numbers

Base Year

Commodity	Price	Weight	Index
A	£5	1	100
B	£4	5	500
C	.50p	10	1000
		16	1600

Index for all items= 100

Base year +1

Commodity	Price	Weight	Index
A	£4	1	80
B	£6	5	750
C	.55p	10	1100
		16	1930

Index for all items= 120.6

Weighting produces an increase in the price level of 20.6%. If commodity A were weighted sufficiently, then the price level would show a fall. The importance of a weighting principle which is a true reflection of quantities bought is demonstrated.

(b) Choice of base year
This should be a year of relative price stability. When inflation is sustained over a long period, it becomes necessary to establish new bases at regular intervals.

(c) Long periods
Following from the above, for several reasons index numbers are of little use in making comparisons over long periods. Changes in taste vary the demand for the items in the 'basket'; new goods enter the market; the age, sex and ethnic composition of the population is subject to change. The composition of the 'basket' must therefore be regularly reviewed.

4.3 THE GNP DEFLATOR   This is the price index used to adjust GNP for inflation and is considered by many economists to be a superior measure to the Retail Price Index since it has a wider coverage. The two indices are based on different 'baskets'. While the RPI is concerned with the purchases of a typical family, the GNP deflator includes every item in the GNP, i.e. all consumer and capital goods and all services produced in both public and private sectors.

This index is applied in accordance with the following formula.

$$\text{Real GNP} = \frac{\text{Nominal GNP}}{\text{GNP deflator}}$$

EXAMINATION PRACTICE 3

Chapter 3 has developed some important quantitative techniques which are commonly used in economic analysis. Clearly, these are not examined in isolation from material to which they are applied. This appears throughout the book, but some sample questions are given, based upon the contents of the chapter.

MULTIPLE CHOICE

The number of passenger journeys per week by train on a certain route is shown by the demand curve QQ' in the diagram below.

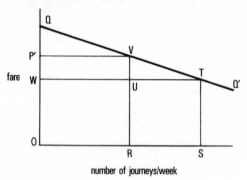

number of journeys/week

Initially the fare is OP, but it is then cut by PW. The loss of revenue from those passengers who would have travelled at the higher fare is shown by the area:

(a)   PVTW;   (b)   VUT;   (c)   QVUW;
(d)   QPV;   (e)   PVUW.

(O & C SEB, June 1984)

Key References 1.1. Answer (e).

DATA RESPONSE

General index of retail prices (15 January 1974=100)

	1974		1978		1983	
	Weights	Index	Weights	Index	Weights	Index
All items	1000	108	1000	197	1000	335
Food	248	106	233	204	203	309
Alcoholic drink	73	110	85	196	78	367
Tobacco	49	116	48	226	39	441
Housing	126	106	113	173	137	367
Fuel and light	58	111	60	228	69	465
Durable household goods	58	108	64	182	64	250
Clothing and footwear	89	109	80	171	74	215
Transport and vehicles	135	111	140	207	159	366
Miscellaneous goods	65	111	70	206	75	346
Services	53	107	56	192	63	343
Meals bought out	46	108	51	208	39	364

Monthly Digest of Statistics

(a) Explain briefly
(i) the principle of weighting
(ii) the principle of index numbers
(iii) how the general index of retail prices is constructed
(b) The price indexes for alcoholic drink and for housing show the same increase from 15 January 1974 to 1983. However, this statement obscures significant differences between the items during the period. Explain these differences and suggest why they occurred.
(c) Identify the significant trends evident from examining the table.   (O & C SEB, 9633/3 & 9635/2, July 1985)
Key References 4.1 & 4.2.

ESSAYS

Is it possible to give a meaningful and precise measure of the change in living standards over a long period? What indicators would help us to assess changes in living standards in Britain over the last 20 years?
(JMB, June 1982)

Key References 2.1; 2.2; 3.1; 3.2; 4.3.

PRODUCTION

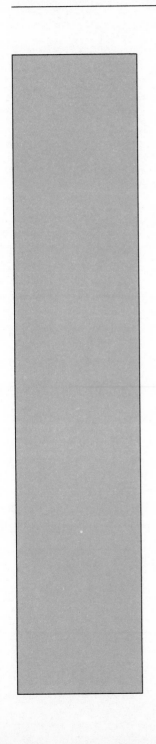

SCALE OF PRODUCTION

CONTENTS

1. MOTIVES FOR EXPANSION

1.1 THE FIRM

This is a business unit which sells its output in the market. In the *private sector*, firms range from the *sole trader* through *partnerships*, *private companies* to giant public *joint stock companies*. The latter are owned by shareholders who have contributed to a joint stock of capital in a company whose shares are quoted on the Stock Exchange.

In the *public sector*, *public corporations* – which include in particular the nationalized industries – also sell their output in the market. In this sense, they too are 'firms'. In contrast, *public services* such as the NHS operate outside the market and are not therefore considered to be firms.

An *industry* comprises a number of firms, large and small, with broadly similar interests.

1.2 PROFIT MAXIMIZATION

To construct a model of the way in which firms organize production, mainstream economics assumes profit maximization to be the sole motivation. (Post-war, a number of alternative theories of a firm's motivation have been constructed. In the extreme, J. K. Galbraith takes the view that for the modern corporation, profit considerations are marginal.) On this general assumption, it will be recognized that the entrepreneur will seek to expand if at the same time he can expand revenue and reduce costs.

1.3 HISTORICAL REASONS FOR THE GROWTH OF LARGE-SCALE PRODUCTION

Over the past two centuries, the scale of production has continued to increase:

(a) Mass markets
As living standards in most of the world have risen above subsistence, there has been an increase in the demand for mass produced goods.

(b) Improved transport
Geographically, the mass markets have been opened up and increasing degrees of specialization made possible.

(c) Increasing specialization
This implies an ever greater substitution of capital for labour, which in turn means organization on the large scale.

(d) Legal considerations
The principle of *limited liability* has encouraged *venture capital* in industrial expansion in a way which would not have occurred if the entrepreneur's total assets had been at risk.

(e) Economies of scale
Lower unit costs to give the firm a competitive edge.

2. ECONOMIES OF SCALE

2.1 INTERNAL ECONOMIES OF LARGE-SCALE PRODUCTION

We distinguish between *external economies* which are enjoyed by the whole industry in consequence of its concentration in a particular area, and *internal economies* which are enjoyed exclusively by one firm because of its own expansion. The latter include:

(a) Better use of the factors of production
Consider the case of the small garage proprietor operating as a sole trader. Alone, he serves petrol, repairs cars and keeps the books. When he expands he employs mechanics and a clerk and installs new equipment, while the garage still occupies the same area of land. This land is now being used more intensively and the unit costs of land have fallen. At the same time, the expanded labour force permits greater specialization and the use of more sophisticated equipment. The unit costs of labour and capital have also fallen in line with the more intensive use of these two factors.

(b) Administrative economies
Of particular significance are the potential economies in the use of this particular form of labour. It is unlikely that if the firm's output doubles, it will be necessary to double the managerial staff.

(c) Research
Only the large organization can afford to maintain its own research establishment. This gives it a significant advantage in markets where innovation and design are important.

(d) Finance
The large organization will be seen as a better risk by banking institutions and will be able to borrow on more favourable terms.

(e) Marketing
Similarly there are advantages, both in bulk buying on better terms

and in national advertising, the unit cost of which is low when sales are high.

(f) Welfare and better labour performance

Only the large firm can afford the sports, recreational and other welfare facilities which may be expected to improve industrial relations and labour's output.

Note: Items (c)–(f) refer strictly to economies in long-run money costs, which is the definition which some writers prefer for the phrase 'economies of scale'. This is to make a distinction from the phrase 'returns to scale'. which refers to the *physical output* of the factors of production (see p.84 below), and to which (a) and (b) relate.

2.2 LIMITS TO ECONOMIES

Economies are limited by several factors:

(a) The market

Ultimately, the scale of production is limited to the output which the market can absorb. However, this consideration may affect the size of the industry rather than the individual firm.

(b) The individuality of the market

The principle of mass production was established with the Model T Ford, of which it was said that you could have any colour provided that it was black. If the market demands variety, the possibility of large-scale production is restricted.

(c) Increasing factor costs *v* falling product price

Other things being equal, as the entrepreneur demands more of any one factor he will have to pay more for it. On the other hand, to market more of the end product price will have to fall.

(d) Increased risk

The greater the scale, the greater the risk of loss from some miscalculation. The entrepreneur may prefer to entrench at his present level of output.

2.3 DISECONOMIES OF SCALE

Expansion beyond a certain size may produce positive disadvantages:

(a) Loss of incentive

The sole trader has the advantage that he alone enjoys the profit or suffers the loss. The larger the organization, the more impersonal it is likely to be. One of the major problems of modern industrial relations is the lack of identification of the interests of the worker and his firm. The result may be low productivity or, at worst, repeated industrial disputes.

(b) Unresponsive bureaucracy

In practice, large organizations have tended to imply unwieldy management bureaucracies with extended lines of communication. The board-room is remote from the shop floor which all too frequently means delay and misunderstanding (as well as mistrust) in the implementation of decisions, also a lack of sensitivity to the response.

2.4 THE OPTIMUM FIRM

This is a useful theoretical concept, although in practice difficult if not impossible to determine. It is the scale of output at which the firm has minimized its unit costs of production. It has no further motive for expansion, nor would a lower output be in its interest. The primary practical difficulty in deciding the optimum output lies in the reconciliation of different optima, e.g. the lowest marketing costs may be achieved at an output which conflicts with the lowest administrative costs.

3. LAWS OF DIMINISHING AND INCREASING RETURNS

3.1 COMBINATION OF THE FACTORS IN DIFFERENT PROPORTIONS

The first observation of the Law of Diminishing Returns was made in the early nineteenth century in relation to agriculture. Land was particularly susceptible to its operation, although modern economics applies it equally to the other factors of production.

The Law states that: 'In any form of production where the quantity of one or more factors is fixed, successive applications of another factor will ultimately lead to a less than proportionate increase in physical output.' In the agricultural context, a fixed area of land combined with a fixed amount of capital (in the form of fertilizer and machinery) is worked by varying numbers of labourers. At first the work-force is expanded towards the point where these three factors are combined in ideal proportions. More efficient organization is rewarded by the operation of the Law of Increasing Returns. With each additional input of labour, there is a more than proportionate increase in output. Inexorably, however, beyond a certain point diminishing returns will apply. This results from *varying* the proportions in which the factors are combined, due chiefly to the difficulty of increasing the factors in *equal* proportions.

3.2 RETURNS TO SCALE

Were it possible to combine the factors of production only in given proportions, the entrepreneur would still have to determine the scale of production. This is illustrated in Table 4.

Table 4. Scale of production with fixed proportions

Firm	Units of land	Units of labour	Units of capital
X	10	40	12
Y	50	200	60
Z	100	400	120

The inputs of Firm Z are twice as great as those of Firm Y, which in turn are five times as great as those of Firm X. In each case, however, the factors are combined in the same proportions. If it is the case that the *output* of Firm Z is *more* than twice that of Firm Y, there will be *increasing returns to scale*. The concept can be illustrated arithmetically with reference to a cubic container made of sheet metal. The dimensions are:

> 2m×2m=4sq m each side×6=24sq m of sheet metal to give a cubic capacity of 2m×2m×2m=8cu m

If the size of each side is doubled:

> 4m×4m=16sq m×6=96sq m of sheet metal to give a cubic capacity of 4m×4m×4m=64cu m

The input has increased fourfold to yield an eightfold increase in output.

Some economists are inclined to doubt whether, in practice, such *pure* returns to scale arise. *N.B.* They are therefore disposed to treat *all* returns to scale as being the result of varying the proportions in which the factors are combined. If we allow the possibility, we can see that there are two sets of laws which govern returns, one resulting from *varying proportions* and the other from the *sheer scale of production*.

In Table 4, it may be that the output of Firm Y is *exactly* five times that of Firm X, in which case there are said to be *constant returns to scale*. If the output of Firm Z is *less* than double that of Firm Y, there are *decreasing returns to scale*. In the example, this may occur because the container has become too unwieldy.

3.3 THE OPTIMUM FIRM AND THE LAWS OF RETURN

Since it is by definition the most efficient firm in the industry, the optimum firm will have expanded to that point where it has maximized its economies of scale and at the same time combined the factors of production in optimal proportions.

4. SCALE OF PRODUCTION AND COST CURVES (SEE ALSO 13.1.1–6)

4.1 SHORT RUN AND LONG RUN

We have examined the *principle of substitution* of one input for another. However, the firm's ability to vary inputs depends very much on the time scale. In the short run, input choices are restricted by past decisions; e.g. if the firm purchased a machine last year, it is committed to that decision for the duration of the machine's life. In the long run, when that life is complete the restriction is removed and there may be a decision to vary the combination of inputs. More precisely, the short run is that period of time in which at least one factor of production is fixed. Output can only be increased by adding more of the variable factor. In the long run, all factors are assumed to be variable and the *scale* of the fixed factor (usually capital) can be increased.

4.2 AVERAGE TOTAL COST (ATC) CURVES IN THE SHORT AND LONG RUNS

The ATC curve is the result of the firm's attempts to minimize costs and this involves the optimal combination of the factors of production which are variable. However, we have just established that the inputs which can be varied depend upon the time scale. The long-run ATC curve therefore differs from that for the short run since more inputs are variable.

In Figure 11, the long-run ATC curve is drawn tangential to a set of short-run ATC curves. In the long run, the firm is able to expand output, moving from one SRATC to another. The shape of the curve depends upon whether the firm experiences economies or diseconomies of scale. Where an increase in all inputs produces a decline in LRATC, there exist economies of scale. This is shown in the movement from $SRATC_1$ to $SRATC_3$. The optimum firm produces output OQ at a cost of OC. Further expansion to $SRATC_4$ incurs diseconomies of scale, reflected in a continuing rise in LRATC.

Figure 11. *Short- and long-run average total cost curves.* The LRATC curve is tangential to a series of SRATC curves. In the long run, all inputs are variable and, at first, economies of scale are enjoyed. Beyond the optimum, diseconomies of scale are incurred.

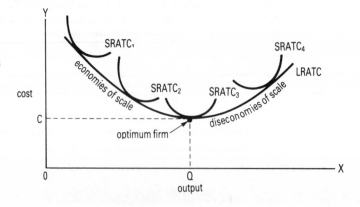

Illustrated is the classic U-shaped LRATC curve. Some industries which are particularly suited to large-scale production may have an

LRATC curve which continues to decline. Other activities, particularly in the service industries, are more suited to small-scale production and the LRATC curve will rise throughout. Some industries are not particularly susceptible to either economies or diseconomies of scale, in which case LRATC will be shown as a horizontal straight line.

EXAMINATION ON PRACTICE 4

MULTIPLE CHOICE

A firm has a fixed amount of land and capital and increases production by employing labour according to the following schedule.

Labour	Output
1	15
2	32
3	51
4	68
5	80
6	90

The Law of Diminishing Returns begins to operate
(a)   after 2 units of labour are employed;
(b)   after 3 units of labour are employed;
(c)   after 4 units of labour are employed;
(d)   after 5 units of labour are employed.

(*AEB, November 1983*)

Key References 3.1. *Answer* (c).

ESSAYS

What is meant by the Law of Diminishing Returns? Show the relationship between this concept and diseconomies of scale.

(*AEB, November 1984*)

Key References 3.1; 2.1; 2.2; 2.3.

How would you use the law of variable proportions to explain the conventional theoretical shapes of a firm's cost curves?

(*O & CSEB, 9635/1, June 1981*)

Key References 3.1; 4.1; 4.2 – and more fully, Ch. 13, 1.1–6.

Explain what is meant by economies of scale and how they arise. What factors are likely to determine the scale of production chosen by a firm? (*JMB, June 1980*)

Key References 2.1; 2.2; 2.3; 2.4; 3.1; 3.2; 3.3.

GROWTH IN THE PRIVATE SECTOR

1. METHODS OF GROWTH

1.1 CHANGES IN INDUSTRIAL STRUCTURE

One of the most significant changes has been the growth of the large-scale firm. Before the First World War, the hundred largest manufacturing companies accounted for only 16% of output. By the late 1940s this had risen to 25% and by the early 1980s to over 40%.

This change has given rise to certain fears, to which governments have responded with their *competition policy*.

(a) Fear of monopoly
Growth may lead to monopoly power, which in private hands will be used to exploit the consumer.

(b) Fear of excessive concentration of socio-economic power
Without public accountability, as firms grow their power over society increases through their pricing, investment and employment policies.

(c) Bureaucratization
The possibility that the decline of the small entrepreneur reduces the dynamism of industry, with consequent economic stagnation.

While it is true that much company growth is still financed by ploughing back profits, the major increases in size – particularly since the 1960s – have been achieved through *takeovers* and *mergers*. There is a takeover when the management of one firm makes an attractive offer to the shareholders of another firm in order to acquire a controlling interest. Mergers are of four main types.

1.2 VERTICAL INTEGRATION

This is combination of firms at different stages of the production process. *Backward integration* towards the source of supply may produce greater security of delivery and closer control over quality. *Forward integration* through wholesaling and retailing gives closer contact with the market and may facilitate improved planning. Vertical integration is fairly infrequent since there is a strong likelihood of infringing monopoly legislation.

1.3 HORIZONTAL INTEGRATION

The majority of mergers are of this type. Firms operating at the *same* stage of production combine. The advantage lies in the economies of scale which may be achieved. *Plant economies* may permit greater specialization and the concentration of production in a smaller number of enlarged plants. *Firm economies* result from the increased scale of the whole business, e.g. financial, marketing, administrative economies, etc. (see 4.2).

1.4 CONGLOMERATES

These are based upon managerial and financial expertise rather than any perceived production or marketing advantages. Firms diversify into non-competing and non-complementary products, e.g. Unilever with interests in detergents, food, chemicals, plastics, plantations, animal feeds and toiletries.

The principal advantage lies in spreading risk for the firm and its shareholders. The major objections are that they may be financed by repeated issues of new shares and lack financial soundness, and that they may practise cross-subsidization policies which distort the efficient allocation of productive resources.

1.5 LATERAL INTEGRATION

Similar to the conglomerate, a term used to indicate some degree of common interest between the combining firms. This may be in respect of labour skills or types of capital employed or in product outlets, e.g. the interlocking of Debenhams, J. Hepworth and Habitat in 1986.

1.6 MEASURES OF SIZE

It is difficult to make a precise distinction between a small firm and a large firm. Today there are about 400,000 private companies and some 11,000 public companies. However, not all private companies could be described as small, nor all public companies as large. In addition, there are many sole traders and partnerships. In 1971, the Bolton Committee of Inquiry into small firms reported that there were 820,000 of them, responsible for 14% of GNP; it employed four principal criteria in its perception of a small firm:

(*a*)   *Number of employees*
(*b*)   *Independence*
(*c*)   *Relatively small market share*
(*d*)   *Personal Management by owner*

In determining what is a large firm, economists frequently use two measures. The *aggregate concentration ratio* refers to the percentage of total manufacturing output produced by the hundred largest firms.

The *five-firm concentration ratio* is a *market concentration ratio* which is frequently used to measure the degree of concentration within a particular industry. It shows that since the late 1960s the five largest firms have accounted for over 90% of the domestic output in 25% of the various manufacturing groups or orders.

Note: The Standard Industrial Classification comprises more than twenty divisions, described as *Orders,* an example being the Food, Drink and Tobacco Group. There is a further sub-division into almost two-hundred *Minimum List Headings.* This classification provides the *official* definition of an industry.

2. FINANCING GROWTH

2.1 SOURCES OF FINANCE

There are several possibilities:

(a) Self-finance
This is a most important source with up to 70% of new investment being financed from ploughed-back profits.

(b) External sources
The remaining 30% of private sector investment comes from sources outside the firm.

(i) Bank loans Traditionally, UK banks have considered their primary function to be the provision of working or circulating capital to agriculture, industry and commerce. About one third of external funds available to firms come from this source.

(ii) Government finance Large sums of public money are administered through a vast number of agencies in the forms of loans, grants and subsidies. Much of it is related to regional development policies (see 6.4.3).

(iii) Trade credit Terms may be negotiated, but in principle a month for settlement is normal.

(iv) Capital market This is the market in long-term loanable funds for periods of years, as distinct from the short-term market in money for periods usually of three months. The market operates through a large number of intermediaries which specialize in particular types of investment. They are concerned with raising fresh capital and with trading in existing financial assets, e.g. insurance companies, pension funds, merchant banks, building societies.

2.2 THE STOCK EXCHANGE

While it is true that the Stock Exchange has a residual role in raising fresh capital through new issues, its primary purpose is implied by its name. It provides the facilities through which existing stocks and shares can be bought and sold. However, in so doing it provides the basis which makes it possible to raise fresh capital from investors. Firstly, investment is more likely when the investor knows that he can always revert to cash by selling his securities through the Stock Exchange. Secondly, before a company's shares are *listed* and a price *quoted*, the Stock Exchange Council will examine the company's credentials very carefully; therefore the investor may have some confidence that he is making a bona fide investment. Thirdly, the market prices of shares quoted gives the investor a fair indication of a company's performance.

Companies may seek to raise long-term capital through *debentures* – which guarantee a fixed rate of interest – or they may sell shares (equity) in the company which yield whatever dividend the company decides to pay from trading profits. A new issue will probably be managed by a merchant bank specializing in this area (an issuing house) which will appeal to the general public, usually through newspaper advertising. It then *underwrites* the issue, i.e. guarantees to absorb any shares not taken up, for later disposal through the Stock Exchange. In this process it may be assisted by *stags*, speculators who specialize in new issues.

An existing public company may decide to raise new share capital through a *rights issue*, which gives current shareholders the right of purchase at a favourable price.

2.3 SMALL BUSINESS FINANCE

In principle, access to the capital market is restricted to publicly quoted companies. The very many sole traders, partnerships and small private companies must rely on bank loans which are expensive and stringently administered for practical reasons.

(a) Gearing

Small firms are likely to be more highly *geared* than large public companies, i.e. a large part of their assets is financed by bank loans, not shareholders' funds. These loans must be serviced regardless of how well the company is performing, whereas with the public company which is experiencing a bad patch, dividends are reduced. The small firm therefore stands a greater chance of failure.

(b) Diversification

The large firm is likely to have more diversified activities and therefore a greater spread of risk.

In 1979, the Wilson Committee reported on *The Finance of Small Firms*, recognizing the problems. It made a number of recommendations.

(i)   *Guarantee Scheme for Bank Loans* State-backed, the scheme was implemented in 1981.

(ii)   *Small Firms Investment Company* (SFIC).

(iii)   *English Development Agency* (EDA).

(iv)   *Small Business Agency.*
The last three were to be state-sponsored intermediaries for the raising of investment capital for small businesses.
(v)   *Unlisted Securities Market (USM).* This was established by the Stock Exchange in 1980 and makes it easier and cheaper for small public companies to raise capital through unlisted shares.

3. MONOPOLY

3.1 IN FAVOUR OF MONOPOLY

One of the central fears of the excessive growth of individual firms, particularly in a society rooted in the presumed benefits of competition, is that monopoly will result. Yet in certain circumstances it can be argued that monopoly gives certain advantages:

(a) Economies of scale
Theory may suggest that in certain industries – e.g. UK steel – benefits can only be fully enjoyed through a very large-scale monopoly enterprise.

(b) International competitiveness
The case above is reinforced if we consider the need to compete internationally with large-scale overseas producers, e.g. steel producers in the USA, Germany and Japan.

(c) Stabilizing influence on the economy
The monopoly firm may be more resistant to fluctuations in aggregate demand than the firm operating on slim profit margins in a highly competitive environment. With a stronger chance of survival, it gives greater security to work-force and shareholders.

(d) Avoidance of uneconomic duplication
Even in the nineteenth-century heyday of laissez-faire, parliament granted monopoly rights to railway companies operating between two destinations. Similarly, the duplication of distribution networks for the utilities – gas, electricity and water – would clearly be wasteful.

(e) Competition costs
Fiercely competitive markets may lead to very high advertising budgets, the cost of which is ultimately borne by the consumer. Moreover, cut-throat competition may so reduce profits that sound enterprises are driven out of business.

(f) Research and development costs
The Austro-American economist, Schumpeter, pointed to the high costs of innovation in an industrial era increasingly dominated by high technology. It can be argued that only the monopoly firm with

an assured market can afford the risk and raise the investment funds.

3.2 AGAINST MONOPOLY   There are countervailing arguments:

(a) Inefficient resource allocation
Economic theory indicates that monopoly power is exercised deliberately to restrict output in order to maximize monopoly profit. While this may be in the interest of the firm, there is a distortion of the allocation of the factors of production, with unit costs higher than they would have been in a competitive market.

(b) Loss of innovation
In the absence of competition, the firm is under no pressure to innovate, either in product design or in production technique. The economy therefore stagnates.

(c) Restriction of consumer choice
For the consumer it is 'take it or leave it' at the price determined by the monopolist.

(d) Unfair discrimination
The monopolist may use his power to discriminate 'unfairly' between segregated parts of his market.

3.3 THREE RESPONSES TO MONOPOLY   The contradictory nature of the traditional arguments for and against monopoly lead to three possible responses.

(a) Pure laissez-faire
On this view, government should *never* intervene in the working of a market economy, even when market forces produce monopolies.

(b) Clear legislative rules
Other free marketeers take the view that there should be non-discretionary rules on the American model, which clearly outlaw monopolies and restrictive practices.

(c) A pragmatic approach
This is the British approach, judging each case on its merits. In this school of thought are those who would concentrate on the way that monopolists behave – on whether their restrictive practices militate against the consumer's interests.

4. RESTRICTIVE PRACTICES

4.1 CARTELS

Price rings agree to charge the same prices. There are none of the economic advantages of full mergers and they are usually illegal. However, informal arrangements are easily made.

4.2 RIGGING TENDERS

The dominant firms in the industry agree in advance who will carry out the work and rig their tenders accordingly, to the detriment of the customer.

4.3 RESTRICTION OF INTERNATIONAL COMPETITION

Monopolists in two countries make a reciprocal agreement not to compete in each other's home markets.

4.4 'FULL LINE FORCING'

The monopoly supplier insists that the wholesaler or retailer takes the full range of his products as a condition of supplying the one which is wanted.

4.5 RESALE PRICE MAINTENANCE (RPM)

In order to secure as wide a market as possible – even through uneconomic low profit outlets – the manufacturer insists upon a minimum retail price as a condition of supply.

4.6 DEALERSHIPS

The product is handled only through specified outlets. Consumer choice is therefore restricted but, more significantly, so is freedom of entry to the market.

4.7 AGGREGATED REBATES

These are paid over a period of years on condition of loyalty to the supplier, which makes it extremely difficult for new entrants to the market.

5. BRITISH COMPETITION POLICY

5.1 MONOPOLIES AND RESTRICTIVE PRACTICES (INQUIRY AND CONTROL) ACT, 1948

This was the first UK legislation. It set up the Monopolies Commission to report on situations in which one firm or group of firms – acting in concert – controlled at least one third of the market. Since it was purely advisory, the Commission lacked teeth and most of its recommendations were ignored.

5.2 RESTRICTIVE TRADES PRACTICES ACT, 1956

The Act separated investigations of unitary monopolies from those of restrictive practices by groups of firms. Such practices had now to be registered with a Registrar of Restrictive Practices. The latter was empowered to bring cases before a Restrictive Practices Court which would determine whether the practices were against the public interest. This would be so unless they could satisfy at least one of seven *gateways*:

(a)　　　*Protects the public from injury*
(b)　　　*Prevents local unemployment*
(c)　　　*Maintains exports*
(d)　　　*Gives special benefits to consumers*
(e)　　　*Operates against existing restrictions on competition*
(f)　　　*Supports other acceptable restrictions*
(g)　　　*Promotes fair trading terms for buyers and suppliers*

Since 1956, over 3,000 restrictive practices have been registered. Relatively few have been brought before the court and when this has occurred, they have usually been dissolved voluntarily in anticipation of an unfavourable decision by the court.

5.3 'INFORMATION AGREEMENTS'

Arrangements whereby firms notified each other formally of their prices and conditions were considered a restrictive practice for the first time in 1968. At the same time, an eighth gateway was added: agreements should neither restrict nor deter competition.

5.4 MONOPOLIES AND MERGERS COMMISSION (MMC), 1965

The name of the Commission was changed and its scope enlarged to include mergers as well as existing monopolies.

5.5 FAIR TRADING ACT, 1973

This established the Office of Fair Trading (OFT), with a Director General (DGFT). It opened the way for restrictive practices legislation to be extended to services in 1976.

5.6 RESTRICTIVE PRACTICES ACT, 1976

This was a consolidating act, with the DGFT now made responsible for bringing cases before the Restrictive Practices Court (RPC).

5.7 COMPETITION ACT, 1980

The existing anti-monopoly arrangements were retained and reinforced and the MMC was given the power to investigate the efficiency of nationalized industries. The DGFT was empowered to deal directly with firms on the subject of restrictive practices, resorting to the MMC only if the company would not respond. Special attention was to be paid to attempts to restrict competition from small firms.

5.8 CURRENT COMPETITION POLICY

The 1973 and 1980 Acts provide the framework of policy in the 1980s, administered through three institutions; the OFT, the MMC and the RPC. The main features are:

(a) A statutory monopoly
This exists when a firm has at least 25% of the market as a buyer or seller (a *scale* monopoly), or when a number of firms in collusion control 25% of the market (a *complex* monopoly) and operate in a way which restricts competition, e.g. price leadership.

(b) Mergers
Proposed mergers can be referred for investigation when the combining firms control at least 25% of the market, or when the merger involves gross assets in excess of £15m.

(d) Monopolies and Mergers Commission
The MMC comprises 26 part–time members and a full-time Chairman, all appointed by government. There is no *automatic* reference of statutory monopolies to the Commission; it is made primarily at the discretion of the DGFT, who collects information on whether a firm's activities fall within the ambit of current legislation. To maintain consistency in his decisions, he observes certain criteria:

(i) Market structure Concentration ratios give a good indication of changes in market structure.

(ii) Performance indicators These provide a useful measure of economic efficiency and include: return on capital; ratio of capital to turnover; profit margins; price changes.

(iii) Conduct indicators These provide a guide to whether the firm's behaviour is in the consumer's interests. They include: evidence of price discrimination or price leadership; customer complaints; evidence of merger proposals; advertising expenditure in relation to sales volume.

The MMC has no powers of enforcement. It reports to government, which decides whether to act. In the extreme, government may make an *order* requiring the divestment of assets or the splitting of firms. In practice, it is more likely that the DGFT will be asked to approach the firms to persuade them to respond voluntarily.

(d) Restrictive practices
A distinction should be made between the restrictive practices of a single firm (see 4. above), and those which are the result of an agreement between firms. There is no separate legislation covering the former case, which the DGFT will take into account when deciding on a reference to the MMC. In the second case, he may refer to the RPC; since this is a court with powers of enforcement, competition policy is sometimes thought to be more effective in respect of collective agreements than in restraining monopoly. The MMC is only an investigative body.

5.9 EEC LEGISLATION

Community competition legislation takes precedence over national anti-trust laws through authority derived directly from the Treaty of Rome:

(a) Article 85
A prohibition of collective agreements which result in the restriction of competition, e.g. price rings and market sharing. However, the article refers only to agreements which affect trade *between* members.

(b) Article 86
This prohibits a dominant firm from using its power to exploit the consumer.

(c) Articles 92–94
Subsidies to firms or industries are prohibited if they pose a threat to competition.

While it is true that Community law takes precedence over national law, these articles apply only to firms engaged in inter-state trade.

A further criticism of the lack of comprehensiveness of EEC policy is its failure to vet mergers and takeovers. However, if the Commission finds that a firm *has* infringed the anti-trust articles, it can ban the practice and impose fines of up to 10% of the sales resulting from the practice. Despite recent evidence that the EEC is adopting a firmer approach to restrictive practices and state subsidies, it is nevertheless clear that the ultimate objective of harmonization of trade law is far distant.

6. EVALUATION

6.1 'BIG IS BEAUTIFUL'?   The 1960s and 1970s were the age of the takeover and merger on the broadly accepted view that 'big is beautiful'. Combinations continue of course but more cautiously, since both firms and governments are more conscious of the diseconomies which can result. In this changed climate of opinion, there have been *de-mergers*, particularly of conglomerates which have divested themselves of extraneous activities to concentrate their management expertise on those areas where they have most experience. This has often resulted in *management buy-outs*.

A further reason for some move to the smaller scale has been the need to respond rapidly to a changing technological environment, e.g. the electronics sector.

6.2 CONCLUSIONS   The available evidence does not in present circumstances suggest that mergers lead to any significant increase in economic efficiency. The most likely motivation would seem to be managerial aspirations for security, status and salary.

In the area of government competition policy, there is still confusion with a blend of the pragmatic approach (the MMC) and the legalistic approach (the RPC). The objective has been to resolve the fundamental problem, i.e. the discrepancy between maximum profit and net social benefit which results from the lack of competition. The manifestation is poor products at high prices. Policy so far does not seem to have been successful in generating dynamism in UK industry, and some economists advocate the tougher legislative and statistical approach to mergers as practised in the USA.

Note. The *Herfindahl-Hirschman Index* is a sophisticated statistical calculation of market concentration which, in conjunction with Justice department guidelines, provides a firm basis for American competition policy.

While still a part of syllabuses, questions based exclusively on the material of Section 2 are now less common.

MULTIPLE CHOICE

A steelmaking firm acquires a company producing iron ore and an engineering company. This is an example of
(*a*)   lateral integration;
(*b*)   horizontal integration;
(*c*)   vertical integration;
(*d*)   diversification.   (*AEB, November 1985*)
Key References 1.2; 1.3; 1.4; 1.5; *Answer* (c).

Which of the following is NOT an activity associated with the long-term capital market?
(*a*)   New issue underwriting;
(*b*)   Discounting bills;
(*c*)   Stockjobbing;
(*d*)   Making 'rights issues'.   (*AEB, November 1983*)
Key References 2.1(b) (iv); 2.2; *Answer* (b).

ESSAYS

What is the theoretical justification for mergers? In the light of recent evidence on the efficiency and performance of merged firms, do you think that it would be sensible for the government to adopt a more stringent policy towards mergers?   (*JMB, Special, June 1982*)
Key References 1.2–5; 3.1; 3.2; 4.1–7; 5.1–8; 6.1; 6.2.

Monopoly is neither good nor bad but has the power to be either.
                                                      (*AEB, November 1985*)
Key References 3.1; 3.2.

LOCATION OF INDUSTRY

CONTENTS

1. LOCATIONAL THEORY

1.1 COMPARATIVE COSTS

In a perfectly competitive economy, the profit maximizing firm must find the location which offers the lowest unit costs. The theory of *comparative cost advantage* used to explain international trade (see Ch. 17. 1.4) is equally applicable to the location of domestic industry. The factors which determine these costs and led to an industry's original location will change through time. Meanwhile, additional cost advantages will accrue to the firm in the form of *external economies of scale*.

1.2 EXTERNAL ECONOMIES OF SCALE

The benefits are not restricted to one firm as a result of its *own* expansion (internal economies), but are enjoyed by all firms in the area as a result of the *industry's* expansion. They include:

(a) Specialization between firms
Just as division of labour within the firm increases output, so specialization between firms is facilitated when they are in close proximity and with similar results.

(b) Pool of skilled labour
Many regions have enjoyed a tradition in a particular type of labour skill because of the concentration of an industry in that area. A new firm entering the industry would know where to find that skill.

(c) Growth of subsidiary industries
A high degree of concentration will lead to the development of subsidiary activities which focus upon supporting and servicing the main industry.

(d) Specialist markets
These are encouraged, to the advantage of the participating firms.

1.3 INDUSTRIAL INERTIA

Even when the original reasons for an industry's location have disappeared and other areas offer lower costs, the external economies may provide an offset which makes firms reluctant to move. Moreover, to the extent that they enjoy supra-normal profit they are cushioned against the effects of higher costs.

1.4 'FOOTLOOSE' INDUSTRIES

The original cost advantages of one area over another hinge chiefly upon the availability of energy and the cost of transport. As these have improved, so cost differentials have been reduced and in general industry has become more 'footloose', i.e. able to locate itself anywhere. Clearly, this will be less true for *bulk reducing industries* such as smelting, and more true for *bulk adding industries* such as brewing where the cost advantage lies in proximity to the market.

2. THE LOCATION OF UK INDUSTRY IN A FREE MARKET ECONOMY

2.1 HEAVY INDUSTRY BEFORE 1914

The locational pattern of nineteenth-century industry in a laissez-faire economy provided the seeds of many modern regional problems. In this period was created the foundation of heavy industry, which was particularly susceptible to comparative cost advantages.

(a) Proximity to coal
Steam was the motive power of the period and it was clearly cheaper to take industry to the coalfields grouped around the Pennines, Central Scotland and South Wales, than to take coal to other locations.

(b) Proximity to raw materials
This was the principal factor in determining specialization between the coalfields, particularly because of the bulk of the materials employed. The West Riding had access to local wool; Lancashire to American cotton via the port of Liverpool; Middlesbrough to iron ore, etc.

(c) Miscellaneous influences
Other lesser factors had some influence upon comparative costs, e.g. Pennine soft water favoured the Lancashire and Yorkshire textile industries; the humid Lancashire climate was suited to cotton spinning etc.

2.2 LIGHT INDUSTRY BETWEEN THE WARS

The old heavy industries continued to be located in the same areas for the original reasons. However, the new industries were very different in character. They were directed to the consumer. For the first time, a whole new range of goods became available, e.g. wireless and domestic electrical equipment; new packaged foods and confectionery; mass-produced furniture.

Different considerations governed comparative costs.

(a) Road transport

In the nineteenth century, localization had been encouraged by the canals and railways. By the 1930s, road transport was well developed; it was often cheaper and certainly more flexible. Moreover, the products of the new industry were less bulky and it was therefore far more 'footloose'. This position was accentuated by:

(b) New forms of energy

While nineteenth-century industry had been directly dependent upon coal, twentieth-century industry turned to gas, electricity and oil which could be transmitted cheaply to any part of the country.

(c) Proximity to the market

For the new consumer industries, the primary consideration was proximity to large centres of population. It might immediately be thought that such centres on the coalfields would have provided an attraction. However, it was the old heavy industries which were first hit by depression, and high unemployment was hardly consistent with high consumer spending power. Consequently, there was a natural gravitation to London and the South East.

The Midlands, which might have been as badly affected as the North, benefited from the new motor vehicle industry, located there for the older cost consideration of coal, steel and engineering expertise.

3. THE UK REGIONAL PROBLEM

3.1 GENESIS OF THE PROBLEM

While it is true historically that there are always some regions which are in decline while others expand, the modern problem can be traced to the inter-war period. As heavy industry declined and light industry grew, there emerged 'two nations', not specifically socially but geographically. The relatively prosperous South was separated from the depressed North by – in today's vernacular – 'the Watford gap'.

3.2 CHARACTERISTICS OF DEPRESSED REGIONS

The evidence of the 1930s and of more recent times points to certain features:

(a) High unemployment

Excessive specialization means that when the key industry declines, there is little alternative employment. Since local income suffers a major reduction, the surrounding service industries will be adversely affected, with further effects upon employment.

(b) 'De-skilling'

In areas of chronic long-term unemployment, the work-force loses the opportunity to develop skills.

(c) Low educational attainment

There is substantial evidence to indicate that pupils are demotivated when they believe that the future offers only unemployment.

(d) Urban decay

When a major city is the centre of a depressed region, e.g. Liverpool (and other cities) in 1986, there is a downward spiral. Depopulation occurs (in Liverpool currently at the rate of 10,000 a year); the housing stock deteriorates, leaving vast numbers of unoccupied derelict premises. Simultaneously, the commercial and industrial infrastructure degenerates, making new investment even less likely.

3.3 SUMMARY OF THE REGIONAL PROBLEM

In 1986, the problem is more complex than it was in the 1930s. In fact, it may be argued that there are several distinct problems which call for a flexible response.

(a) The structural problem

This is the original problem reflected in the North/South divide.

(b) The congestion problem

In the South-East, this is the mirror image of the North's problem of decline.

(c) The rural problem

The isolation of, for example, the Scottish Highlands and Islands as well as parts of the South West, usually restricts employment opportunities to small farming and fishing and seasonal tourism.

(d) The inner city problem

This is not restricted to the North, but is now also found in London and the Midlands.

(e) A regional problem or a national problem?

In the 1950s, the age of 'the affluent society', the original regional problem was not so acute. However, it began to re-emerge during the late 1960s, the broad drift of government's policy response being to transfer resources from the prosperous South and Midlands to the depressed North as a means of economic regeneration. By the mid-seventies, however, previously prosperous areas – particularly in the Midlands – were also suffering from recession and this response no longer seemed so appropriate. Subsequently, *de-industrialization* has increasingly become a national rather than a regional problem. The focus has therefore shifted from policies aimed at specific regions to a broader national industrial policy.

4. POSSIBLE GOVERNMENT RESPONSES

4.1 WHAT ARE THE OBJECTIVES?

With its emphasis upon the maximization of e.g. profits, revenue, returns and consumer satisfaction, conventional economic theory does little to clarify the objectives of regional policy. There are many desirable socio-economic goals, but precisely what does regional policy seek to maximize? Is it income, welfare, educational opportunity or even happiness? Since employment is measurable and is politically as well as economically desirable, this would seem to have been the principal objective. There are two possible approaches:

4.2 IMPROVE THE GEOGRAPHICAL MOBILITY OF LABOUR

A free marketeer might advocate the encouragement of wage differentials, which would attract labour to areas where presumably job opportunities existed. In government circles today, there is some disposition to this point of view, which in the extreme would deny the need for any regional policy. However, the mainstream view has been that the regional problem is the *consequence* of the free market. Moreover, the social and economic costs of migration are high. Family life is disrupted; new housing and social facilities must be built, while that which is left behind falls into disuse.

There are other objections:

(a) The multiplier effect (see Ch. 13, 2.1).
A substantial migration may so reduce aggregate demand within the region that the percentage rate of unemployment remains unchanged.

(b) Reduction of skilled workers
Those most likely to find employment elsewhere will be skilled. The region therefore loses those it needs most.

(c) Congestion elsewhere
Experience shows that this is the likely result of large population movements.

4.3 IMPROVE THE MOBILITY OF CAPITAL

In practice, the basis of regional policy has been to take industry to the worker. With a 'carrot and stick' approach, government has attempted to encourage investment in the regions. However, this approach also raises problems:

(a) Nullification of comparative advantage

If industry is not located in areas to which market forces would have drawn it naturally, there is a loss of efficiency and competitiveness.

(b) The branch factory syndrome

When large companies are persuaded to expand into the regions, they do so with branch factories. In recession, it is the branch which is the first to close.

(c) The excessive attraction of grants

There are a number of cases where it has been suspected that companies have opened a branch to collect the government grant, only to close it shortly after.

(d) Capital intensive industry

When subsidies are directed towards capital investment rather than directly to employment, the incentive is biased to capital intensive industry with a low demand for labour.

5. CHRONOLOGY OF REGIONAL LEGISLATION

5.1 RELIEVING REGIONAL UNEMPLOYMENT, 1934–1966

Two strategies can be detected in the approach to the regional problem. In the first period, 1934–66, the perceived problem was the structural North/South divide. The understandable – if in retrospect negative – strategy was to focus solely upon the relief of unemployment, considered in isolation from the economic side effects which the policies might produce.

(a) Special Areas Act, 1934

This Act saw the birth of regional policy. Four particularly depressed areas were designated and given some financial assistance, but with little response from industry.

(b) Distribution of Industry Act, 1945

The adoption of the new Keynesian approach to unemployment was matched by the development of a policy designed to even out the discrepancies between the regions. The 1934 areas were enlarged and renamed Development Areas, while the Board of Trade was empowered to build new factories for lease at favourable rents. The thrust of this Act was reinforced by the *New Towns Act 1946*, and the *Town and Country Planning Act 1947*. The underlying concept was that there should be a planned and concerted development of housing with industry. The 1947 Act introduced the Industrial Development Certificate (IDC), which remains the principal 'stick' amongst government's persuasive techniques. Required for planning permission for developments above a certain size outside the development areas, it is issued by the Department of Trade.

(c) Local Employment Act, 1960

While it is true that until the 1960s unemployment in the regions had continued to be in excess of the national average, in a period of national high employment it was not seen as an acute problem. When the discrepancies increased, regional policy was revamped. The Act replaced earlier legislation and substituted narrow *development districts* (unemployment black-spots) for the old, wider development areas. Capital for new buildings and assistance to local authorities in improving the economic infrastructure was therefore more highly concentrated.

(d) Local Employment Act, 1963

The same approach was continued, but with aid being extended to places within commuting distance of the development districts. Capital assistance was increased and now made available for the purchase of machinery.

(e) The National Plan, 1965

For a short period there was an attempt to co-ordinate the development of the whole national economy. The greater part of the country was divided into eight regions, each with a Planning Board of senior civil servants and a Planning Council of local representative. Each region would have its own development plan, co-ordinated with national economic policy. This approach was short-lived, although the Councils survived until 1979.

5.2 GROWTH AREA STRATEGY, 1966–86

At this time, there was a shift of emphasis from simply endeavouring to relieve unemployment to the more positive approach of trying to sow the seeds of growth which would itself resolve the unemployment problem.

(a) Industrial Development Act, 1966

Development districts were abolished in favour of five very wide *development areas.* This recognized the wider economic consideration that unemployment black-spots resulted from high cost locations and that to pour aid into them simply gave temporary protection from competition without resolving the underlying problem. Within the wider development areas there might be potential growth points – albeit away from existing centres of population – which would serve as magnets and this is where financial assistance would be concentrated.

(b) Special Development Areas, 1967

Under the pressure of increasing regional unemployment, there was a partial return to the earlier strategy. Localities, with particularly acute unemployment usually within the development areas, qualified for more extensive aid.

(c) Regional Employment Premium (REP), 1967

Employers in development areas received subsidies for the labour they employed. Since it was payable not only for new jobs but also for existing ones, it was criticized, but since it proved to be of some value it was retained for a number of years, finally being abolished in 1976.

(d) Hunt Report, 1969

Some regions of low growth, depopulation and deteriorating economic infrastructures complained that they received no aid. The Hunt Commission investigated and recommended some financial assistance at a reduced level. The government accepted in principle, and new *intermediate (grey) areas* were established.

(e) Conservative policies, 1970–74

There was at first little enthusiasm for increasing the degree of government intervention. However, by 1972 – with national unemployment above 1 million for the first time since the 1930s – government felt obliged to make a 'U-turn' in both its macro- and microeconomic policies. *The Industry Act, 1972* made available substantial investment assistance across the country. Differentials for the regions were maintained by increasing the level of aid which they received.

(f) Labour policies, 1974–79

By the mid-1970s world recession, rising inflation and unemployment, coupled with balance of payments crises, appeared to translate a purely regional problem into a national problem. Government made a series of *ad hoc* responses to what appeared to be the disintegration of the industrial structure, using the powers to dispense financial assistance embodied in the 1972 Act, reinforced by their own *Industry Act 1975*.

(g) Conservative policies, 1979–

The basic framework of regional aid which had been established by 1970 was maintained. Special Development Areas, Development Areas and Intermediate Areas qualify for assistance – but at diminishing levels, in that order. The pattern of assistance is similar throughout but, unsurprisingly in a period of public expenditure restraint, grants have been cut.

Selective aid is still available under the 1972 Act. Consistent with a free market philosophy, while IDCs are still in force there is now a less stringent requirement for them. The one major innovation has been the establishment of *Enterprise Zones*. These are sites of about 500 acres, the attraction of which is the reduction of bureaucratic 'red tape'. There are no training board requirements, planning procedures are simplified, factories are exempt from industrial rates and there are tax advantages. This approach reflects the government view that economic problems are better resolved by the market operating in a favourable environment rather than by government intervention which results in market distortion.

6. EVALUATION OF REGIONAL POLICIES

6.1 FAVOURABLE ASPECTS

Department of Employment figures, certainly until the early 1980s, show quite clearly that by comparison with the 1930s, discrepancies in unemployment have been reduced. Policies have also had a significant effect in either creating or saving jobs. Moore and Rhodes (1977), suggested that since the mid-1950s regional policies had produced 350,000 jobs in manufacturing. For a similar period, Tyler, Moore and Rhodes (1979) concluded that manufacturing *output* was 20% higher in the regions than it would have been without government intervention.

Beyond the *direct* effects on employment and output, there may be *indirect* effects through the operation of the *regional multiplier*. (For an explanation of the multiplier, see Chapter 13, 2.1.) These effects will be reduced to the extent that government expenditure within a region leads to 'imports' from the rest of the country. Nevertheless Gudgin, Moore and Rhodes estimate that if the multiplier is allowed for, between 450,000 and 525,000 jobs were created.

Further, the Cambridge Economic Policy Group (CEPG) suggest that up to the late 1970s, 15% of all manufacturing jobs in the assisted areas were there because of regional policy. Other statistical studies indicate that in the period when regional policy was 'passive' – until the early 1960s – employment in the assisted areas was lower than expected, while in the following period to the late 1970s a strong, active policy was accompanied by employment higher than expected. An active policy is defined as the liberal use of the 'carrot' of financial incentives and the 'stick' of reduced issues of IDCs in the more prosperous regions.

6.2 UNFAVOURABLE ASPECTS

Critics point to the continued expansion of the number of areas receiving assistance and conclude that the overall situation has worsened. By the early 1980s, about 45% of the population lived in such areas. Supporters of the free market criticize the enormous cost of intervention and suggest that the extra burden of taxation and government borrowing destroys more jobs than are created.

Finally, it is a matter of speculation as to how many firms have been persuaded into unsuitable and uneconomic locations.

7. THE URBAN PROBLEM

7.1 DECLINE OF CONURBATIONS

From the early 1960s, there has been a continuing decline in manufacturing employment and population in all the major conurbations. Both have moved to small industrial towns, county towns and rural areas. For example, between 1959 and 1975 employment in the first two categories increased by an average of 23%, while in London *manufacturing* employment fell by 37.8% and in the conurbations, by 15.9%.

Several factors have contributed:

(a) Congestion
Urban expansion has made factory expansion difficult.

(b) Cost of urban land
This is high relative to other areas.

(c) Urban rates
With more environmental and social problems to deal with, rates are substantially higher.

(d) Footloose industry
Some surveys suggest that 60% of UK industry is now footloose.

7.2 INNER CITY DECAY

Movement out of conurbations has left the core of many cities with significant problems, since the shift was primarily out of the centre rather than the suburbs. The residual population has largely been low-income, unskilled or semi-skilled, often with substantial ethnic minorities and council accommodated. These factors imply a high degree of labour immobility.

7.3 URBAN POLICY

Three periods can be distinguished:

(a) Limiting urban growth, 1945–mid-1960s
The New Towns Act introduced 'green belts' around conurbations in an attempt to prevent the kind of 'ribbon' development which had occurred in the 1930s. This approach was reinforced by IDCs.

(b) Focus on social problems, mid-1960s–1977
Evidence of educational deprivation and the concentration of immigrants in city centres led in 1968 to an Urban Programme. The *Local Government Grants (Social Needs) Act, 1969* provided funds for a four-year period. In the same year, *Educational Priority Areas (EPAs)* were

established, as was the *Community Development Project* to look into ways of solving social problems.

(c) Focus on economic problems, 1977–1986

A government White Paper, *Policy for Inner Cities 1977*, marked a new phase in which the attempt would be made to renew the physical infrastructure of inner cities. The *Inner Urban Areas Act, 1978*, empowered local authorities to designate *improvement areas* and to give financial assistance to companies moving there. This approach was continued by the 1979 government which introduced *Enterprise Zones* (see 5.2 (g) above), and *Urban Development Corporations, (UDCs)*, whose task was to acquire and reclaim land for development and to attract private sector involvement.

8. EEC AND REGIONAL POLICY

8.1 THE EEC REGIONAL FUND

As a general principle EEC is opposed to subsidies which promote unfair competition. However, Article 92 of the Treaty of Rome states that: 'Aids intended to promote the economic development of regions where the standard of living is abnormally low or where there exists serious under-employment are compatible with a Common Market.' Such aids are provided through the Regional Fund, established in 1975.

The main criterion for assistance is unemployment rates. It is channelled through national governments as a supplement to their own regional assistance programmes.

In EEC terminology, Special Development Areas and Development Areas are classified as *European Peripheral Regions* and qualify for a higher level of assistance than other areas which are designated *Central Regions*.

There is a general disposition towards selective rather than automatic aid and towards investment rather than the support of operating costs.

8.2 THE EUROPEAN SOCIAL FUND

Funds are available for training, re-training and job creation. Britain has been a major beneficiary, with grants being used to support the Youth Opportunities Programme, the Youth Training Scheme, computer training programmes and employment subsidy schemes.

8.3 OTHER EEC SOURCES

There are two other significant sources of Community funds:

(a) European Investment Bank

This was set up by the Treaty of Rome as a non-profit-making bank, with capital subscribed by member states and funds borrowed in the world's capital markets. It makes loans, particularly for projects which improve the economic infrastructures of the depressed regions. Britain has accounted for about one-third of the total loans made, some 75% of this going to the assisted areas.

(b) European Coal and Steel Community Fund
The EEC has a fund which in certain circumstances can be used to assist redundant workers in these industries.

9. CONCLUSIONS

9.1 DE-INDUSTRIALIZATION UNDER LABOUR GOVERNMENTS, 1974–79

We have noted that by the mid-1970s, there was ample evidence of Britain's declining capacity to compete in international markets, reflected in a continuing reduction of manufacturing capacity. The government's response lay in an industrial strategy which assumed greater powers of planning and control through a *National Enterprise Board (NEB)*, envisaged both as a merchant bank and a state holding company. It was originally funded with a capital of £1,000m. of public money with a brief to buy into not only 'lame duck' firms, but also those with genuine commercial prospects. The 1975 Industry Act also introduced the concept of *planning agreements*, to be made voluntarily between industry and government but with development grants and selective financial assistance being contingent upon their successful conclusion.

9.2 DE-INDUSTRIALIZATION UNDER CONSERVATIVE GOVERNMENTS, 1979–86

The 1979 government was elected on the platform of 'pushing back the frontiers of the state'. It considered that many of the country's economic problems were self-inflicted, interventionist policies having distorted the market and become the primary source of economic instability.

The approach has therefore been one of disengagement. Industrial policy for the nation as a whole has sought to create an environment in which the market could function more effectively, on the general view that politicians and civil servants should not be engaged in activities of which they have no experience. Industry should therefore regenerate itself, encouraged by tax incentives favourable to profits – particularly of small businesses – and to the individual worker. This approach has been supported by making social security payments less attractive in order to reduce 'the poverty trap'. This is the situation in which the low-paid worker finds that additional earned income is immediately offset by reductions in his social security entitlement.

There has also been a continuing reduction in government's direct involvement in industry. This has meant a substantial narrowing of the scope of the NEB, of which government disapproved, and has also been expressed in a massive programme of *privatization*. In 1986, government promises that if re-elected the remainder of publicly owned industry – including the utilities coal, steel and railways – will be returned to the private sector.

EXAMINATION PRACTICE 6

MULTIPLE CHOICE

One or more of the options may be correct. Code –
- (*a*)   if 1, 2 & 3 are all correct;
- (*b*)   if 1 & 2 only are correct;
- (*c*)   if 2 & 3 only are correct;
- (*d*)   if 1 only is correct.

External economies of scale in the motor vehicle assembly industry may be possible where

1   a number of different car companies are geographically close to each other.

2   a car assembly company takes over a rival company operating at the same stage of production.

3   the growth of a car assembly company enables the greater use of division of labour.   (*AEB, November 1985*)

Key References 1.2 Contrast with Ch.4, 2.1 & 1, 2–5. *Answer* (d).

One or more of the options may be correct. Code as above. External economies of scale can be seen in

1   specialized services available to the car industry in the West Midlands.

2   the introduction of more sophisticated capital to double output in the chemical industry.

3   a large car firm's bulk purchases of components at favourable terms.
                (*AEB, November 1983*)

Key References 1.2 Contrast with Ch. 4.2.1 & 1.2–5. *Answer* (d).

ESSAYS

Evaluate the changes in regional policy in the United Kingdom since the Second World War.   (*JMB Special, June 1982*)

Key References Some background attention to 2.1–2; 3.1–3; 4.1–3; 5.1–2; 6.1–2.

Discuss what is meant by 'deindustrialization' in the British context. Is a policy to combat deindustrialization possible or desirable?
                (*JMB, June 1984*)

Key References 9.1–2; 3.3 and particularly 3.3(d); 5.1–2 and particularly 6.1–2.

Outline the influences which are chiefly responsible for the pattern of urban and regional unemployment in Britain. Does economics give any guidance as to whether or not it is desirable or possible to do anything to change this pattern?   (*JMB, June 1985*)
Key References 2.1–2; 3.1–3; 4.1–3; 6.1–2.

NATIONALIZED INDUSTRIES AND THE PUBLIC SECTOR

CONTENTS

1. PUBLIC FINANCE

1.1 THE PUBLIC SECTOR

The student who wishes to focus upon the *microeconomic* aspects of public finance which are dealt with below should first read section 1, Chapter 13, which outlines the purposes of a system of public finance. That chapter then goes on to concentrate upon *macroeconomic* aspects. Broadly, the public sector comprises those activities of central and local government whose product is not sold in the market and – with some important qualifications – certain aspects of the activities of public corporations. The most important of these corporations are the nationalized industries.

1.2 PUBLIC REVENUE

There are several sources:

(a) Central Government

Taxation is the major source, with borrowing in the capital and money markets covering any excess expenditure. Additionally, government has receipts from loans which it has made and from certain services – e.g. overseas military services – which it does sell.

(b) Local Government

Local revenue derives chiefly – and increasingly so in the 1980s – from the *local rates*. These comprise an *industrial rate* and· a *domestic rate*, levied upon the notional rentable value of all property. This valuation is made by the Inland Revenue and a *poundage* calculated by the local authority, sufficient to cover its anticipated expenditure: e.g. total rateable value £500; anticipated expenditure £100; poundage 20p in the £. However, such is the scale of modern local authority expenditure that it has to be assisted by central government through the *Rate Support Grant* (RSG). In 1986, this averages 46% of total local expenditure. Like central government, local authorities also borrow in the money and capital markets and sell certain services, e.g. car parking.

(c) Public Corporations

There is a diversity of public corporations, ranging from the BBC, the Forestry Commission and the Church Commissioners to the nationalized industries. Their funding is equally diverse and we shall later concentrate upon the financing of the latter. In principle, however, the amount of public funding is reflected in the degree of *public accountability* of these organizations.

2. CENTRAL GOVERNMENT TAXATION

2.1 SMITH'S CANONS OF TAXATION

Adam Smith suggested four principles which remain useful in evaluating a system of taxation.

(a) Equity
A 'fair' system should relate to the taxpayer's ability to pay, which implies that the rich should pay more. The application of the principle will, however, vary with society's notion of fairness. For example, the nineteenth-century principle of *proportionality* left rich and poor in the same relative position after tax as they had been before. In the twentieth century, the principle of *progressive taxation* taxes the rich more than proportionately.

(b) Economy
The tax yield should be great relative to the collection cost.

(c) Convenience
Tax should be raised in a way which is most convenient to the taxpayer rather than the tax collector.

(d) Certainty
Tax liability should be clearly understood in terms of amount, date and method of payment. Additionally, when considering the *efficiency* of a complete fiscal system attention must be given to the incidence and effects of different types of tax.

2.2 STRUCTURE OF UK TAXATION

Taxes are usually classified as:

(a) Direct
The tax is paid and the burden carried at the point at which it is levied:
(i)   Income Tax;
(ii)   Employees' National Insurance Contributions;
(iii)   Corporation Tax;
(iv)   Capital Gains Tax;
(v)   Capital Transfer Tax (CTT) – a gift or inheritance tax;
(vi)   Employers' National Insurance Contributions – a 'payroll tax';
(vii)   Stamp duties.

(b) Indirect

The burden is frequently shifted from the point at which the tax is levied. Such taxes are usually, but not always, *expenditure taxes*:

(i)   Value-added Tax (VAT) – an *ad valorem* (calculated on value) tax;

(ii)   Customs and Excise Duties – these may be *ad valorem* but are often *specific*, i.e. the tax is levied on quantity, not value.

Other specific taxes are direct, e.g. television and motor vehicle licences.

3. TAX INCIDENCE

(*Note:* It is recommended that the student be fully conversant with the operation of the price mechanism, covered in Part 3, before proceeding with this and the following section.)

3.1 SIGNIFICANCE OF TAX INCIDENCE

Some economists question the usefulness of an examination of the incidence of taxation in isolation from broad tax *effects* to which incidence is closely related. Nevertheless, it is of practical value to have some idea of the distribution of the *direct money burden* of taxation, with which a study of incidence deals.

3.2 ELASTICITY AND THE INCIDENCE OF EXPENDITURE TAXES

There are two fundamental propositions:

(a) The more inelastic the demand, the greater the incidence on the consumer

Where the Chancellor is looking for a predictable revenue as the primary purpose of a tax, he will look for a commodity in inelastic demand, e.g. petrol and tobacco.

(b) The more inelastic the supply, the greater the incidence on the producer

In general, the shorter the time scale, the more inelastic is supply. After a period of adjustment, it becomes more elastic. It follows that while in the short run the incidence of a new tax will be on the supplier, in the long run it moves to the buyer.

These two propositions indicate that the direct money burden of a tax is split between buyer and seller in accordance with the strength of their relative bargaining positions.

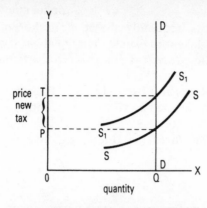

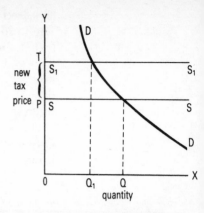

Figure 12(a). Expenditure tax with supply relatively elastic and demand perfectly inelastic.

Figure 12(b). Expenditure tax with supply perfectly elastic and demand relatively inelastic.

Figure 12(a) and (b) shows two limiting cases. In the first case, demand is perfectly inelastic, the same quantity OQ being bought, irrespective of price. With a starting price of OP, a new tax PT is imposed. The full burden is borne by the consumer, who now pays a new price OT

In Figure 12(b), while not *perfectly* inelastic, demand is inelastic relative to supply which is *perfectly elastic*. With an original equilibrium of OP, a new tax PT is levied. Supply is immediately cut from OQ to OQ_1. At the higher price OT the consumer again bears the full burden of the tax.

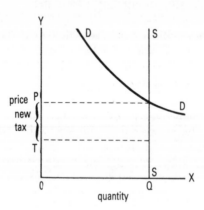

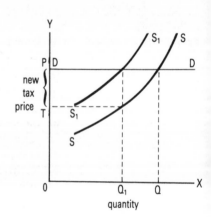

Figure 13(a). Expenditure tax with supply perfectly inelastic and demand relatively elastic.

Figure 13(b). Expenditure tax with demand perfectly elastic and supply relatively inelastic.

The opposite two limiting cases are illustrated in Figure 13(a) and (b). In the first example demand is *relatively* elastic, while supply is perfectly inelastic. The original equilibrium is at OP with quantity OQ. A new tax PT is borne solely by the supplier since he is unable to adjust his supply, and the buyer is only willing to pay OP for OQ. In Figure 13(b), supply is inelastic relative to demand which is perfectly elastic. The buyer will still only pay OP, so that the incidence of a new tax PT is entirely on the supplier, i.e. OP is now inclusive of tax.

*Note:*The analysis of tax incidence in respect of expenditure taxes on domestic trade can equally be adapted to a consideration of customs duties on international trade. What is important here is the relative elasticities of demand and supply for imports and exports.

3.3 INCIDENCE OF INCOME TAXES

For three reasons, it can be argued that the normal incidence of an income tax is upon the income recipient.

(a) The market determines the price and quantity of the end product

Particularly in recent years, it has been believed that a rise in income tax would be recouped through further wage claims which would be handed on in higher prices. The businessman may attempt to do so, but must recognize that he can only secure the price that the market will pay.

(b) Income tax is not a production cost

As far as corporate taxation is concerned, it cannot be treated as a cost which is built into the price structure. This is because profit is a realized surplus (or indeed a loss), which cannot be calculated in advance.

(c) Inelastic supply of factors for general use

The most telling argument rests on the observation of the generality of income taxes. While the supply of the factors of production to *particular* uses may be elastic, the supply for *general* use is inelastic, i.e. there is no more favourable use to which resources can be put after tax than existed before tax.

3.4 CONCLUSION

With figures available which, with an analysis of incidence, show the distribution of the direct money burden of income and expenditure taxes, it becomes possible to construct a tax system which pays attention to the principle of *equity*. Moreover, this analysis will be valuable in examining the *effects* of taxation.

4. EFFECTS OF TAXATION

4.1 EFFECTS ON PRODUCTION

Our concern here is to determine whether a particular tax system will have adverse effects on economic efficiency. There are two major considerations:

(a) Ability to work, save and invest

In principle, taxation of low incomes or of necessities may impair the physical capacity of the work-force, although in practice it will be difficult to establish what ought to be a net national minimum wage. *All* taxation will necessarily affect personal savings. Corporate saving will be less impaired since equity does not require that corporate taxation should be progressive. In respect of investment, *all* taxation reduces the funds available to the private sector.

(b) Incentive to work, save and invest

The presumed disincentive effect of taxation should not be taken for granted. For example, if all taxes were scrapped it might reasonably be assumed that, with increased net incomes, we would be more disposed to leisure and less to work. At the same time, we would be inclined to consume more and to save more and increased consumption would prompt more investment. In short, as a very broad generalization lower taxation would militate in favour of saving and investment but against work. In particular, however, individuals will respond to various taxes in different ways.

4.2 ELASTICITY OF DEMAND FOR INCOME

The individual's response to a reduction in net income will depend on his personal situation. His elasticity of demand for income is governed by:

(a) Elasticity of personal commitments

Where these are inelastic, higher taxes may provide a positive incentive to more work, particularly for the lower income groups.

(b) Inelastic demand for savings

This may be pertinent to middle income groups with a strong desire to save for *future* income. This implies inelastic demand for *present* income.

(c) Status

For upper income groups, the elasticity of demand for income may be zero, since their desire for income is related to the need for status rather than consumption or saving.

(d) Marginal rates of taxation and marginal units of income

Where there is tax liability, it is the rate applicable to the marginal unit of income which may have a disincentive effect. However, where hours of work are determined by collective agreement, any disincentive effect is nullified.

4.3 EFFECT ON PRODUCTION OF SPECIFIED TAXES	Three situations are assumed:

(a) A 'windfall tax'
Elasticity of demand for income is irrelevant in a situation where there is, for example, an unanticipated capital gain. Such situations offer considerable scope for taxation.

(b) Where there is an elastic demand for income
The effects will be:

(i) Income Tax There is a disincentive effect on earning and therefore work and saving.

(ii) Expenditure Taxes Since spending, not earning, is taxed, there is a lower disincentive effect. It will be still lower when only a small part of marginal income is spent on the taxed commodity.

(c) Where there is an inelastic demand for income
On this assumption, income and expenditure taxes will have an *incentive* rather than disincentive effect.

So far we have considered tax effects on the *volume* of production without reference to the effects on structure.

4.4 EFFECTS OF TAXATION ON THE STRUCTURE OF PRODUCTION	*Perfect competition* without taxation will produce a particular allocation of productive resources which it is desired to leave undisturbed. In this case:

(a) Taxes with least re-allocative effect
These will be used when taxation is introduced. Otherwise, resources will be diverted to untaxed or lower taxed uses.

(i) General taxes on income and expenditure These are non-selective and will therefore have no diversionary effects.

(ii) Taxation of monopoly profit Since the monopolist has, by definition, optimized his output, he has no incentive to reallocate resources. Monopoly profit absorbs the whole tax.

(iii) 'Windfall taxes' Since windfall gains are unanticipated, when taxed there will be no diversionary effects.

(iv) Non-selective taxation of land values Since the land is taxed without regard to the use to which it may be put, there is no diversionary effect.

(b) Taxation with the purpose of reallocating resources
Circumstances may arise in which there is a deliberate intention to divert resources from one use to another.

(i) Constraint of domestic demand A country with balance of payments difficulties may wish to focus upon the export trades.

(ii) Products with health hazards The taxation of tobacco at ever higher levels has not only the objective of raising revenue, but also of discouraging smoking.

(iii) Protective duties Such duties against imports will have the objective of encouraging the redeployment and fuller use of domestic resources.

(iv) Redeployment between regions Discriminatory taxation may be used to encourage growth in depressed regions.

5. CONTROL OF PUBLIC EXPENDITURE

5.1 PROBLEM OF RESTRAINING PUBLIC EXPENDITURE

Orthodox Keynesian thinking at one time took the view that it was possible to 'fine tune' aggregate demand, not only through the manipulation of taxation but also through adjustment of public spending. In practice, *demand management* proved to have an inflationary bias. It was much easier to increase public spending in the downswing of the business cycle than to decrease it in the upswing.

(a) Political reasons
Without any constitutional requirement for a balanced budget, in a democracy political popularity can be bought by spending more than is taken in tax revenue and financing the difference through borrowing. Moreover, Keynesianism taught that deficit financing of public spending was positively desirable in recession.

(b) Difficulty of checking departmental spending
Even within government's own spending departments there exist problems. In Cabinet, a function of ministers is to fight for an increased shared of total spending for their own departments. In this they will be assisted by their own civil servants and health, education, social services and defence are all likely to find very good reasons to resist cuts.

(c) Difficulty of controlling local authority and nationalized industry expenditure

Government has little direct control although it may seek to impose broad limits.

(d) Cyclical expenditure

Here government has no control, e.g. in recession there is an automatic increase in social security expenditure.

5.2 PARLIAMENTARY CONTROL

Only government may propose expenditure to Parliament and does so through *estimates* for the *supply services* (civil and defence), which the Commons debates and then *votes* sums for agreed purposes. To ensure that these are adhered to, an *Appropriation Act* is passed. Each spending department is then responsible for its own *Appropriation Accounts* which are audited by the *Comptroller and Auditor General*. His task is both to verify the technical accuracy of the accounts and to look for waste and inefficiency. The accounts are finally referred to the *Public Accounts Committee*, a very powerful cross-bench committee which publishes a report on which the Treasury must act.

By the early 1960s, it was apparent that this annual cycle of procedures was unequal to the task of long-range planning and control. In 1961, the *Plowden Committee* observed that 'the central problem is how to bring the growth of public expenditure under better control'.

5.3 PUBLIC EXPENDITURE SURVEYS

On the Committee's recommendation, a new series of annual White papers, *Public Expenditure*, began in 1969. These surveys were 'five-year plans' – rolled forward each year with appropriate modifications – which estimated the growth of public spending in all sectors, set against the anticipated growth in national income.

Before 1976, these surveys were made at *constant prices* or volume terms. In other words, the intention was to regulate the volume of *real* rather than *money* resources devoted to public sector use.

In a period of escalating inflation, the result was that as the price of inputs rose, more cash was allocated to the departments to enable them to sustain the volume of their programmes. Budgets were overspent, occasioning a steady rise in the size of the Public Sector Borrowing Requirement.

5.4 CASH LIMITS

In the sterling crisis of 1976, with inflation trending above 25%p.a., the limits to volume in real terms under the public expenditure survey system were reinforced by cash limits on spending programmes.

The transition was completed in 1981, when government decided to plan all spending in cash rather than volume terms. By this time, cash limits applied to about 60% of all public spending. In the construction of these plans, some allowance is made for the *anticipated* rate of inflation. If the *actual* rate is greater, then the *volume* of resources used must be reduced.

This approach to cash control has been extended in 1986 with the selective *'rate capping'* of those local authorities which government considers to have been profligate spenders. A ceiling is placed upon the percentage increase in its rate which the authority is permitted to make.

5.5 CONCLUSION

So far, we have been concerned with that part of the public sector whose activities are financed from public revenues. There remains to be considered those publicly owned industries which, while in receipt of public subsidy, still operate in the market like their private sector counterparts.

6. NATIONALIZED INDUSTRIES

6.1 DEFINITION

In 1976, the National Economic Development Office (NEDO), defined nationalized industries narrowly as public corporations whose assets are in public ownership; whose boards are not civil servants, but are appointed by the relevant Secretary of State; and which are primarily engaged in the market sector of the economy. The definition therefore excludes the activities of government departments, municipal undertakings and even those trading companies such as British Leyland in which the state has a large or complete shareholding, since these are not run by public corporations.

6.2 CASE FOR NATIONALIZATION

The arguments are wide-ranging and are not restricted to economic issues.

(a) Political
Clause 4 of the Labour Party constitution calls for 'the public ownership of the means of production, distribution and exchange' as a necessary step towards the attainment of socialism. In practice, after 1945 this was translated into a policy of nationalizing 'the commanding heights of the economy', interpreted as transport, power, iron and steel. Control of the economic infrastructure, it was thought, would assist planning.

The application of Clause 4, however, has remained controversial even within the Labour Party and in 1986, there appears to be no firm commitment to nationalization as it has been so far implemented.

There remain, perhaps, other forms of public ownership to be explored.

(b) Public interest
In the private sector, the profit motive means the aim to maximize the private or internal interest. No account is taken of external costs which must be borne by the public. Nationalized industries, on the other hand, must take account of the social interest; e.g. railways seek to make an overall profit while taking account of rural and commuter services, which do not easily pay their way. They are therefore cross-subsidized from more profitable services.

(c) Natural monopolies
Railways and public utilities may be considered natural monopolies in that duplication of services would be clearly wasteful of resources. The theory of the firm in monopoly tells us that supply will be regulated to maximize monopoly profit, to the social detriment. Such natural monopolies are therefore only safe, it is argued, in the hands of the state.

(d) Economies of scale
Some industries – such as coal, iron and steel – lend themselves to very large-scale production. Faced with international competition from giant producers in the USA and Europe after 1945, this seemed to imply the rationalization of such industries in the UK to create single national organizations. Moreover, these were the industries which had suffered from a lack of investment in private hands pre-war. Only the state could afford the scale of investment now required and to take the long-term view in waiting to reap the benefit of this investment.

(e) Improved industrial relations
The hope was expressed that the conflict of interest between labour and private employer would at least be reduced when the employer became the state.

6.3 CASE AGAINST NATIONALIZATION

There are equally forceful arguments:

(a) Monopoly power always neglects the consumer interest
The state is in a more powerful position than any private monopolist to reinforce its monopoly in any industry through, for example, protective duties and discriminatory taxation. Critics then argue that the consumer is even more exploited since his only recourse is to some impersonal, long-drawn-out and bureaucractic complaints procedure.

(b) Diseconomies of scale

By their nature, nationalized industries must operate on a very large scale, even when this proves uneconomic. The chief danger of diseconomies lies in unwieldy bureaucracy and an inflexibility of response to changing market conditions.

(c) Absence of market disciplines

The objectives of the nationalized industries suffer from having seldom been clearly defined. In the private sector, the incentive of profit is accompanied by the spur of loss; sooner or later the firm goes into liquidation. In the public sector, losses are absorbed in public subsidies; the organization is thus shielded from inefficiency and resources continue to be misallocated

(d) Political dangers

There is always the danger that the government of the day will use the nationalized industries for electoral advantage, e.g. employment or investment policies. This cannot be consistent with sound economic management.

6.4 PRICING POLICY

The early acts of nationalization simply required the corporations to make available supplies in appropriate quantities at prices which seemed to be in the public interest. There was a general expectation that in the long run the industries would break even. These vague objectives were clarified by three White Papers in 1961, 1967 and 1978.

The 1967 White Paper instructed the Boards to adopt *marginal cost pricing policies*. Since nationalized industries operate in a condition of imperfect competition, their prices tend to be *higher* than marginal cost, indicating that to improve allocative efficiency output should be increased. However, there are certain difficulties in accepting that marginal cost pricing will necessarily improve allocative efficiency by producing a closer simulation of perfect competition.

(*a*)   Should price be related to short-run or long-run marginal cost?

(*b*)   How will an organization like British Rail, providing various goods and services, raise adequate information to enable it to marginal cost each?

(*c*)   Marginal cost pricing will only improve the allocation of resources across the economy provided that all other prices equal marginal cost.

(*d*)   When long-run marginal costs decline over a very large output due to the economies of scale, losses will result if price is so determined.

6.5 FINANCIAL TARGETS

The 1967 White Paper also introduced investment appraisal techniques which distinguished those activities which were expected to produce a commercial rate of return from those which were considered to be provided as a social service. Initially, commercial projects were required to pass a Discounted Cash Flow test parallel to that employed in the private sector. However, difficulties arose and the 1978 White Paper introduced three criteria for the assessment of performance.

(a) Medium term financial target

These are set as returns per annum on capital employed for a 3–5-year period and take account of all the factors which affect the industry. Consequently, they vary from industry to industry.

(b) Required rate of return (RRR)

Beyond the target for the industry as a whole, any new programme of investment must show a return on capital of 5%, the RRR. This is seen as the opportunity cost of what the capital might have returned in the private sector. Within this constraint upon *broad programmes*, there is flexibility for management to establish its own investment criteria for *specific projects*.

6.6 NON-FINANCIAL TARGETS

To avoid the monopoly exploitation of the consumer as a means of achieving financial targets, other performance targets are set for each industry. Basically, these revolve around the stabilization or reduction of operating costs.

6.7 CONFLICTING CRITERIA

One criterion may conflict with another, particularly where the attainment of lower operating costs requires investment which does not meet financial criteria.

6.8 PUBLIC ACCOUNTABILITY

There is continued unease that the nationalized industries are insufficiently accountable to the electorate. The system as it has so far developed is as follows.

(a) Corporate boards

The chairman and board of each industry are appointed by the Secretary of State for that industry to which they are responsible for day-to-day operations. At least in theory the Secretary does not interfere and is only concerned – in consultation with his Cabinet colleagues – with long-term strategic decisions. Government is then responsible to Parliament, which is in turn responsible to the electorate.

(b) Parliamentary Select Committees

All-party select committees have observed the nationalized industries since 1951, and from 1956 the *Parliamentary Select Committee on Nationalized Industries* has investigated board reports and accounts.

Since 1979, this responsibility has been divided between Select Committees which oversee the activities of government departments. The objection to the select committee system is that MPs lack the personal expertise, the time and the professional administrative back-up to carry out the job thoroughly.

(c) Consultative Councils

These are organized on a regional basis for each industry, composed of laymen and with the responsibility of advising the boards, particularly in the representation of the consumer interest. Their weakness is that few amongst the general public are aware of their existence or the machinery for approaching them.

7. A FOOTNOTE ON PRIVATIZATION

7.1 MEANING

It should be noted that the term 'privatization' runs beyond denationalization, although this is perhaps its most significant aspect. It may also mean the sale of a portion of a nationalized industry while government retains a substantial shareholding, e.g. British Aerospace. It can also be construed as the development of some activities to a joint enterprise with the private sector, e.g. the formation of Allied Steel and Wire by British Steel and GKN.

Outside the area of nationalized industry, it also means the sale of shares in companies in which the NEB had an interest. Additionally, work previously carried out exclusively by municipal authorities and the NHS – e.g. refuse collection, hospital laundry and catering services – is now being put out to tender.

7.2 BROAD CASE FOR PRIVATIZATION

The Conservative government's case is based on the view that the market economy optimizes the allocation of productive resources. Additionally it is seen as a mechanism for widening share ownership, particularly amongst employees, and therefore of encouraging public rather than state ownership. It is also a means of rapidly reducing the PSBR. Instead of having to fund the investment programmes of public industries through its own borrowing, in private hands these industries become responsible for their own finance, competing in the capital market with other industries.

7.3 CASE AGAINST PRIVATIZATION

Beyond the arguments in favour of nationalization already discussed, there are certain specific objections.

(a) 'Selling the family silver'

This was the criticism levelled by Harold Macmillan, a former Conservative Prime Minister. It is a legitimate criticism to the extent that in the year of sale of a major industry, government receives windfall revenue which disguises the true size of the PSBR. It is less valid when it is understood that it is a sale *within* the family, from state to citizens.

(b) Will there be wider share ownership?

While the financial institutions (pension funds and insurance companies) are major purchasers, there is considerable doubt as to whether there will be any sustained increased in small shareholding, especially amongst employees.

(c) Strain on the Capital Market

In the year of sale of a major industry, vast new funds must be raised for the purchase of existing assets when these might have been used to finance new ventures.

MULTIPLE CHOICE

A progressive tax is defined as one which
(a)   falls more heavily on the rich than the poor;
(b)   increases proportionately with income;
(c)   increases more than proportionately with income;
(d)   redistributes income by taking from the rich and giving to the poor.   (*AEB, June 1985*)
Key Reference 2.1(a). *Answer* (c).

A local council, planning current expenditure of £500 million, receives 60% of its requirements from central government, 30% from rates and the remaining 10% from rents and other charges. The total rateable value of the local government district is £120 million. What general rate in the pound will have to be levied to raise the necessary rates revenue, assuming all ratepayers are assessed equally?
(a)   30p;
(b)   80p;
(c)   125p;
(d)   150p.   (*AEB, June 1984*)
Key Reference 1.2(b). *Answer* (c).

If price elasticity of demand is infinitely elastic and supply relatively inelastic, then the incidence of taxation will fall
(a)   entirely upon the buyer;
(b)   entirely upon the seller;
(c)   partly upon the buyer and partly upon the seller;
(d)   wholly upon the final consumer.   (*AEB, June 1984*)
Key References 3.2 and particularly Fig. 13(b). *Answer* (b).

ESSAYS

Examine and comment on the effects on the market for a good of the imposition of a specific tax.   (*O & CSEB, July 1984*)
Key References 2.2(b) (ii); 3.1–2; 4.4.

'We need to strengthen incentives, by allowing people to keep more of what they earn.' (Sir Geoffrey Howe, Budget Speech, 1979.) Give a broad outline of the UK tax system and say whether or not you agree with this statement.   (*JMB, June 1985*)

Key References For the first part, 2.2; then, 3.3; 4.1; 4.2; 4.3.

Discuss the main objectives of taxation, illustrating your answer with reference to the United Kingdom's system of taxation.

(AEB, June 1985)

Key References First read 1.1, then refer to Ch.13. 1.1–3, followed by 2.1 and 2.2, to *illustrate* your answer.

Nationalization

Since an active advocacy of nationalization no longer appears to be on the political agenda, questions specifically directed to the nationalized industries have been fairly rare in recent years. *Indirectly,* however, a knowledge of their structure and financial operation is important because of their significance to the Public Sector Borrowing Requirement and the money supply. (Initially, refer to Ch.13, 4.3.) *Direct* questions may be slanted to broader issues of allocative efficiency.

Define profits and outline their function in a free enterprise economy. How useful are measures of profitability as indicators of the efficiency of nationalized industries?   *(JMB, June 1980)*

Key References Ch. 11.7–3; 6.2–7.

Discuss the arguments for and against the closure of 'uneconomic' coal mines.   *(O & CSEB, 9633/3 & 9635/2, July 1985)*

Key References Ch. 13.1.1; 6.1–8, keeping in mind that you must focus on the idea of 'uneconomic'.

'Privatization represents by far the most effective means of extending market forces and in turn improving efficiency.' (Lord Cockfield, 1981.) Explain what is mean by efficiency in economics and discuss whether or not you agree with this statement about British industry.

(JMB, June 1983)

Key References 7.2; Ch.10, focusing on whether or not the market economy optimizes resource use, particularly in monopoly. Consideration then to 6.2–8.

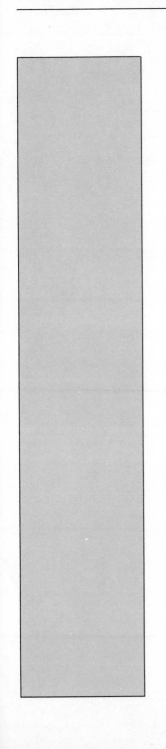

THE PRICE MECHANISM

THE INTERACTION OF DEMAND, SUPPLY AND PRICE

CONTENTS

144 Contents

1. THE EQUILIBRIUM PRICE

1.1 DEMAND AND SUPPLY DEFINITIONS

By the end of the nineteenth century it had been clearly established that no theory of value could be complete unless it took equal account of both demand and supply (See Ch.1, 1.8.).

(a)   *Demand* is the quantity of a commodity which a consumer is willing and able to buy *at a given price*.

(b)   *Supply* is the quantity of a commodity which a producer is willing and able to offer for sale *at a given price*.

The key phrase is 'at a given price', since it is impossible to envisage any quantity which will be bought or sold without postulating some price. This leads to two important conclusions. Firstly, demand and supply determine price and a change in one or the other will immediately induce a change in price. Secondly, demand and supply are themselves conditioned *by* price. These observations provide the twofold basis for our analysis.

1.2 DEMAND AND SUPPLY DETERMINE PRICE

This can be illustrated using tables of figures or graphs.

(a) Demand schedules

On the assumption of adequate market information it would be possible to formulate a schedule which showed how buyers in a particular market reacted to price changes. We would normally expect that the lower the price, the greater the quantity which would be bought.

Table 5. Demand schedule

Price per carton	Demand per month (millions)
£2	1.4
£1.60	2.2
£1.20	3.8
£0.80	6.1
£0.60	8.6

(b) Demand curves

The same information can be represented graphically as in Figure 14 (*cf* Ch.2, Fig 3). Note that in this example the curve flattens rapidly below point (b) and the graph will not accommodate any fall in price below 60p. This is a *normal* demand curve and is negatively sloped.

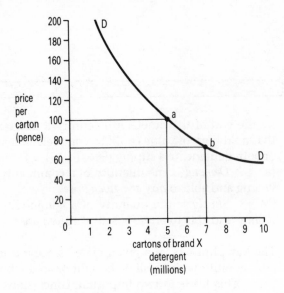

Figure 14. *Normal demand curve.* The curve portrays graphically the figures in Table 5.

(c) Exceptional demand curves
In certain circumstances the demand curve may be positively sloped, i.e. the higher the price, the greater the quantity bought. The following are some reasons:

(i) **Price rise of basic goods** When there is a rise in the price of, for example, staple foods, the lower income groups have less to spend on luxuries and may now substitute more of the higher-priced staple.

(ii) **Snob appeal** Some items like perfumes and fashion goods derive their attraction from their exclusiveness which is associated with a high price.

(iii) **Anticipated further price rises** It is commonly the case (and in fact pressure selling often depends on it) that when the price of an item is expected to *continue* to rise, as it does so sales increase.

(d) Supply schedules
In a similar way to demand, a schedule can be constructed which illustrates the observation that normally, the higher the price, the greater the quantity the producer is willing and able to offer to the market.

Table 6. Supply schedule

Price per carton	Demand per month (millions)
£0.75	1
£0.80	3
£1.20	6.4
£1.60	8.2
£2.00	9.2

(e) Supply curves

Once again this information can be reported graphically in a supply curve which normally slopes positively. Note that at a price of 70p, producers are unwilling to enter the market and supply is zero. Moreover, since the curve is concave we see that price must rise more than proportionately as supply is extended. The reasons for this will be examined in Chapter 10.

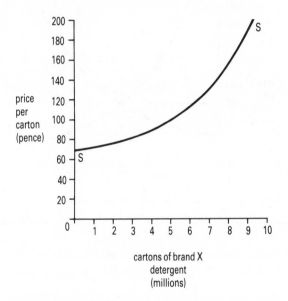

Figure 15. *Normal supply curve.* The higher the price, the greater the quantity the producer is willing to offer for sale.

(f) Exceptional supply curves

In some situations the slope of the supply curve may be reversed.

(i) Regressive supply In this case, the higher the price within a certain range, the smaller the amount offered to the market. This may occur for example in some labour markets where above a certain level, higher wages have a disincentive effect.

(ii) Fixed supply Where the commodity is rare or unique, e.g. the 'Mona Lisa', the supply remains the same regardless of price. This will be true in the short term of the supply of all things, particularly raw materials and agricultural products, since time must elapse before it is physically possible to increase output.

(g) Demand and supply in harmony

The *equilibrium price* brings demand and supply into balance. It is the price at which consumers are willing and able to take from the market exactly the amount which producers are willing and able to supply at that price. This process of adjustment is continuous, since no sooner has one equilibrium been achieved than forces are at work to disturb it and move the market to a new equilibrium. It is therefore a long-term concept; i.e. in the long run the market is perceived to be in balance. There is also the assumption of a flexible price, capable of moving down as well as up so that the market is always harmonized and cleared, i.e. there are no long-term surpluses either of end products or factors of production such as labour.

The concept is illustrated in Figure 16. The equilibrium price is £1 with 5 million sales.

Figure 16. *Equilibrium price.* Demand and supply are in balance at a price of £1 with 5 million sales.

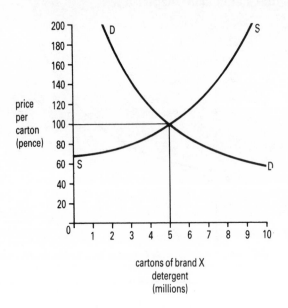

cartons of brand X
detergent
(millions)

---

2. CHANGES IN MARKET CONDITIONS

2.1 CHANGES IN DEMAND AND SUPPLY AFFECT PRICE: CHANGES IN PRICE AFFECT DEMAND AND SUPPLY

It is important to distinguish between the two; for example, a consumer may buy more or less detergent because of a change in his valuation of the product or because of a change in its price. Similarly, the entrepreneur may offer more or less detergent for sale because of a change in the circumstances in which he produces, or because of a change in market price.

The circumstances of valuation or production are described as the *conditions* of demand and supply. A change in these conditions will result in a movement of the whole curve to the right (an *increase*) or to the left (a *decrease*), with a resulting change in price.

Secondly, demand and supply themselves are affected by price changes and this is shown by movements *along the same curve*. This is the concept of *elasticity* which is revealed in the *slope* of the curve (see section 4). In order to avoid confusion, it is better to reserve the term *'extension'* to describe a movement to the right *along* the curves and *'contraction'* for a movement to the left.

2.2 AN INCREASE OR DECREASE IN DEMAND

This tells us that at any price selected on the vertical scale a greater of lesser quantity will be bought in consequence of a changed valuation by the consumer. In Figure 17, the original demand curve DD shows that at price OP, quantity OQ will be bought. Demand increases and shifts to the right to D_1D_1, with OQ_1 now purchased at price OP. Demand decreases and the curve shifts to the left to D_2D_2 with OQ_2 purchased at OP.

Figure 17. *An increase or decrease in demand.* At OP, demand increases from DD to D_1D_1 with OQ_1 purchased, or decreases to D_2D_2 with OQ_2 purchased.

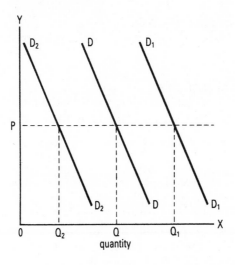

2.3 REASONS FOR A SHIFT OF THE DEMAND CURVE

For several reasons a consumer may change his valuation of a good or service.

(a) Changes in fashion or taste
It is difficult to give a full account of the reasons why some products capture the public imagination and secure a place in the market while others do not. Much market research aims to explain this, while advertising will apply the results in an attempt to increase the popularity of a product, i.e. shift its demand curve to the right. Similarly, campaigns such as those against smoking seek to move the curve to the left.

(b) Obsolescent products and new technology
Progress implies the replacement of dated goods with new.

(c) Taxes

Excise duties on tobacco and alcohol have the effect of restricting demand. Progressive income taxes redistribute income, with the result that the pattern of demand is affected. Demand is increased in the direction where the lower income groups concentrate expenditure and decreased for the higher income groups.

(d) Variations in purchasing power

This will occur because of changes in the level of nominal incomes or because of changes in the value of money. If the effect is to increase purchasing power demand will increase, and vice-versa.

(e) Anticipated profits

The entrepreneur's decision to invest in new equipment is conditioned by the return which he anticipates.

(f) An anticipated rise in price

To avoid the higher price, the demand curve immediately shifts to the right.

(g) Population structure

If the population is ageing, then the demand curve for those products consumed by the elderly moves to the right and vice-versa.

2.4 AN INCREASE OR DECREASE IN SUPPLY

By parallel reasoning, an increase or decrease in supply implies a movement of the supply curve to the right or left. At any given price the producer is prepared to supply more or less. Initially, at OP, he supplies OQ. A change in conditions produces an increase in supply to OQ_1 at the same price. With an opposite change he is able to supply only OQ_2 (see Figure 18).

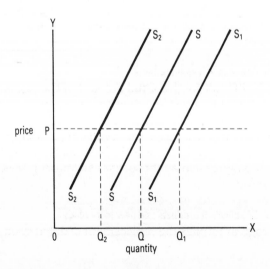

Figure 18. *An increase or decrease in supply.* At OP supply increases from SS to S_1S_1 with OQ_1 purchased or decreases to S_2S_2 with OQ_2 purchased.

2.5 REASONS FOR A SHIFT OF THE SUPPLY CURVE

There are several:

(a) Production costs
The cost to the producer of land, labour and capital will vary, as will their productivity.

(b) Unpredictable events
Supply may be interrupted by natural catastrophes, strikes or revolutions. Conversely, a bumper harvest may produce an unexpected increase in supply.

(c) Taxes
When an increased tax cannot be passed on to the consumer, production costs are raised.

2.6 THE IMMEDIATE EFFECTS OF CHANGED MARKET CONDITIONS

(a) The demand curve shifts
In Figure 19 the original equilibrium price is OP with OQ sales. An increase in demand to D_1D_1 raises price to OP_1, which *extends* supply to OQ_1. Conversely, a decrease in demand to D_2D_2 reduces price to OP_2, thus *contracting* supply to OQ_2.

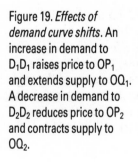

Figure 19. *Effects of demand curve shifts*. An increase in demand to D_1D_1 raises price to OP_1 and extends supply to OQ_1. A decrease in demand to D_2D_2 reduces price to OP_2 and contracts supply to OQ_2.

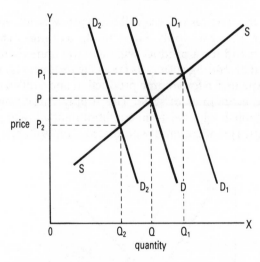

(b) The supply curve shifts
In Figure 20, conditions of demand remain unchanged while supply increases from SS to S_1S_1, inducing a *fall* in price to OP_1 and an extension of demand to OQ_1 where a new equilibrium is established. Conversely, a decrease in supply to S_2S_2 produces yet another equilibrium at OP_2 with sales of OQ_2.

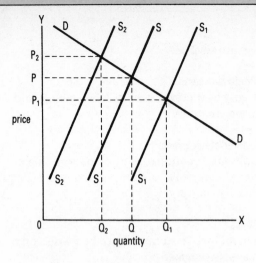

Figure 20. *Effects of supply curve shifts.* An increase in
supply from SS to S_1S_1 lowers price to OP₁ and
establishes a new equilibrium with OQ₁ bought.
A decrease in supply to S_2S_2 establishes equilibrium at OP₂
with OQ₂ bought.

2.7 THE LONGER-TERM EFFECTS OF CHANGED MARKET CONDITIONS

In the long term there will be an interaction between the conditions of demand and supply. For example, a change in fashion which increases demand for a product will have the immediate effect of raising price and extending supply as far as the producer is able. In the longer term, he gears up for volume production and unit costs are reduced through the economies of scale. The supply curve now shifts to the right to establish a longer-term equilibrium at a lower price than the original, with a greater quantity produced. This is illustrated in Figure 21.

Figure 21. *Long-term effects of changed market conditions.* From the original price equilibrium at OP demand increases to D_1D_1 to raise price to OP₁ and extend supply to OQ₁. Subsequently, the supply curve shifts from SS to S_1S_1 to *lower* price to OP₂ and extend supply still further to OQ₂.

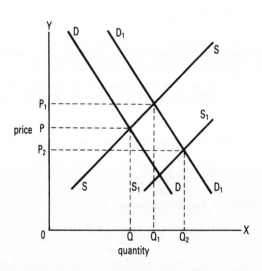

2.8 RELATIONSHIPS BETWEEN THE DEMAND FOR DIFFERENT GOODS

It is commonly the case that a change in the conditions of demand for one product will effect the conditions of demand for another.

(a) Competing demand

When two goods substitute easily for each other, e.g. two brands of ballpoint pens, they are in competing demand. An increase in the demand for one will lead to a decrease in the demand for the other.

(b) Joint demand

When two goods are complementary to each other, an increase or decrease in the demand for one will be accompanied by an increase or decrease in the demand for the other, e.g. motor vehicles and petrol.

(c) Composite demand

The demand for some products, particularly raw materials and semi-finished goods, comes from a variety of sources. Therefore, when there is an increase in the demand, for example, for sheet steel for refrigerators, the manufacturers of washing machines will also have to pay the increased price.

(d) Derived demand

In some markets, the demand for one good derives directly from the demand for another, e.g. the demand for most raw materials and semi-finished goods derives from the demand for the end product.

2.9 RELATIONSHIPS BETWEEN THE SUPPLY OF DIFFERENT GOODS

In a similar way, it is often the case that a change in the supply of one product will affect the supply of another.

(a) Joint supply

Depending on the state of technology, it is not possible to vary the supply of the main product without varying the supply of its by-products, e.g. beef and hides.

(b) Competitive supply

Observing the basic economic principle of opportunity cost, all things that we do not produce are in competition with those things which we do produce. In the more specific sense, specialized resources devoted to one use are in competition with the same resources which might be devoted to another, e.g. builders may build houses or hospitals.

3. INTERVENTIONISM

3.1 INTERFERENCE WITH THE MARKET MECHANISM

Throughout history, for moral or political reasons politicians have frequently been dissatisfied with the results produced by the market. However, market forces in all societies have continued to be resistant to attempts to artificially influence price through legislation, subsidy or taxation. Legislative controls in particular have proved markedly unsuccessful and have invariably had the same consequences.

(a) Shortages

Price controls are followed by reduced supply, queuing and rationing as a substitute for the distributive process of the price mechanism.

(b) 'Black markets'

Even in the most politically constrained societies, black markets continue to meet unsatisfied demand. Prices which they establish are likely to give a truer picture of demand and supply for that product.

3.2 RENT CONTROLS

A classic example of the consequences of intervention is the various attempts by post-war UK governments to provide protection for the tenant against excessive rents. The long-run result has been to establish a theoretical level of rents for accommodation which is no longer available. This is illustrated in Figures 22(a) and (b).

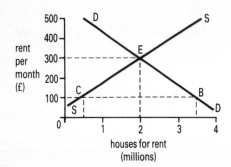

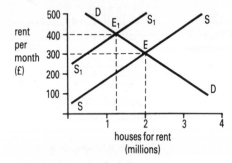

Figure 22(a). *Short-term effect of rent controls*. At equilibrium E, 2 million houses rented at £300 per month. A rent ceiling of £100 per month produces a shortage between B and C.

Figure 22(b). *Long-term effect of rent controls*. Disenchanted landlords decrease supply of rented houses, i.e. supply curve moves to left. A much higher equilibrium level of rent is established which is likely to influence actual rents even if government persists with rent restrictions.

In Figure 22(a), the equilibrium free market rent is £300 per month with 2 million houses for rent (point E). When a rent control of £100 per month is imposed, the number of houses available shrinks to .5 million (point C), while the number demanded is 3.5 million (point B). There is a shortage of 3 million.

In the long term, Figure 22(b) shows the volume of rented houses shrinking as they are abandoned in a state of disrepair, demolished and the land sold or converted to other uses, i.e. the supply curve shifts to S_1S_1 to a new market equilibrium, E_1. There are now only 1.25 million houses available at a rental of £400. Even if controls succeed in keeping actual rents below this figure, they are likely to be higher than if there had been no intervention.

3.3 SUBSIDIES

The market will also be distorted with undesirable results by attempts to sustain an artificially high price. Figures 23(a) and (b) illustrate the results of two different approaches to farm subsidies.

Under the deficiency payments system which operated in the UK prior to entry to EEC and shown in Figure 23(a), farm output of OQ was sold on the market at price OP. Each unit of output was then subsidized by PP_1 to give farmers the revenue they desired.

Under the EEC system there is intervention to ensure that a market price of OP_1 is sustained. At that price, the market itself will only absorb OQ_1. The Commission therefore purchases the surplus QQ_1 which is produced at this price, and butter and beef mountains accumulate.

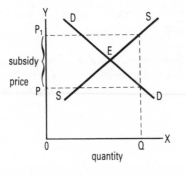

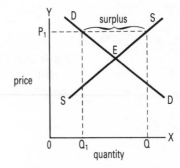

Figure 23(a). *Deficiency payments system.* At price OP, OQ will be demanded but not supplied. To guarantee farm revenue of $OP_1 \times OQ$, a subsidy of PP_1 per unit is paid.

Figure 23(b). *Intervention price.* Under the EEC system, the Commission intervenes in the market to guarantee price OP_1. Only OQ_1 is demanded at this price with the Commission taking the surplus, QQ_1.

4. PRICE CONDITIONS DEMAND AND SUPPLY

4.1 CONCEPT OF ELASTICITY

The second aspect of the analysis of demand, supply and price relationships lies within the concept of elasticity. This can be defined as the responsiveness or sensitivity of demand or supply to a change in price.

4.2 ELASTICITY OF DEMAND

Demand is said to be elastic when a small change in price leads to a more than proportionate change in the quantity bought. Conversely, it is inelastic when a substantial price change produces a less than proportionate change in the quantity bought. Elasticity of demand is thus revealed in the shape or slope of the demand curve itself, as demand *extends* or *contracts* in response to a fall or a rise in price (see figure 24).

In practice, the demand curve is unlikely to slope evenly throughout its length but will vary within different price ranges.

Elasticity can be quantified in accordance with the following formula:

$$\frac{\% \text{ change in the quantity bought}}{\% \text{ change in price}}$$

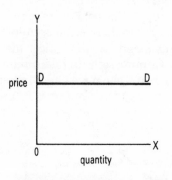

Figure 24(a). *Perfectly elastic demand.* At a given price an infinite quantity will be bought.

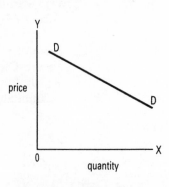

Figure 24(b). *An elastic demand curve.* Quantity bought is more than proportionate than the fall in price.

Figure 24(c). *Inelastic demand curve.* The quantity bought is relatively unresponsive to price change.

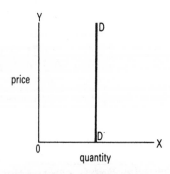

Figure 24(d). *Perfectly inelastic demand curve.* Quantity bought is wholly unresponsive to price change.

When quantity is exactly proportionate to price change, there is an elasticity of 1. Less than unity indicates inelastic demand. Greater than unity tells us that demand is elastic.

4.3 SUBSTITUTABILITY

Elasticity is governed by the ease or difficulty with which one good can be substituted for another. The practical considerations which govern this are dealt with below. However, it should be remembered that ultimately – due to our limited incomes – all things that we do not consume are substitutes for those that we do, e.g. the demand for petrol will be inelastic for as long as we drive motor cars, but if the price rises sufficiently we will be obliged to give up the car and substitute a pair of shoes. For this reason, the perfectly inelastic demand curve illustrated in Figure 24(d) is purely hypothetical.

(a) Necessities and luxuries
By definition a necessity is a good which cannot easily be foregone and for which demand will be inelastic. Conversely, the demand for luxuries will be elastic.

(b) Age group
With advancing age, substitution is likely to become more difficult, while at the same time goods which were luxuries now become necessities. Demand for the restricted range of goods consumed becomes increasingly inelastic.

(c) Income group
The higher the income, the more inelastic becomes the demand curve.

(d) Irrational expenditure
The economist makes the assumption of rational economic man. In practice expenditure may – at least in the short term – conform to set patterns, regardless of price change.

(e) Closely similar products
Substitution becomes easy when there are readily available alternatives, e.g. different brands of cheap ballpoint pens.

4.4 ELASTICITY OF SUPPLY

By parallel reasoning, elasticity of supply will be defined as the degree to which supply extends in response to a price rise or contracts in response to a fall in price. It will be shown in the upward slope of the supply curve.

Similarly, it can be quantified on the formula:

$$\frac{\% \text{ change in the quantity supplied}}{\% \text{ change in price}}$$

4.5 FACTORS GOVERNING ELASTICITY OF SUPPLY

In general, the supply of all things is inelastic in the short term, since time must elapse before the producer can respond to the new price. The ability to respond depends upon two basic considerations.

(a) Nature

Primary products such as minerals, foodstuffs and other raw materials have natural limitations upon their supply and, certainly in the short term, there will be little response to a rise in price.

(b) Flexibility of industrial organization

Manufacturing industry will offer a greater elasticity of supply, depending upon the ease with which the factors of production can be substituted for each other. Where by its nature industry is capital intensive, e.g. steel production, it will be more difficult to adjust output to either a rise or a fall in price. In the long period, however, a rise in price will induce an extension of supply for two reasons. Existing firms will produce more and new firms will be drawn into the industry. A fall in price will have the opposite effect.

4.6 PRACTICAL APPLICATIONS

The concept of elasticity can give some useful insights.

(a) Marketing

Market research will seek to discover the effect upon demand of a price change. It should then be noted that in practice all that is ever likely to be discovered is something of the slope of the curve immediately to either side of the existing market price. The full length of the curve will remain hypothetical.

(b) Expenditure taxes

Chancellors will be concerned to estimate the effect upon revenue of a given change in an expenditure tax. The more inelastic the demand for the product, the more predictable will be the effect upon tax revenue.

(c) 'Supply side' policies

Having in 1979 abandoned the attempt to 'fine tune' the economy with Keynesian 'demand side' policies, government has aimed to improve the elasticity of supply of both the factors of production and the end product, i.e. to create an economic environment in which supply extends more readily to a small rise in price. This has implied policies designed to increase competition and to increase mobility in the labour markets. In contrast to government-promoted movements of the aggregate demand curve which can produce a rapid effect upon output *or price*, supply side policies are less predictable in their results and most certainly require a longer time to work their way through the economy.

MULTIPLE CHOICE

The diagram below shows the market supply and demand curves for a particular agricultural product. The government guarantees producers a minimum price of OX for their output, but allows the market price to be freely determined by demand and supply.

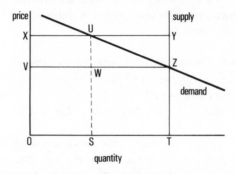

Which area in the diagram represents the total subsidy payments made by the government to producers? (*a*) OXUS; (*b*) UYTS; (*c*) UYZW; (*d*) XUWV; (*e*) XYZV.   (*O & C SEB, June 1985*)
Key Reference 3.3 *Answer* (*e*).

The following table shows a linear demand schedule for a particular commodity.

price (pence)	quantity demanded (units)
2	12000
3	10000
4	8000
5	6000
6	4000

Within what range does the value of the price elasticity of demand (defined as a positive number) at a price of 4 pence lie?
(*a*) 0.0 to 0.6; (*b*) 0.7 to 1.3; (*c*) 1.4 to 1.6; (*d*) 1.7 to 2.0; (*e*) 2.1 to 2.5.
                    (*O & C SEB, June 1983*)
Key References 1.2(a); 4.1–2. *Answer* (*b*).

One or more of the options may be correct. Code – (*a*) 1.2.3. all correct; (*b*) 1,2 only correct; (*c*) 2,3 only correct; (*d*) 1 only correct. A shift in the market supply curve for a commodity may be caused by

(1)   a reduction in the price of raw materials used by producers;
(2)   an increase in the number of firms supplying the market;
(3)   an increase in the price of the commodity.

(AEB, June 1984)

Key References 2.1; 2.4; 2.5. *Answer* (*b*).

ESSAYS

This chapter has introduced the broad analytical framework within which a free market economy functions, adding to the propositions which were made in Chapter 1.3.1 (*The Free Market Economy*). This basic apparatus is used throughout the subject and will be applied to questions in many areas. Those which point most directly to the contents of this chapter revolve around an understanding that *all* economies are 'planned'. What is debated are the merits of the 'planning' mechanism.

Explain the meaning of 'consumer sovereignty'. What effect, if any, might the privatization of parts of the public sector have on consumer sovereignty in Britain?   (*JMB, June 1984*)
Key References Ch.1.3.1; Sections 1, 2 & 3. Ch.7.7.1.

The market has been described as a good servant but a poor master. Explain what you think is meant by this statement and discuss whether or not other economic systems are superior to the market in your opinion.   (*JMB, June 1983*)
Key References Sections 1, 2 & 3; Ch.1.3.1–3.

How do individuals pursuing their own interests determine the price and quantity of a commodity traded in a free market economy?

(O & C SEB, 9635/1, June 1981)

Key References Sections 1 & 2.

Define the supply curve of a single product firm. What are the main determinants of its elasticity in the short and the long run?

(O & C SEB, 9633/1(b), June 1980)

Key References 1.2(d) & (e); 4.1; 4.4; 4.5.

Explain why it is thought that more of a product is normally supplied at a higher price per period.   (*London, Paper 1, January 1982*)
Key References 4.4; 4.5; Ch.10.2.5 and in particular, Fig 31.

THE THEORY OF CONSUMER BEHAVIOUR

CONTENTS

1. MARGINAL UTILITY

1.1 THEORIES OF DEMAND AND SUPPLY

So far, our analysis has assumed as a matter of common sense that normally a demand curve will slope down from left to right, i.e. that the lower the price, the more we will buy. Equally, we expect that a supply curve will slope upward from left to right, i.e. the higher the price, the more the supplier will wish to put on the market. In each case, we must now look for explanations of this 'common sense'.

1.2 DEMAND, THE MARGIN AND UTILITY

The first attempt to explain consumer behaviour was made in the late nineteenth century and was based upon two new concepts: an analytical tool, *the margin*; and a psychological notion, *utility*.

(a) Utility

In the economist's special sense, this is not to be confused with the word 'usefulness'. It means simply, 'the ability to satisfy a human want'. There are no moral implications, e.g. a casino may yield greater utility than a hospital. Further, like happiness it is an entirely subjective concept and no good will yield precisely the same utility to two different individuals, nor even to the same individual at different points in time. Most importantly, the utility yielded by a good diminishes as we acquire more of it. We are now able to formulate a *Law of Diminishing Utility* which states that 'successive units of consumption add progressively less utility to that yielded by the whole supply'. This observation is illustrated in Figure 25.

Unit 1 yields ten units of utility and unit 2 yields slightly less. At unit 4, the utility returned has fallen to nine units. The curve is likely to be concave, since additional units consumed see marginal utility diminishing more than proportionately.

(b) The margin

Reference has been made to this analytical device in Chapter 3. In this context it is applied first to consumption. Additional units are consumed to the point where the buyer subjectively equates the marginal unit, six, with the price which he is willing to pay. It is not a fixed margin, since it will move in or out as the ruling market price rises or falls.

This is also the *margin of transference*, the point at which marginal

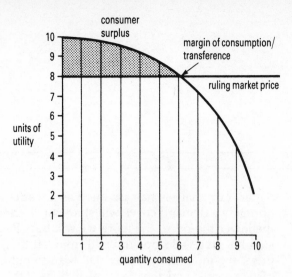

Figure 25. *Diminishing marginal utility.* Successive units consumed yield progressively less utility. The consumer makes purchases to the point where, at the margin of consumption/transference his estimate of marginal utility equates with the price he pays.

expenditure is switched to some other form of consumption which yields higher utility. The consumer strives to reach the point of *equi-marginal utility*, i.e. the position in which his income is so allocated that the utilities yielded at the margin in all lines of expenditure are equal.

(c) Total utility and marginal utility

Figure 25 shows that with increased consumption, total utility (the whole area below the curve) increases, while marginal utility – unit by unit – diminishes. It is *marginal* and not *total* utility which the buyer attempts to equate with price (see ch.1 1.8). From this contrast derives the notion of a *consumer surplus*. If for some reason supply had been restricted to fewer than six units, the buyer would have been willing to pay more. As it is, six interchangeable units are consumed as a whole supply. He therefore enjoys a bonus utility from all of the infra-marginal units.

1.3 DEMAND CURVES AND MARGINAL UTILITY

The normally sloped demand curve is now explained. As the margin of consumption moves outward, so marginal utility diminishes and with it the price which the buyer is willing to pay.

1.4 CRITICISM OF MARGINAL UTILITY ANALYSIS

While this analysis provides the economist with some extremely useful insights, in the twentieth century a major criticism was levelled at the form of its presentation. Figure 25 may be criticized for implying that it is possible to measure the utility yielded by consumption. It is not of course possible to quantify qualities such as happiness or satisfaction; the best we can do is to compare the satisfaction derived from one form of consumption with that from another, i.e. the strength of our preference for each, measured in terms of the other. 'Value is relative and expresses the relation between two things at a particular place and time', (Alfred Marshall). We conclude that in allocating our expenditure between two goods we exercise our preferences in a way which establishes an exchange ratio between them. These observations led to a restatement of marginal utility theory in terms of the *marginal rate of substitution*: this is to say the rate at which, at the margin of consumption (or transference), we are willing to substitute units of one good for units of another.

Another concept with a variety of applications is used for this analysis. It is the *indifference curve*.

2. INDIFFERENCE CURVE ANALYSIS

2.1 WHAT IS AN INDIFFERENCE CURVE?

It indicates the relative preference of the consumer for two goods. For example, with a given income to be allocated between apples and oranges, he may be perfectly content with a combination of ten apples and one orange or five apples and three oranges or a variety of other combinations, each of which gives him the same satisfaction. These combinations can be shown in the form of an indifference curve, as in Figure 26.

The consumer is *indifferent* to which position he occupies on the curve. However, he would clearly be better off if he had more of *both* goods. Assuming higher levels of income, we can now construct more indifference curves on the same principle, to construct a '*contour map*'. Note that the concept of the consumer indifference curve is similar to that of the *production indifference curve* (see Figure 8).

The question, 'What are all the combinations of apples and oranges which give you the same satisfaction?' is similar to the question to the farmer, 'What are all the possible combinations of land and labour which will produce a given quantity of wheat?' There is one major difference. In the case of an *isoquant* for wheat, it is possible to attach a numerical quantity for output. It is not possible to attach a numerical quantity for utility to each of the consumer's indifference curves. The difference between curves 1, 2 and 3 lies in the assumption that the consumer prefers more rather than less, that he would prefer to reach the highest point possible on his contour map. It follows that it is equally impossible to measure *how much* better off he is by moving from one curve to another. Another point of similarity between production isoquants and consumer indifference curves is that they are both drawn convex to the origin. In the case of the consumer curve, this tells us that with ten apples and one orange, it is at first easy to give up apples in order to enjoy more oranges. As we are left with

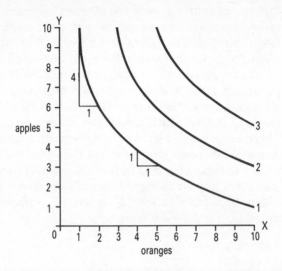

Figure 26. *An indifference curve map.* Each curve represents combinations of apples and oranges. At any point on a curve, the consumer is equally well off. He is indifferent to which point he adopts but will prefer to climb to a higher curve where he will be better off. We cannot measure how much better off. Diminishing marginal rate of substitution is shown in the diminishing number of apples the consumer will give up to enjoy more oranges (4<1).

progressively fewer apples, we need proportionately more oranges in compensation. In nineteenth–century terms, the marginal utility of oranges is falling as that of apples rises. In the modern analysis, we speak of a *law of diminishing marginal rate of substitution in consumption.* The marginal rate of substitution of oranges for apples is the number of apples we will give up in order to have one more orange while still enjoying the same satisfaction.

The marginal rate of substitution is measured by the slope of the indifference curve. Referring again to curve 1 in Figure 26, the upper triangle shows that at first substitution is easy and we are prepared to forego four apples in order to have one more orange. As the curve flattens out and substitution becomes more difficult, in the lower triangle we are only willing to give up one apple for one more orange.

2.2 THE DEMAND CURVE AND THE INDIFFERENCE CURVE

In explaining the nature of consumer behaviour, our specific purpose has been to relate consumer tastes and preferences to the demand curve. What we must do is to take a consumer with a given income and show how many oranges he will buy at a given price. Then we must demonstrate how his purchases will be affected by a change in the price of oranges. In this way we extrapolate his demand curve for oranges. Assume that his income is fixed at £1 and that there are only apples and oranges on which to spend it; the price of an apple is given at 10 pence and *initially* oranges are 20 pence each. Figure 27 represents his indifference curve map, showing RES as his *budget line*, i.e. the different combinations of apples and oranges which he can buy with his fixed income. At the prevailing prices, he can have ten apples or 5 oranges, or any combination in between and along his budget line RES. Which combination will he choose? Only at point E, a combination of six apples and two oranges, will he attain the highest possible indifference curve on his contour map. Any other combination will move him to a lower curve, i.e. reduce his total satisfaction. We now know that for this particular consumer, when the price of oranges is 20 pence each, he will buy two.

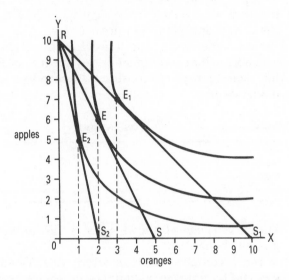

Figure 27. *The demand curve and the indifference curve.* The initial budget line RES shows all combinations of apples and oranges which can be bought for £1 when an apple costs 10p and an orange 20p. Satisfaction is only maximized when the highest indifference curve has been reached, point E at which the budget line is tangent. A lower or higher price for oranges takes the consumer to a higher (E_1) or lower (E_2) indifference curve with more or fewer oranges bought.

Note: equilibrium E lies at the point where the budget line is just tangent to the indifference curve – that is, the point where the slope of the budget line and the slope of the indifference curve are exactly equal. We have already established that the slope of the indifference curve is the marginal rate of substitution of oranges for apples. The slope of the budget line is the price of oranges divided by the price of apples. Where the two slopes are equal, we are saying that:

$$\frac{\text{Price of Oranges}}{\text{Price of Apples}} = \begin{array}{l}\text{The marginal rate} \\ \text{of substitution of} \\ \text{oranges for apples}\end{array}$$

Generalized, the conclusion must be that the consumer will only be in equilibrium when the ratio of the prices of all the commodities he purchases is equal to the relevant marginal rates of substitution. Presented as a formula for any goods, n and m:

$$\frac{P_n}{P_m} = MRS\ (n \text{ for } m)$$

Having fixed one point on this consumer's demand curve, we must now repeat the process in respect of other prices for oranges. Graphically, changes in the price of oranges, still assuming a fixed income of £1 and the price of apples given at 10 pence, requires us to rotate the budget line from the fixed point, R. In Figure 27, RS_1 is the new budget line when the price of oranges has fallen to 10 pence. Allocating all his income to oranges, he can have ten, or alternatively to apples he can also have ten. Observe that a lower price of oranges moves the budget line to the right along the X axis. Conversely, RS_2 is the budget line when the price of oranges rises to 50 pence. As before, the consumer will locate himself on the highest indifference curve available to him at different prices, i.e. at E_1 or E_2. From this information, we can begin to construct a demand schedule and from that, a demand curve.

Table 7. Demand schedule for oranges

Price per orange	Quantity bought
50p	1
20p	2
10p	3

The curve is *normal*, showing that the lower the price, the greater the quantity bought.

For a complete analysis which established the total consumer demand for oranges, it would be necessary to include the alternative not only of apples, but of all the other goods and services in the economy. We would also have to aggregate the demand curves of all the consumers of oranges. However, the analysis is sufficient to demonstrate the relationship between consumer preference and consumer demand. It also gives us a greater insight into the reasons why a normal demand curve slopes down from right to left when we extend it to consider income and substitution effects.

2.3 INCOME AND SUBSTITUTION EFFECTS

When price of one good falls, two distinct things happen. First, the consumer is better off since with the same fixed income he can now buy more of all goods. Second, the price of this particular good is cheaper relative to all others. Both of these effects will cause the consumer to buy more of the good whose price has fallen. These two effects are shown in Figure 28.

(a) Income effect
The reduction in *one* price reduces the *general* or *average* price level.

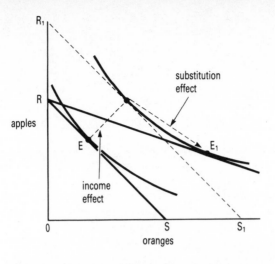

Figure 28. *Income and substitution effects.* When the price of oranges falls, there is an income effect which takes the consumer from E to a higher indifference curve. The substitution effect takes him along the curve to E_1 as he substitutes oranges for apples.

This is the equivalent of an increase in income, as though the budget line had shifted from RS to R_1S_1. The income effect therefore takes the consumer from his equilibrium at E to a higher indifference curve.

(b) Substitution effect

The consumer substitutes cheaper oranges for apples (or all other goods), and there is a second movement along the indifference curve to a new equilibrium E_1.

For both reasons, the consumer will buy more as price falls, i.e. the demand curve normally slopes down from left to right.

MULTIPLE CHOICE

In the diagram below I_1 and I_2 are indifference curves; MS is an individual's initial budget line, and MT is his budget line following a reduction in the price of good Y.

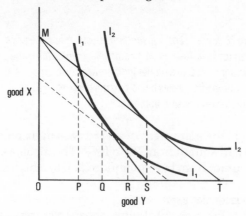

Which difference represents the increase in the quantity demanded of good Y which is attributable to the *income* effect of the price reduction?

(a) PQ; (b) PR; (c) QR; (d) QS; (e) RS.   (O & C SEB, June 1985)
Key References 2.1–3. *Answer* (e).

A basic assumption of demand theory is that households allocate their incomes in order to maximize:

(a)   present consumption;
(b)   the quantities of all goods bought;
(c   their wealth;
(d)   total utility;
(e)   marginal utility.   (O & C SEB, June 1983)
Key References 1.2, particularly 1.2(b) and the concept of equi-marginal utility. *Answer* (d).

The diagram below shows the marginal utility derived from the consumption of successive units of commodity X.

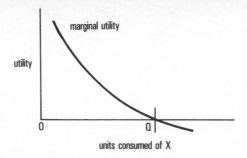

When a person is consuming OQ units of X we can conclude that, for units of X consumed:
(a) total utility is at its minimum;
(b) total utility is at its maximum;
(c) the consumer derives no satisfaction at all;
(d) the consumer is in equilibrium with respect to purchase of X.
(*AEB, November 1983*)
Key References 1.2, particularly Fig 25 and 1.2(c). *Answer* (b).

ESSAYS

How far can the pattern of consumer expenditure in an economy be explained by the theory of consumer demand? What part does advertising play in determining the level and pattern of consumption?
(*JMB, June 1985*)
Key References The first part of the question requires a full understanding of the whole of Chapter 9 and the derivation of the demand curve. The second part requires reference to Chapter 8, in particular section 2, looking first at 2.3(a).

What is meant by the 'substitution effect'? Why is this not sufficient to determine the actual shape of the demand curve for a specific good or service? (*O & C SEB, 9635/1, June 1981*)
Key References 2.2; 2.3.

What are the main differences between the utility and indifference approaches to the analysis of consumer behaviour?
(*O & C SEB, 9635/1, June 1983*)
Key References 1.2–4 (utility approach); 2.1–3 (indifference approach).

Discuss and illustrate the relevance of total and marginal utility for the determination of consumer demand in the cases of water and gold. (*London, Paper 1, June 1984*)
Key References 1.2; 1.3; Ch.1.18.

THE THEORY OF THE FIRM

CONTENTS

1. COSTS OF PRODUCTION

1.1 THE UPWARD SLOPING SUPPLY CURVE

Just as the theory of consumer behaviour explains the downward sloping demand curve, so the theory of the firm explains why a normal supply curve slopes upward. Originally, we took it for granted that as price rose the supplier would be 'willing and able to offer more for sale'. The link between supply and price lies in costs of production.

First, it should be emphasized that there is no single cost of production. Costs vary with output. Moreover, the different components of total cost behave differently as output varies.

1.2 AVERAGE FIXED COST

By definition, *total* fixed costs remain unchanged regardless of output. They include all capital investment and overheads. When *averaged* over an expanding output, the average fixed cost curve declines steeply at first, gradually flattening out and continuing to decline to infinity. For example, the first motor car off the assembly line at a new car plant bears the whole fixed cost. When two are produced, the average per unit is halved. This is illustrated in Figure 29(a).

1.3 AVERAGE VARIABLE COST

By definition, these vary with output. At first, the Law of Increasing Returns applies as economies of scale are achieved with expanded output. In due course, this trend is reversed with the application of the Law of Diminishing Returns. These costs include labour, raw materials and energy. The characteristic shape is illustrated in Figure 29(b).

1.4 AVERAGE TOTAL COST

This is illustrated in Figure 29(c). The curve is the aggregation of the two preceding curves. Unit costs will decline more steeply and rise less steeply than average variable costs, due to the beneficial influence of fixed costs being averaged over an expanding output.

1.5 MARGINAL COST

This is defined as the addition to total cost of one more unit of output. Like variable costs, it includes such items as labour, raw materials and energy. The presentation is different since it deals with *extra* costs, unit by unit, while the other curves illustrate *average* unit costs for different outputs.

1.6 THE AVERAGE TOTAL COST CURVE AND THE MARGINAL COST CURVE

By definition, the two curves must intersect at the lowest point on the average total cost curve. As long as the extra cost of one more unit is less than the average total cost per unit, it is pulling the average down. When it is greater, it pulls the average up. This is shown in Figure 29(d).

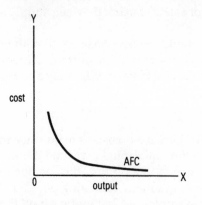

Figure 29(a). *Average fixed cost.* The curve slopes steeply at first and then gradually flattens out.

Figure 29(b). *Average variable cost.* The curve declines and then rises rapidly due to the Law of Diminishing Returns.

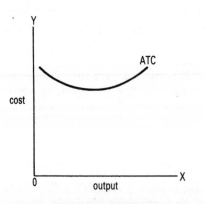

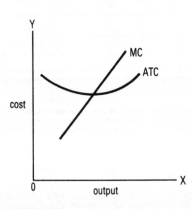

Figure 29(c). *Average total cost.* The aggregation of the preceding two curves, it is characteristically saucer shaped.

Figure 29(d). *Marginal cost.* Comprises variable costs BUT expressed as the *extra* cost, unit by unit.

2. COMPETITIVE CONDITIONS

2.1 A RANGE OF ENVIRONMENTS

The way in which the individual firm behaves in relating outputs to costs and price will depend upon the competitive environment in which it operates. The possibilities range from the concept of *perfect competition* at one end of the scale to *monopoly* at the other. In between, there are varying shades of *imperfect competition*, categorized in different ways and covering the majority of cases in the real world.

2.2 PERFECT COMPETITION

This concept was implicit in the way that nineteenth-century economists thought markets worked. However, it was only with the more closely analytical approach of twentieth-century economists that the attempt was made to prescribe the conditions necessary to perfect competition. This has sometimes led to confusion. In making an analysis with real world examples, some writers have described highly competitive market conditions which fell short of *absolute* perfection, while still using the term 'perfect competition'.

To avoid such confusion this analysis will follow Stigler, who distinguishes two degrees of perfect competition to which he gives the labels 'market competition' and 'industrial competition'.

2.3 MARKET COMPETITION AND INDUSTRIAL COMPETITION

Two conditions must be fulfilled.

(a) Many buyers and many sellers
No individual buyer or seller must be in a position to influence price by boycotting the market. This is normally the case for buyers who compete with each other, thus bidding up price. Exceptionally there may exist *monopsony*, where a single buyer absorbs the whole output. He is therefore individually in a strong position to bring pressure to bear upon price.

The degree of competition and the number of competitors on the supply side varies considerably from industry to industry.

(b) A perfect market
Frequently, this concept also causes confusion amongst students. It should be stressed that it is *not* synonymous with 'perfect competition'; it is only ONE of two necessary conditions. Since its principal characteristic is a *single ruling market price*, in practice there is a greater likelihood of a perfect market where there is monopoly.

A perfect market requires the following conditions.

(i) **A homogeneous commodity** All units of the product are identical and interchangeable. There is therefore no reason to pay more for one unit than for any other.

(ii) **Perfect knowledge** All offer and bid prices are immediately known to all participants in the market.

(iii) **Portable commodity** The product must be freely available in all parts of the market.

(iv) **Rational choice** Once again there is the assumption of 'economic man' who, given the preceding three conditions, will make his decision on price alone and buy the cheapest.

(v) **Free entry and exit** There must be no impediments, social or political, to the free movement in and out of the market of the factors of production. They will respond to shifts of the demand curve.

When all of the conditions specified so far have been met, there exists in our analysis market competition. This is what many texts describe as perfect competition and for which there are examples such as the stock market, the commodity markets and the foreign exchange markets. For the *absolute* case of industrial competition, two further conditions need to be met.

(vi) **Perfect mobility in the factor markets** At least in the short term, this is a hypothetical concept. There is an assumption that land, labour and capital can move *between industries* without difficulty, in response to changes in the pattern of demand. Labour, for example, is capable of moving geographically and occupationally from areas and jobs where demand and wages are falling into uses where demand is rising.

(vii) **Divisibility of the factors of production** This is an extension of the preceding point. Not only must the factors be perfectly mobile, they must also be capable of movement in precisely the quantities required. While the concept of industrial competition may appear purely academic, it has two uses. First it establishes an *absolute* against which various imperfections can be measured. Second, while it is clearly hypothetical in the short term, it nevertheless describes trends in a market economy in the long term, e.g. an elderly unemployed miner in South Wales is unlikely to become an electronic engineer in Newbury – but his son or grandson may do so.

2.4 THE FIRM IN PERFECT (MARKET) COMPETITION

Since most texts do not make the distinction made in 2.3, for the moment we shall revert to the generally used term, perfect competition.

It should also be noted that this analysis follows the traditional, neo-classical assumption of *profit maximization* as the sole motivation of the firm. (Since the 1950s, a number of alternative 'theories of the firm' have been put forward which suggest other motives.)

In perfect competition, the *individual* firm is faced with a perfectly elastic demand curve. Such is the strength of competition from the vast number of other suppliers that for this firm the market price is a datum. It must adjust its output policy accordingly, in the certain knowledge that the demand or price curve for its own product is identical to its marginal revenue curve, i.e. every unit sold will add exactly the market price to revenue. In this situation, in order to maximize profit the firm has no choice but to pursue its marginal cost curve to the point where *marginal cost equals marginal revenue*. Short of this point, there are still profits to be made from further production. Beyond this point, marginal cost is greater than marginal revenue (see Figure 30).

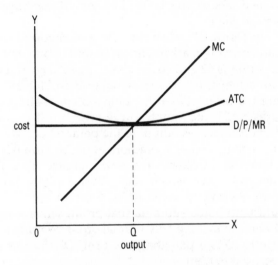

Figure 30. *The firm in perfect (market) competition.* The demand curve is perfectly elastic. The market price is a datum which the firm is unable to influence. The same curve also shows marginal revenue, i.e. each unit adds to revenue exactly its own selling price. Only output OQ maximizes profit, where MC = MR. Observing the ATC curve, any other output would be produced at a loss.

In the case of the *marginal* or least efficient firm in the industry, this is also the lowest point on its average total cost curve. This is the firm illustrated in Figure 30. It was shown in 1.6 above that by definition, the MC curve must intersect the ATC curve at its lowest point. For the *marginal* firm, this is also the point of intersection of the demand or price curve. Any output less than or greater than OQ leaves ATC greater than price and in the long run the firm cannot survive. Moreover, for this marginal firm the D/P curve cannot lie at a lower level, since at no output would its average total costs be covered. Neither can the D/P curve lie at a higher level, since the intensity of competition would force it down. In this position, the firm is said to be *in equilibrium*. Why should it continue to operate when it is only just covering its average total costs? The answer lies in the concept of *normal profit* – the minimum profit necessary to persuade the firm to stay in business. In this sense it is a cost and the concept is incorporated in the ATC curve.

2.5 THE INDUSTRY IN EQUILIBRIUM

In *market competition*, not all firms make only normal profit; some have ATC curves which lie at a lower level on the graph. This springs from impediments to the free movement of the factors of production (see 2.3 (b) (v) above). Some firms, at least in the short run, are able to retain the exclusive use of better quality management, more highly skilled labour and better location. These advantages lead to *supra-normal profit*.

In Figure 31, when the ruling market price lies at £2, only Firm A can enter the market with an output of one unit. The marginal cost of this unit is £2 and so is its average total cost, the lowest that the firm can achieve. It is the marginal firm and for the moment, makes only normal profit. When the demand curve shifts to the right and price rises to £3, the supply curve *extends* to four units for two reasons. Firm A increases output to the point where MC again equals MR and in so doing makes supra-normal profit. Firm B is now able to enter the market and becomes the new marginal firm. A further shift of the demand curve which establishes a ruling price of £4 extends the supply curve to seven units. Firms A and B have increased output and both make supra-normal profit, while firm C becomes the marginal firm making only normal profit. Waiting in the wings for a price rise to £5 is a potential new firm, D. *Thus the supply curve slopes* up from left to right.

Figure 31. *The industry in equilibrium*. In market competition, due to differences in cost levels, Firms A and B make supra-normal profit. Only Firm C, the marginal firm, makes normal profit. The ultra-marginal firm D awaits a rise in price to £5 before it can enter the industry.

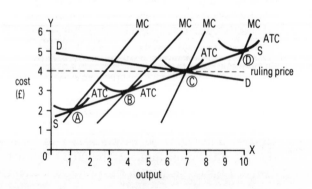

When there is no tendency for firms to enter or leave the industry, there is equilibrium. Due to impediments to entry and exit, this equilibrium may be imperfect, with the result that *in the short term* even Firm C may make supra-normal profit or even a loss.

2.6 THE INDUSTRY IN PERFECT EQUILIBRIUM

In the very long run, there is a tendency towards the conditions of *industrial competition* as the factors of production become more mobile between different uses. The owners of the factors will seek to equate the marginal net returns which can be secured from these different uses, e.g. capital will not be deployed in one industry if a higher return can be gained in another. As this movement occurs, cost differences between firms are reduced. In the extreme case where the industry is in perfect equilibrium, all firms have identical cost structures. They are all marginal firms and make only normal profit, operate at the optimal scale of production i.e. the lowest point on the ATC curve – and contribute equal outputs to the supply of the industry. Consequently, the supply curve of the industry is perfectly elastic and extensions of supply are at constant cost.

Note: It is this largely hypothetical concept of wholly perfect competition which provides the rationale for a laissez-faire economy. All firms are obliged to operate with maximum efficiency and the benefits are immediately handed on to the consumer in the lowest possible price.

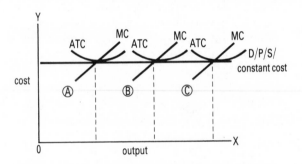

Figure 32. *The industry in perfect equilibrium.* Firms A, B and C have identical cost structures and contribute equal outputs, operating at the lowest points on their ATC curves. The supply of the industry is perfectly elastic at constant cost.

3. THE MONOPOLY FIRM

3.1 THE NATURE OF MONOPOLY

The behaviour of the firm will differ when the market environment changes. Like industrial competition, absolute monopoly is a largely hypothetical concept. First it implies complete control over the whole supply, a feature which is sometimes found; second, it implies the impossibility of substitution, which due to the limitations of our incomes is never wholly true (see Ch.11, 4.3). Nevertheless, to the extent that substitution is difficult, the monopolist is able to influence price by regulating output. What he cannot do is control the slope and position on the graph of the demand curve, which is determined by consumer preferences. He must accept that if he wishes to restrict output he may enjoy a high price but that if he increases output, he will be obliged to accept a lower price. In contrast to the *individual firm* in perfect competition which is faced with a perfectly elastic demand curve, the increased sales of the monopolist are accompanied by a declining price, i.e. the demand curve slopes down. In using his power to regulate output, the monopolist will have two objectives between which he will need to make a compromise. He will seek that output which maximizes revenue, while at the same time looking for the output which minimizes total costs. If he succeeds, he will maximize *monopoly profit*.

3.2 REVENUE AND INCREASING OUTPUT

The effect on *total* revenue of increasing output will depend upon the elasticity of demand for the product. This is illustrated in Figures 33(a) and (b). When demand is inelastic and output is restricted to two units, a price of £6 per unit is achieved to give total revenue of £12. If output is increased to four units, price falls to £1 per unit to give total revenue of £4. Conversely, when demand is elastic, an increase in output will increase total revenue. From an original output of two and a revenue of £12, there is an increase to six units to produce a revenue of £24.

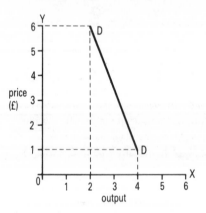

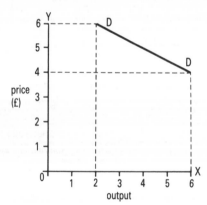

Figure 33(a). *Total revenue and inelastic demand.* An increased output reduces revenue.

Figure 33(b). *Total revenue and elastic demand.* Increased output increases revenue.

The effect on *marginal* revenue of increased output is even more significant to our analysis. It was shown in 2.4 above that in perfect competition, the D/P and MR curves are identical. However this is not so with monopoly, whether the demand curve is elastic or inelastic. The MR curve slopes more steeply than the D/P curve, i.e. *each successive unit adds less than its own price to total revenue*. This is shown in Figure 34, and can be explained in a simple table of figures.

Table 8. Marginal revenue declines more steeply than average revenue/price

Output	Average revenue/price	Total revenue	Marginal revenue
1	£10	£10	£10
2	£8	£16	£6
3	£6	£18	£2

When output is increased to two units, *both* sell at the reduced price of £8 to give a total revenue of £16. The advantage of the extra sale is not the £8 for which it sells, but the £6 which is added to revenue.

3.3 COSTS AND INCREASING OUTPUT

As in other market environments, the ATC curve of the monopolist will at first decline and then rise due to the economies of scale, followed by the diseconomies of scale. Ideally, he would like that output to be consistent with lowest ATC, but this will not coincide with the output which maximizes his total revenue.

3.4 THE COMPROMISE

The monopolist will follow the same rule as the firm operating in perfect competition. He will produce that output consistent with MC = MR and for the same reasons. In Figure 34, if he produces less or more than OP, either there is more profit to be made or else extra units add more to cost than they add to revenue. At OP, total revenue is OPQR and total cost is OPTS. Only in this position is monopoly profit – the difference between the two – maximised. This is the

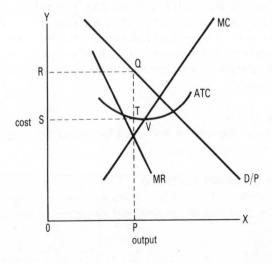

Figure 34. *The monopoly firm.* Only when MC = MR are monopoly profits maximized. This is the rectangle, STQR, the difference between total revenue, OPQR and total costs, OPTS.

rectangle STQR. It is the return to the monopolist's power to restrict output short of V, the lowest point on the average cost curve, and the output which perfect competition would have enforced (*cf* Figure 30).

Observe that this artificial restriction of output implies a less than optimal allocation of resources, with production taking place at a higher point on the ATC curve. It provides an economic justification for government intervention in the free market.

3.5 DISCRIMINATING MONOPOLY

From the monopolist's point of view, the compromise he makes is not entirely satisfactory, since clearly he would prefer to increase output and move to a lower point on his ATC curve. He can do this to advantage when he is able to segregate different parts of his market. In his primary market, he still *sells* that output consistent with MC = MR, but he has increased production and moved to a lower point on his ATC curve, e.g. point V in Figure 34. The total cost of output OP is reduced, and monopoly profit STQR correspondingly increased. He has now to dispose of his surplus output in his secondary market, and this he can do at any price whch covers *marginal* cost. This price does not even need to cover average *total* cost, since a return to fixed capital investment is not an imperative.

Examples of *price discrimination* are protected home markets with surpluses 'dumped' overseas; and the tariffs for gas, electricity and telephones.

4. THE FIRM IN IMPERFECT COMPETITION

4.1 ITS NATURE

In the spectrum of competitive conditions, we have established that the extreme case of industrial competition is hypothetical – at least in the short run although there are examples of the lesser market competition. Equally, the opposite extreme of absolute monopoly is hypothetical, although not uncommonly supply is controlled by a single or a few suppliers who exercise some degree of monopoly power. The concept of imperfect competition covers the range of possibilities in between and is characterized by the absence of one or both of the two fundamental conditions necessary to perfect competition (see 2.3 above).

(a) Oligopoly
There are only a few suppliers who are able to influence price by regulating output.

(b) Monopolistic competition
In consequence of the absence of one or more conditions necessary to a perfect market, there is not a single market price.

4.2 OLIGOPOLY

Where the supply of the whole industry is controlled by only a few producers, each will be able to exercise a degree of monopoly power and will regulate his output accordingly. The extent of that power will be reflected in the difference between marginal cost and price, which can be illustrated graphically as for the monopoly firm in Figure 34. Oligopoly is of two kinds.

(a) Perfect oligopoly

There are several suppliers and a *perfect market* with a single market price. Any supplier who attempts to increase his revenue through an expanded market share at a lower price must expect a quick response from his competitors. Since only the cheapest product will be sold, they too must reduce price. Commonly, the dominant firm will assume the role of price leader, with its competitors following the price which it establishes in its own interest. The higher-cost firms are likely to find that this results in a narrowing of the gap between their marginal costs and price. Their surplus profits are correspondingly reduced.

(b) Imperfect oligopoly

There are several suppliers and an *imperfect market* with consequent price variations. The supplier may deliberately seek to increase this imperfection – and therefore his monopoly power – through, for example, the practice of branding. Much advertising is designed to foster the idea not that Brand X is better than Brand Y, but that it is unique and without substitute. To the extent that this is successful, the demand curve for the product becomes more inelastic, the gap between marginal cost and price is widened and surplus profits increased.

Even with product differentiation which gives each supplier some independence in pursuing his own output policy, he may still be tempted to enlarge his market share by price cutting. Retaliation is to be expected and a 'price war' may follow. As prices are forced closer to marginal costs, so surplus profits diminish. The end result is likely to be that each of the major competitors retains his original market share and the price competition has been in vain. Rather than 'spoil the market' in this way, the supplier may resort to 'service competition' in the form of free gifts, games of chance, coupons or better sales service. The petroleum industry is characteristic of imperfect oligopoly; the major companies engage alternately in price and service competition.

Note: With price cutting the intention is to *extend* output along the demand curve, in contrast to service competition where the intention is to *increase* demand by shifting the curve to the right.

4.3 MONOPOLISTIC COMPETITION

This differs from both forms of oligopoly since there are many suppliers. It is similar to imperfect oligopoly in that there is an imperfect market with price variations. This is quite commonly the case in retailing where a number of the features of a perfect market may be absent, e.g. although a homogeneous product is offered by different retailers, the *service* they offer is far from homogeneous. The corner shop has a geographical advantage over the town centre supermarket; it may also open for longer hours and personal contact and service may encourage loyalty. Consequently there is some element of monopoly power which enables such retailers to sustain rather higher prices.

This power is likely to lead to excess capacity in the industry rather than large surplus profits. In other words, the small high-cost firm is able to survive in the face of competition from large organizations which enjoy the economies of scale.

MULTIPLE CHOICE

A firm discovers that if it either increases or reduces output, its short-run average cost increases. It follows that
(a)   the firm is maximizing its profits at its present output;
(b)   the firm is minimizing its marginal costs at its present output;
(c)   the firm is producing at the point where marginal cost equals average cost;
(d)   diseconomies of scale are present;
(e)   total costs are at a minimum.   (O & C SEB, June 1983)
Key References 1.2–5 but especially 1.6. Answer (c).

For a firm in equilibrium in perfect competition, average revenue is
(a)   less than marginal revenue, and both are positive;
(b)   equal to marginal revenue, and both are zero;
(c)   equal to marginal revenue, and both are positive;
(d)   greater than marginal revenue, which is zero;
(e)   greater than marginal revenue, which is positive.
                                        (O & C SEB, June 1985)
Key Reference 2.4. Answer (c).

Which one of the following is an example of price discrimination?
(a)   A bus company charges less than British Rail to take passengers from London to Manchester;
(b)   Men's hairdressers charge less than women's;
(c)   Greengrocers in different neighbourhoods charge different prices for apples;
(d)   British Telecom charges reduced rates for telephone calls made by government agencies;
(e)   The National Coal Board charges less per tonne for coke than coal.   (O & C SEB, June 1984)
Key Reference 3.5. Answer (d).

The diagram below shows the short-run supply curve (S) for the product of an industry operating in a competitive market.

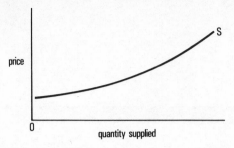

The supply curve is derived by adding horizontally the individual firm's schedules of
(*a*)   average costs;
(*b*)   marginal costs;
(*c*)   average revenues;
(*d*)   marginal revenues.   (*AEB, November 1984*)
Key References 1.1; 2.5 and particularly Figure 31.

Oligopoly is best described as a market situation where there
(*a*)   is a large number of competing firms with similar products;
(*b*)   is a large number of competing firms whose products differ slightly;
(*c*)   is a small number of competing firms;
(*d*)   are only two competing firms.   (*AEB, June 1984*)
Key References 4.1(a); 4.2. *Answer* (*c*).

ESSAYS

Explain briefly, with the aid of cost and revenue curves, when it becomes uneconomic for a competitive private firm or plant to remain in business. Discuss whether or not the future of nationalized plants or firms should be governed by the same criteria.
                                        (*JMB, June 1985*)
Key References 2.4–5; Ch.7.6.1–7.

Compare and comment on the long-run equilibrium positions of a perfectly competitive industry and of a monopoly.
                                        (*O & C SEB, 9635/1, July 1984*)
Key References 2.4–6; 3.1–4.

Describe briefly how price and output are determined by
(*a*)   a firm operating under conditions of perfect competition;
(*b*)   a monopolist.
How is the consumer likely to be affected by such decisions?
                                        (*AEB, November 1983*)
Key References (*a*) 2.4; 2.6; (*b*) 3.1–4. For elaboration of the last part of the question, Ch.5.3.1–2.

Describe the characteristics of an oligopolistic industry and examine the different explanations of oligopolistic price and output determination.   (*AEB, June 1985*)
Key References 4.1; 4.2; Figure 34.

PRICING THE FACTORS OF PRODUCTION

CONTENTS

1. THE CONCEPT OF MARGINAL PRODUCTIVITY

1.1 THE DISTRIBUTION OF INCOME

Our purpose is to discover the principles which govern the distribution of the value of the end product between the factors of production which have contributed to it, i.e. how we apply economic analysis to the pricing of the factors of production. These prices are returned to the owners of the factors as income in the form of wages, interest, rent (to labour, capital and land) and something which is rather more elusive – profit as a return to enterprise.

There are great differences on the supply side of the factor markets, but on the demand side the principle of marginal productivity has a general application.

1.2 MARGINAL PHYSICAL PRODUCT (MPP) AND MARGINAL REVENUE PRODUCT (MRP)

The marginal *physical* product is the addition of total output which results from the application of one more unit of any one factor while the inputs of the other factors remain constant. Following the Law of Increasing Returns, MPP will at first increase as the factors are combined in more efficient proportions, but ultimately the Law of Diminishing Returns will apply, MPP will increase more slowly and finally become negative.

The marginal *revenue* product of an input is the addition to total sales revenue which results from the sale of the MPP of that input.

These principles are illustrated in Table 9.

Table 9. The MPP and MRP of Applications of Fertilizer to a Given Area of Land with a Fixed Quantity of Labour

Tons of fertilizer	MPP (tons of potatoes)	MRP (£)
1	10	200
2	15	300
3	20	400
4	15	300
5	10	200
6	5	100
7	2	40
8	0	0
9	−5	−100

The MPP column shows how many additional tons of potatoes are produced using one more ton of fertilizer. In the MRP column, potatoes are assumed to sell at £20 per ton; the sixth ton therefore adds a total of £100 to revenue. If fertilizer is assumed to sell at £100 per ton, then the optimal application will be 6 tons. Short of this, the cost of fertilizer is less than its MRP and there is still profit to be made. In excess of this, MRP is less than the cost of the input. At 9 tons, over-intensive farming makes MRP negative.

These observations may be stated as a general principle.

In competitive factor markets, a profit-maximizing firm will employ that quantity of any input for which the marginal revenue product is equal to the cost of the input.

The obvious extension to this line of reasoning is that the quantity of the input employed will vary with its price, e.g. if the price of fertilizer doubled to £200 per ton, then the optimal input would be 5 tons. It follows that for the factors as for end products there is normally a downward sloping demand curve.

1.3 DERIVED DEMAND

The demand for any factor of production (in our illustration, capital in the form of fertilizer) derives from the demand for the end product. If a decrease in demand caused the price of potatoes to fall to £10 per ton, then at each level of use the MRP of a ton of fertilizer would be halved. The demand curve for fertilizer would shift to the left.

In general, a shift to the right or left of the demand curve for the end product will be accompanied by a similar shift of the demand curves for the factors engaged in that production.

2. WAGES IN COMPETITIVE LABOUR MARKETS

2.1 DEMAND FOR LABOUR

Initially, we assume fully competitive conditions with no attempt by government to regulate labour markets and wages. Equally, there are no unions capable of exercising monopoly power.

The MRP curve for labour, as for the other factors, is downward sloping. The derived demand curve for labour will therefore behave similarly.

2.2 THE SUPPLY OF LABOUR

The analysis is based on the simple observation that the supply of labour and the demand for leisure are two sides of the same coin. If, for example, a man has 100 waking hours to allocate between work and leisure, the decision to work for 40 hours has an opportunity cost in the leisure foregone. Conversely, the decision to have 60 hours' leisure implies the cost of extra wages foregone. Leisure has a price and the demand for it – as for other commodities – varies with price.

In Chapter 12, 2.3, we saw that a price change has two effects on the quantity of a good demanded. The same is true of the demand for leisure, i.e. the supply of labour.

(a) The income effect
When wages are raised, the worker is better off and his demand for all things, including leisure, will increase: i.e. *he will want to work less*.

(b) Substitution effect
When wage rates rise, leisure becomes more expensive relative to other goods. We would therefore expect other goods to be substituted for leisure and the *worker will work longer*.

We are left with a paradox which cannot be resolved precisely. When wages rise, some workers will work more, others will work less and many may have little choice, being committed to a fixed working week. However, empirical studies suggest that low wage-earners are sensitive to the substitution effect and they will work more when wages rise, while for high wage-earners income and substitution effects more or less offset each other.

2.3 HIGHER WAGES AND A SHORTER WORKING WEEK

Trends in the twentieth century towards an ever-shorter working week accompanied by higher wages – both money and real – seem to run counter to the concept of an upward sloping supply curve. Part of the answer lies in the observation that the income effect has outweighed the substitution effect. The income effect is illustrated in the backward-bending supply curve shown in Figure 35.

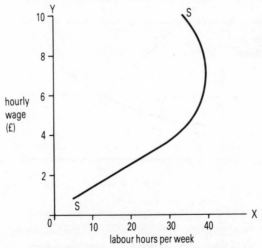

Figure 35. *Backward-bending supply curve.* The curve for the individual worker may bend backwards, indicating in this case that he will work longer hours up to a 40-hour week and a rate of £7 per hour. Higher rates produce an 'income effect' and he works fewer hours.

2.4 SHORT-RUN AND LONG-RUN CONSIDERATIONS

Turning from the supply of labour of an individual to the total supply of labour to a specific market, we observe that it is not just a question of the number of hours one man works but also of the number of workers. From this point of view, we would expect the supply of, say, car mechanics to be inelastic in the short run, since their skills are not quickly acquired. In the longer run, higher wages will persuade those workers in trades with lower wages to retrain, and the supply curve becomes more elastic.

2.5 EQUILIBRIUM IN A FULLY COMPETITIVE LABOUR MARKET

In Figure 36, the curve L_s represents the supply of labour of a specific kind in the medium run. It is of moderate elasticity. At its intersection with the demand curve L_D lies the equilibrium wage w_o, and the equilibrium quantity of labour hired Q_o. At this point, the firm is content, since it is hiring labour to the point where $MRP=W_o$. Labour is equally content, since its supply curve incorporates not only the decisions which have been made between work and leisure and different wage rates, but also the movements in and out of this specific labour market in the medium term. At this wage, labour will offer Q_o to the market, precisely the same quantity that the firm is willing to employ.

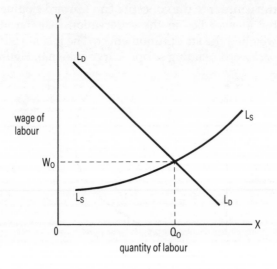

Figure 36. *Equilibrium in a competitive labour market.*
At the intersection of the supply curve, L_s and the demand curve L_D the equilibrium wage, W_o, is set. It equals the MRP of labour.

**2.6 WAGE
DIFFERENTIALS**

When in a particular labour market demand is strong and supply is weak, the equilibrium wage will be high and vice-versa. This is obvious and for a greater insight we must examine the particular nature of the demand and supply curves for labour.

(a) Demand for labour

This is governed by the MRP of labour, which in turn depends upon *labour's MPP* and *the price of the product*. Anything that influences either of these will influence wages.

Labour's MPP is in part determined by a worker's own ability and effort. However, this is likely to be less significant than the way in which labour is combined with the other factors of production. Industries – and indeed countries where production is capital-intensive – will give labour a high MPP and therefore a high wage.

Further, we remember that the demand for labour is derived from the demand for the end product. Anything which influences that demand will influence the demand for labour.

(b) Supply of labour

There are three distinct considerations.

(i) Size of workforce The total work-force available in an area relative to the scale of industrial activity will affect the general level of wages.

(ii) Job satisfaction Agreeable work in pleasant conditions (some might suggest teaching as an example) will attract more labour and consequently a low wage. Conversely, unpleasant dangerous work is consistent with high wages.

(iii) Ability and skill Certain highly specialised jobs require not only natural ability but also lengthy and costly training. Supply will be limited relative to demand and therefore wages will be high.

We should now distinguish the relationship between ability and wages and skills and wages. Apart from arduous training, Caruso had a unique operatic talent which enabled him to command high fees. In these payments lay an element of *economic rent*, a return to this uniqueness. Other skills can be duplicated through intensive training and enjoy no economic rent. The decision to undertake such training is akin to an investment decision, since it involves the sacrifice of present income in the expectation of a higher future income. Like all investment, however, these expectations may or may not be fulfilled.

3. UNIONS AND THE MONOPOLY SUPPLY OF LABOUR

3.1 COMPETITIVE PRODUCT MARKET AND MONOPOLY LABOUR SUPPLY

We assume that firms are in market competition, having neither monopolistic nor monopsonistic power while the supply of labour is monopolized by a trade union. Through mechanisms such as the closed shop, demarcation lines between crafts, the delegated power from management to recruit labour and various other restrictive practices, the union has total control of this particular type of labour. It will then behave in a way closely analogous to the monopolist in the product market.

In Chapter 13, 3.4, we saw that the latter will restrict output to the point consistent with MC=MR. In a similar way, the union is faced with a downward sloping demand curve which corresponds to the MRP curve of the competitive firm. Again like the product monopolist, the MR curve for labour will slope more steeply than its demand or price curve (*cf* Table 8). Following the monopoly rule, labour will be supplied to the point where MC=MR. The marginal cost of labour will be the cost to each worker of the last hour of work supplied, conceived in terms of an hour's leisure foregone. Where MC=MR, that cost will be exactly balanced by the addition to total income from one more hour's work. To offer more labour would be to incur additional costs which exceeded the additional reward.

The contrast between this monopoly equilibrium and the competitive equilibrium illustrated in Figure 36 is shown in Figure 37.

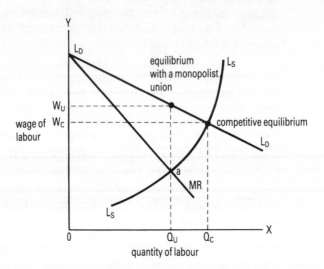

Figure 37. *Monopoly labour supply.* In a fully competitive labour market, the equilibrium wage will be W_c and the equilibrium labour supply Q_c. When a union exercises monopoly control of supply, equilibrium will lie at point a, the intersection of MC and MR. Supply is restricted to Q_u to achieve a higher wage, W_u. The difference between W_c and W_u is the return to the monopoly power of the union and is analogous to the power of the monopolist in the product market.

L_DL_D is the demand curve for labour from firms operating in market competition. L_SL_S is the competitive supply curve of labour, each worker being unable *individually* to influence his wage rate. In a competitive labour market, the equilibrium wage will be W_c and the equilibrium supply of labour Q_c. When labour is now unionized and the union exercises monopoly power, the supply of labour will be restricted to Q_u to secure a higher equilibrium wage W_u.

3.2 VARIOUS UNION OBJECTIVES

There is one major difference between the analysis of the monopoly labour market and that of the monopoly product market. In the latter, profit maximization is assumed to be the sole objective. For the union, there are several possible objectives.

(a) Wage maximization
Characteristically, this has been a major goal of craft unions which through the terms of apprenticeship seek to control admission to the craft. In Figure 37, they will tend towards a restriction of labour supply to Q_u. Note that fewer workers are employed than would have been the case in a competitive market.

(b) Expanding the union
If increasing the size and power of the union is the objective, which may be the case with unskilled and semi-skilled labour unions, there will be a tendency to increase the labour supply towards the point of competitive equilibrium at Q_c. In this situation, the union will have done nothing to raise wages above the competitive level.

(c) Set the wage
This is comparable with wage maximization, but instead of achieving the desired wage through the restriction of the labour supply, the union sets the wage while the employer determines how much labour he will employ at that wage.

(d) Maximizing wages AND employment
The union will only be able to use its monopoly power to secure wage gains *without* sacrificing employment if it can induce a shift to the right of the demand curve. In the UK there is a good deal of evidence to suggest that, at least until the 1980s, major unions were able to exercise sufficient industrial and political muscle to achieve this objective, e.g. the car, print and coal industries.

4. BILATERAL MONOPOLY

4.1 MONOPSONY AND MONOPOLY

The preceding analysis will be applicable in many cases, a monopoly union supplying labour to a competitive industry – e.g. the Transport and General Workers' Union in relation to the many small haulage firms. On the other hand, the giant union is frequently faced with a giant employer who has *monopsony* power (i.e. sole control) over the *demand* for that type of labour – e.g. the National Union of Railwaymen in relation to British Rail. Such a situation is described as *bilateral monopoly*.

The starting position is one in which the union will look for a wage above the competitive rate and the firm for one below that rate. In between lies an indeterminate area in which conventional economic analysis can offer little assistance in predicting the outcome.

4.2 COLLECTIVE BARGAINING

This well-known phrase is difficult for the economist to define with any precision, since the framework within which it takes place varies considerably from industry to industry and is largely dependent on institutional and historical factors. Equally, it embraces many goals other than wage gains such as hours, paid holidays, sick leave, incremental scales and promotion, pension schemes, recreational and canteen facilities and a vast range of other fringe benefits. While economic analysis may assist in establishing minimum and maximum positions in financial terms, the outcome of the negotiations will depend partly on economic logic, partly on the relative strengths of management and labour in the context of their respective finances and current labour law, and partly upon the skills and personalities of the negotiators. When all else fails and an impasse is reached, labour may resort to a strike or management to a lock-out.

4.3 CONCILIATION AND ARBITRATION

In the event of deadlock, union and firm may agree to call in an impartial mediator – in the UK at the present time the Arbitration and Conciliation Advisory Service (ACAS), whose function it is to suggest avenues of negotiation through which agreement may be reached.

If this proves fruitless, both parties may agree to go to impartial and binding arbitration. Beyond this, there lies only a trial of strength.

5. CAPITAL AND INTEREST

5.1 INVESTMENT AND CAPITAL

Capital is the stock of physical goods such as factories and machinery which contribute to further production. It is created by a process in which the firm first decides to enlarge its stock of capital and then raises the funds to finance the expansion. Inputs of the various factors are then hired to produce this physical capital. This is the process of investment which involves the transformation of money into capital.

If the money was borrowed, the investor will have to pay interest for its use. If it was his own money, he will expect a similar return.

5.2 THE DEMAND FOR FUNDS

As for labour, the demand for capital is determined by its MRP. However, since capital is a *durable* good which contributes not only to today's but also to tomorrow's production, the calculation of its MRP is rather more complicated than for other inputs. In order to determine whether the MRP of capital is greater than the cost of financing it, it is necessary to make a comparison of money values received at different times. The calculation involves a procedure called discounting, which hinges upon two important points:

(*a*)   Money received today is worth more than money received at some future date.

(*b*)   The difference in values is greater when the rate of interest is higher.

These points are easily demonstrated. Consider the difference between £1 received today and £1 received a year hence. If the going interest rate is 10%, today's pound can be invested to produce £1.10 in a year's time. If the interest rate rises to 20%, then the pound will be worth £1.20 at the end of the year. In other words, in order to forego today's pound we require a larger sum in the future.

These two points explain why the demand curve for funds has a negative slope. It *derives* from the demand for investment in capital goods, but most of the MRP of these goods will be received *in the future*. It follows that the value of this MRP measured in today's money contracts as the rate of interest rises. Therefore, what seems a profitable investment at 10% becomes positively unprofitable at 20%. The demand to borrow investment funds thus declines as the interest rate increases.

5.3 THE SUPPLY OF FUNDS

Similar principles govern the supply of funds. Exercising what is sometimes called *consumer time preference*, the consumer evaluates present income in relation to future income. The possibility of future income from capital accumulation is limited by capital's marginal productivity. A rate of interest above the equilibrium rate would represent an overestimate of marginal productivity – a promise to the saver of a future income which cannot be fulfilled with the current state of technology. A rate below the equilibrium rate implies a failure by society to recognize the full possibilities of translating present income into future income through more capital-intensive production.

We will therefore expect the supply curve for funds to slope upwards as the rate of interest rises. At its intersection with the downward sloping demand curve lies the equilibrium rate of interest.

Note: This basic analysis has abstracted from the complications of the real world in which account must be taken of *liquidity preference* and the role of money in the economy, as well as of the part played by the financial institutions. These matters will be considered later. Nevertheless, it demonstrates the fundamental truth that society has a basic choice between present and future consumption and shows how, through the mechanism of capital accumulation, this choice is made.

6. LAND AND RENT

6.1 LAND IN FIXED SUPPLY

The principal feature of land is observed on the supply side. The nineteenth century classical economist, David Ricardo, defined land as 'the original and indestructable powers of the soil'. The implication is that land and natural resources are given once and for all, i.e. they are in perfectly inelastic supply, even in the long run. While this is not absolutely true since mineral resources, for example, will be depleted over time and land can be reclaimed, their supply is certainly highly inelastic by comparison with the other factors.

Figure 38 therefore reasonably represents the supply curve for land (*or indeed any other factor which is in inelastic supply*).

The classical economists referred to the payment to land as rent which was determined solely from the side of demand operating against a fixed supply. When, initially, land is in abundant supply, only the most fertile is cultivated and it pays no rent. As the demand for land increases, resort is made to less fertile areas with a lower yield. This new marginal land pays no rent; the more fertile land does. It is the difference between the two yields.

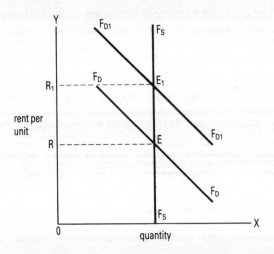

Figure 38. *Rent.* When the factor is in perfectly inelastic supply, the equilibrium rent is determined entirely by demand. F_sF_s is the supply curve and F_DF_D the demand curve which gives an equilibrium rent RE. The demand curve shifts to $F_{D1}F_{D1}$ to establish a new equilibrium R_1E_1.

6.2 ECONOMIC RENT

This concept can be extended to other factors which are in fixed supply. Two interesting characteristics are revealed and illustrated in Figure 38.

The supply curve of the factor F_sF_s is inelastic. The demand curve F_DF_D produces an equilibrium economic rent of RE. Demand increases to $F_{D1}F_{D1}$ and economic rent rises to R_1E_1 without any response from supply. This tells us first that since the demand for land – like the demand for other factors – derives from the demand for the end product; if this varies so will rent. Second , it is apparent that rent is in a sense a surplus or unnecessary payment. Payments are normally made to the other factors to call forth a supply. *Economic rents* are by definition paid to a factor in inelastic supply, i.e. the payment made has no effect on the amount supplied. For example, the services of a particular pop-star can be represented by the supply curve in the diagram. He might well be persuaded to sing for a return of RE but as his popularity increases, the demand curve moves to the right and he enjoys an increased economic rent without any increase in the number of performances.

6.3 OVERLAPPING PAYMENTS

In examining how the three factors of production – land, labour and capital – are priced, we have very broadly established how income is distributed to the owners of those factors as rent, wages and interest. We have also seen that this analysis is not wholly precise, since the pop-star may earn rent – and indeed, physical capital of specific kinds which is in inelastic supply in the short run will also earn a *quasi-rent*. There is also a considerable overlap when we consider the fourth and more elusive category of income, profits.

7. PROFITS

7.1 THE PROFIT MOTIVE IN A MARKET ECONOMY

The theory of the firm assumes profit maximization to be the sole motivation. In long-run *industrial competition*, all firms make only *normal profit* or, as it is sometimes called, *the wages of management*. This concept is built into the average total cost curve. In the short run, due to frictions in the factor markets which impede free movement, abnormal profit may be made but in due course will be competed away. Note, however, that to the extent that anticipated profits are a cost, then there is a profit element in the returns to land, labour and capital.

7.2 MONOPOLY PROFIT

The theory of the firm in monopoly or imperfect competition shows that monopoly profit is the return to the power of the monopolist to restrict output of the end product. Similarly, monopoly control of the supply of the factors will secure some monopoly profit element in the payments made to them. This was shown to be the case in respect of wages (see 3.1 above).

7.3 PURE PROFIT

The residual element in profit is the return to enterprise without which the other factors would remain unused. There are two aspects to these payments made to the entrepreneur or businessman.

(a) Innovation

The great Austrian economist, Joseph Schumpeter, stressed this aspect. The role of the entrepreneur, he said, is to innovate, to discover new techniques of production and organization, to find new products and materials, to open up new markets and marketing techniques. He is the agent of change; he innovates and leads the field and thus enjoys large profits. Competitors shortly follow him and as his original advantage disappears, so do these profits. However, in a dynamic economy there is always innovation somewhere and therefore someone making such profits.

(b) Risk

The return to innovation is uncertain and therefore the higher the risk, the greater the *anticipated* profit necessary to the entrepreneur. It is often forgotten that *realized profit* can be negative as well as positive. It is therefore also to be seen as a return to risk-bearing. In this sense also there is an element of profit in the return to the other factors. In work where prospects of secure employment are lower, it will be expected that wages will be higher. Equally, in risky capital investment projects interest rates will be higher.

MULTIPLE CHOICE

When a person earns more than the wage just sufficient to keep that person in a job, the excess income is called
(a)   an economic rent;
(b)   overtime pay;
(c)   a transfer payment;
(d)   surplus value.   (*AEB, June 1985*)
Key Reference 6.2. *Answer* (*a*).

The marginal revenue product of a factor of production employed by a firm operating in an imperfectly competitive product market must eventually decline as more of the factor is employed because
(a)   its marginal physical product alone declines;
(b)   its marginal physical product and the marginal revenue of the product both decline;
(c)   the marginal revenue of the product alone declines;
(d)   its supply price alone rises;
(e)   its supply price rises and its marginal product declines.
                                    (*O & C SEB, June 1983*)
Key Reference 1.2. *Answer* (b).

Economic rent is defined as a payment to a
(a)   factor, in excess of its transfer cost;
(b)   factor, equal to its opportunity cost;
(c)   factor for successful risk bearing;
(d)   firm for the lease of capital equipment;
(e)   landlord for the use of rented property.
Key Reference 6.2. *Answer* (*a*).

ESSAYS

Briefly outline a theory of wage determination. Nurses and health service ancillary workers are widely acknowledged to be providing essential services. In view of this, why do you think they have relatively low pay?   (*JMB, June 1983*)
Key References 1.2; 1.3; 2.1; 2.2; 2.5; 3.1; 3.2; 4.1; 4.2 provide the theory of wage determination; see 2.6 on wage differentials.

Outline a theory of interest rate determination. Discuss whether, when demand in the economy is low, falling interest rates are a sign of further depression or possible recovery in economic terms.

(JMB, June 1983)

Key Reference 1.2; 1.3; 5.1–3 for a theory of interest rate determination. For the second part of the question, refer to Chapter 14, 2.1–5.

Explain what determines
(*a*)   the demand for loanable funds;
(*b*)   the demand for money.
What is the role of each in the determination of the rate of interest?

(AEB, November 1983)

Key References 5.2; 5.3; 1.2; 1.3 for (*a*). Chapter 14, 2.1–4 for (*b*).

Outline and evaluate a theory of profit.

(O & C SEB, 9635/1, June 1983)

Key References 7.1–3, but also Chapter 10.3.1–4 for a view of *monopoly* profit.

MACROECONOMICS

NATIONAL INCOME DETERMINATION

CONTENTS

1. MACROECONOMIC PROBLEMS

1.1 KEYNES AND THE PROBLEMS OF THE ECONOMY IN THE AGGREGATE

Our analysis so far has been concerned with an examination of *particular* firms, industries, jobs and markets. This is the substance of *microeconomics* and was indeed what economic theory had primarily concerned itself with until the 1930s. Macroeconomics looks at the problems of the economy in the aggregate and seeks to explain not why a specific firm or industry has problems, but why all industries are in difficulty. It asks not why some prices are rising relative to others, but why all prices are rising.

The significance of Keynes's contribution to economic theory is that it provides the key to much of modern macroeconomic analysis. The theory of national income determination is rooted in his work (see 1.1.10).

1.2 THE UNEMPLOYMENT PROBLEM

Any historical observation of the UK economy (or other industrial economies) shows that progress is spasmodic and that periods of prosperity are followed by periods of hardship.

(a) Industrial fluctuations
Variations in economic activity can be classified:

(i) Secular trend Since the Industrial Revolution the long-term tendency has been towards growth.

(ii) Seasonal variations For climatic reasons there are variations throughout the year.

(iii) Erratic fluctuations Crop failures, natural catastrophes, revolutions all cause unpredictable fluctuations.

(iv) Cyclical variations The business or trade cycle was observed throughout the nineteenth century. With a periodicity of 8–11 years for the whole cycle, an 'upswing' or expansionary phase was followed by a 'downswing' with contraction and rising unemployment.

These observations give some insight into the nature of unemployment.

(b) Types of unemployment

Appropriate remedies depend upon correct analysis of causes.

(i) Structural unemployment In the long term, technological advance causes permanent contraction in some industries, with resulting unemployment for men whose skills are no longer in demand.

(ii) Frictional unemployment In a competitive economy less efficient firms will be continuously replaced by more efficient firms, but the skills of the employees will remain in demand. Such employment is likely to be short-term.

(iii) Seasonal unemployment Corresponds to seasonal variations in economic activity.

(iv) Cyclical unemployment This results from the downswing of the business cycle.

(v) Voluntary unemployment The preceding categories relate to involuntary unemployment. However, in modern times there may be a significant element of voluntary unemployment which is difficult to quantify. It will arise for several reasons, e.g. 'the poverty trap' – where there is little difference between social security benefits and low wages; 'the black economy', where employment is concealed for tax or social security reasons; early retirement on occupational pension while still registering as unemployed. The figures will be artificially distorted in the opposite way when unemployed married women do not register as unemployed.

This classification leads us to conclude that the concept of 'full employment' cannot mean a zero measure of unemployment. In a dynamic economy there must always be at least some transitional unemployment. Making the *major* assumption that remedies are available to government, how much is acceptable will be decided on social and political grounds.

(c) Cost of unemployment

There are obvious social costs. Additionally, there is a very real economic cost in terms of potential output of goods and services lost for ever.

1.3 THE INFLATION PROBLEM

The seriousness of inflation as a macroeconomic problem is unlikely to be appreciated until it has been experienced. In the twentieth century, most nations have had this experience, the classic example being the hyperinflation in Germany in 1923 which destroyed the currency. It is characterized by a continuing rise in the general or average price level. There are both social and economic costs.

(a) Social costs

In the twentieth century, in advanced societies, there is general agreement that it is desirable to achieve some redistribution of income and wealth on a planned basis through the fiscal system. Inflation does this in a random and arbitrary way.

(i) Income redistribution As the price level rises, the purchasing power of a fixed nominal income diminishes. When money incomes are unable to respond – which may be the case with for example retired people, non-unionists or members of weak trade unions – *real* incomes are permanently reduced. Other sections of society – e.g. members of powerful trade unions – are able to keep money incomes abreast of or even ahead of the rate of inflation. Real income is redistributed from weaker to stronger.

(ii) Wealth redistribution There is a redistribution of *real* wealth (purchasing power) from lender to borrower; e.g. a nominal interest rate on savings of 10%, with an inflation rate of 25%, means a real rate of −15%. This is the same as saying 'lend us £100 this year and we will repay you £85 next year'.

(b) Economic costs

When the inflation rate of one country exceeds that of its international competitors, its balance of trade and payments will be adversely affected. This is likely to lead to restrictive economic policies which will slow down its growth.

Further, while it is generally supposed that a mild upward movement in the price level which encourages profits and business confidence is to be welcomed, when it escalates (and it will) the unit of account – i.e. the currency unit – becomes so unstable that the entrepreneur finds it increasingly difficult to conclude business contracts. Confidence is lost and recession looms.

2. THEORIES OF INDUSTRIAL FLUCTUATIONS AND UNEMPLOYMENT

In general, the English classical economists had ignored the possibility of a macroeconomic problem of unemployment. Given competitive markets, unemployment could only be frictional and short-term. In the long term, the downward flexibility of wages would ensure full employment equilibrium. This reasoning was supported by Say's Law of Markets (see Chapter 1, 1.5). Nevertheless, towards the end of the nineteenth century, more attention was being given to the phenomenon of the *trade cycle* and a great many theories emerged. They can be conveniently classified.

2.1 PSYCHOLOGICAL THEORIES

An upswing or downswing will initially be rooted in more objective causes, but once they have taken hold, they will be augmented by alternating waves of over-optimism and over-pessimism.

2.2 MONETARY THEORIES

Since cyclical fluctuations date from the advent of the market economy, at which point money assumed a much more important role, explanations are given in terms of deficiencies in the operation of the interest rate and the responsiveness of investment and stockholding.

2.3 OVER-INVESTMENT THEORIES

The essence of these theories is the disequilibrium which occurs when capital goods industries are expanded at a more rapid rate than the consumer goods industries from which they derive. The evidence indeed supports the view that the former are more sensitive to cyclical fluctuations. When consumer demand does not keep pace, the downswing is triggered by the failure of investment.

2.4 UNDER-CONSUMPTION THEORIES

Disequilibrium between production and consumption occurs because of excessive saving. This line of thinking paved the way for Keynes.

3. KEYNES, THE BUSINESS CYCLE AND UNEMPLOYMENT

3.1 A GENERAL THEORY

Keynes considered the work of his predecessors and allowed that their theories had some contribution to make to an understanding of the whole problem. However, in his own work he was looking for something more fundamental. His 'general theory of employment, interest and money' is *general* since it seeks to explain economic equilibrium at *any* level of employment. The classical analysis could only explain one particular equilibrium, at *full* employment. In this sense his thinking was 'revolutionary'. If remedial action by government could stabilize the economy at the desired level of employment, then simultaneously the problem of the business cycle was resolved.

3.2 THE PRINCIPAL FEATURES OF THE KEYNESIAN ANALYSIS

The chief characteristics of Keynes's work are:
(*a*)   The whole emphasis is upon the examination of the aggregates which affect the economy as a whole. This macroeconomic approach contrasted with the microeconomic focus of the preceding era.

(b)   The key to the analysis is the concept of *aggregate demand* which in market economies is recurrently deficient relative to aggregate supply. He thus rejects Say's assertion that supply creates its own demand.

(c)   When, at the full employment level of activity, aggregate demand falls short of aggregate supply, entrepreneurs cut back on production and jobs to the point where supply is again in equilibrium with demand. In this way, persistent mass unemployment could be explained.

(d)   Classical economics had distinguished the monetary world from the real world. In conformity with Say's Law, real output and employment would be determined by real factors such as climate, fertility, ingenuity and enterprise. Money determined only the price level. A most important aspect of Keynes's work is his attempt to produce a synthesis of the real and monetary economies in which money plays a pivotal role. Unlike his predecessors who saw money as simply a medium of exchange, he attributed to it an additional and vitally important quality, *liquidity*. 'Instant purchasing power', a characteristic unique to money, means that people will wish to hold it for its own sake and this can explain the possibility of a discrepancy between aggregate demand and aggregate supply.

(e)   Since market economies were susceptible to such a discrepancy, there was a role for 'pump priming', compensatory government finance to stabilize aggregate demand at the desired level of employment.

4. AGGREGATE DEMAND

4.1 THE COMPONENTS

In Chapter 3.3, the concepts of national income and the circular flow of income were introduced. The three main categories of income are consumption expenditure, investment expenditure and government expenditure. If any of these are deficient, aggregate demand will fall below that necessary to sustain full employment equilibrium. Conversely, if it rises above this level, inflation will result.

4.2 THE CONSUMPTION FUNCTION

Consumption is the most important element of aggregate demand, so for practical policy purposes its accurate estimate is of great importance. For Keynes in 1936, consumption was simply related to current disposable income, a position which was accepted for many years. In the 1950s, however, evidence began to emerge of a divergence between long-term and short-term consumption functions, the latter being much flatter. This led to the development of alternative explanations, the *permanent income, life cycle* and *relative income hypotheses*.

Keynes postulated in the 'general theory' that, 'the fundamental psychological law . . . is that men are disposed, as a rule and on the average, to increase their consumption as their income increases, but not by as much as the increase in their income. The Keynesian consumption function can therefore be stated as: $C = c_0 + bY$ where C is consumer spending, c_0 is a constant, b is the marginal propensity to consume (m.p.c.) – i.e. the amount spent from each additional unit of income – and Y is national income.

We conclude that when income rises, so does consumption, but by less than the amount of the increase; in other words m.p.c. is less than 1. Keynes further asserted that 'a higher absolute level of income will tend, as a rule, to widen the gap between income and consumption'. That is to say, the *proportion* of income consumed will fall as income increases. (In the equation, the positive constant c_0 ensures that this happens.)

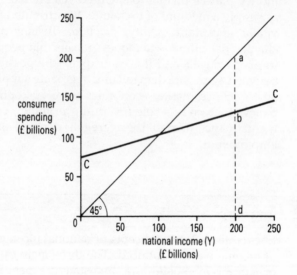

Figure 39. *Consumption function.* National Income is shown as *ad* with anticipated savings of *ab*. As income increases, savings rise more than proportionately.

In Figure 39, the 45° line to the horizontal axis will be the measure of national income at its intersection, in this case £200 billion. Note that *ab* measures anticipated savings at this level of income. When national income falls to £100 billion there are no savings. At still lower levels of income (to the left of the intersection of CC and the 45° line) there is *dissaving* to support spending. To the right of the intersection, consumption rises with income but savings increase as a percentage of income.

In the short run, Keynes believed the main influence upon consumption to be current disposable income, i.e. income less direct taxes. As this varied, so would consumption, but to a lesser degree since m.p.c. was less than 1. However, these predictions did not prove reliable. In years of recession, when real incomes rose at a rate below the long-term trend, m.p.c. was frequently greater than 1, i.e. real consumer spending rose at a rate greater than the rise in real disposable income.

Problems of this kind led to new theories of aggregate consumer behaviour.

4.3 PERMANENT INCOME (PIH) AND LIFE CYCLE (LCH) HYPOTHESES

Friedman's PIH and Modigliani's LCH approach the problem at a more fundamental microeconomic level. Both hypotheses break the link between consumption and *current* disposable income, taking the view that consumers plan their expenditure on a much longer-term view of income. In a world in which it is possible to borrow and lend freely, consumption during any time period need not be tied too closely to the income earned in that period. In other words, consumers will attempt to even out spending in the face of fluctuating income over the long period.

The PIH focuses upon the notion of a long-run average or normal income which the individual can depend upon. The LCH stresses the age of the consumer who tries to even out spending over a lifetime in which a smaller proportion of a relatively high income is consumed in middle life, while the young and the old support consumption on relatively low incomes by drawing on past savings.

4.4 RELATIVE INCOME HYPOTHESIS (RIH)

The focal point of Duesenberry's RIH is that m.p.c. does not depend upon absolute income, as suggested by Keynes, but upon relative income over different time periods for the same individual and between individuals within the same time period. Over a period, consumers become used to a certain level of consumption and if income falls – e.g. in recession – they will resist cuts in their standard of living and sacrifice a much greater proportion of potential savings.

Similarly, as living standards in general continue to rise some families will tend to lag behind. Rather than lose too much relative status, they will save less.

4.5 CONCLUSIONS

These modifications to the original Keynesian consumption function suggest that in the short term it will be flatter than in the long term, i.e. the marginal propensity to consume will be lower in the short run than the long run. Secondly, it should be stressed that while the problem of distinguishing between long- and short-term effects is recognized, the evidence to support any of the above hypotheses remains inconclusive.

Nevertheless, the general view that consumption depends substantially upon level of income has remained durable.

4.6 THE INVESTMENT FUNCTION

While there is a consistency in the relationship between income and consumption, investment is far more volatile and less predictable. It was this instability which Keynes considered to be the major problem of free market economies.

The rate of investment depends on several factors:

(a) Business expectations
Keynes used the phrase *marginal efficiency of capital* to denote the relationship between the *prospective* yield of one more unit of capital investment and the rate of interest which must be paid for it. The difficulty is that these expectations are largely psychological and therefore not amenable to economic analysis. Keynes considered that the entrepreneur was too prone to excessive pessimism due to an imperfect view of the future.

(b) Rate of interest
The cost of borrowing will affect the willingness of firms to invest. Since government is able to influence the interest rate, it has a mechanism for affecting aggregate demand.

(c) Level of innovation
In a period of much innovation and rapid technological change, the marginal efficiency of capital (m.e.c.) will be high and therefore conducive to investment.

(d) Rate of growth of demand
When sales are expanding and inventories reducing, business expectations and m.e.c. will be high and investment increases. Government can influence this situation by increasing aggregate demand.

(e) Company taxation
Government can also influence the investment climate through various forms of tax incentive.

5. DEMAND SIDE EQUILIBRIUM

5.1 CONCEPT OF EQUILIBRIUM GNP

In Figure 40, still assuming a simplified private closed economy, we have added an investment function, I, of the order of £50 billion throughout its length, i.e. it runs parallel to the consumption function. (For reasons examined in 4.6 above, it might in practice run more steeply than the consumption function, investment rising more rapidly as national income increases.) The economy is in equilibrium at e, with consumption and investment expenditure of £175 billion reflected in the same measure of national income. Any point to the left of e is unsustainable, since aggregate demand exceeds national income (Y). The manifestation would be the depletion of inventories, to which firms would respond by increasing output. They might later decide to raise prices as well. Equally, national income at points to the right of *e* cannot be sustained, since aggregate demand is insufficient. Inventories now accumulate and production and jobs are cut back. Firms will normally do this rather than cut prices to stimulate demand until they are certain that the low level of demand is not of a temporary nature.

Equilibrium therefore lies at the point where aggregate demand equals aggregate supply; inventories are at appropriate levels and there is no inducement for firms to vary output or prices.

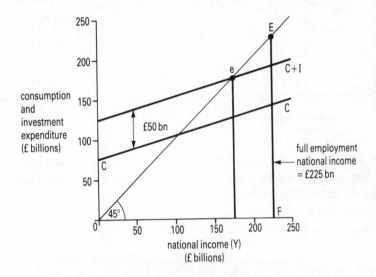

Figure 40. *National income equilibrium in private closed economy.*
Equilibrium lies at the intersection of C+I with the 45° line, point *e*,
(£175bn.). Points to left or right are unsustainable. Point *e* is £50bn.
short of the full employment national income equilibrium of £225bn.
at FE.

5.2 EFFECT ON THE AGGREGATE DEMAND CURVE OF VARIATIONS IN THE PRICE LEVEL

The impact on purchasing power or real wages of changes in the price level has been referred to in 1.3(a) (i) above. We can now relate this to our income/expenditure analysis.

A rise in the price level by reducing real purchasing power will lower consumption and therefore the aggregate demand curve C+I. The opposite will be true when the price level falls. The equilibrium level of national income is correspondingly lowered or raised, as shown in Figure 41 (a).

With stable prices and aggregate demand of C_0+I, equilibrium national income is Y_0. A lower price level shifts the expenditure schedule up to E_2 and a new national income equilibrium of Y_2. A higher price level lowers aggregate demand to E_1 and equilibrium Y_1.

In Figure 41(b), points E_0, E_1 and E_2 are plotted to give an aggregate demand curve for real national income. This tells us that the higher the price level, the lower the equilibrium level of national income. It also tells us that *a 45° line income/expenditure diagram can only be drawn for a specific price level.* This point is crucial to an understanding of unemployment and inflation.

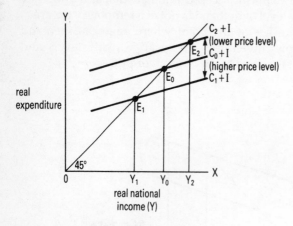

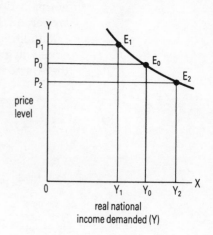

Figure 41(a). *Effect on aggregate demand of changes in the price level.* A lower price level equates with increased purchasing power. C_0+I rise to C_2+I and vice-versa.

Figure 41(b). *Derivation of the aggregate demand curve.* The curve slopes down from left to right.

5.3 FULL EMPLOYMENT NATIONAL INCOME EQUILIBRIUM

So far it has been demonstrated that equilibrium can lie at any level of national income, at whatever point aggregate demand intersects the 45° line, and it is in this sense that Keynes put forward a *general* theory. Referring back to Figure 40, *full employment* national income equilibrium will only be achieved at FE, £225bn. The horizontal distance between *e* and FE (£50bn) represents a *deflationary gap*. This has occurred either because consumers and investors have been unwilling to spend enough or because the price level was too high. Conversely, if C+I were to rise to establish equilibrium to the *right* of E, *an inflationary* gap would emerge. Aggregate demand exceeds the present possibility of increasing output at full employment.

5.4 SAVINGS EQUAL INVESTMENT

In our simplified economy, a deflationary gap would seem to originate in a leakage from the circular flow of income in the form of savings (see Figure 10) which have not been offset by sufficient investment. The problem is that decisions to save and decisions to invest are taken by two different sets of people and for two different sets of reasons. These considerations were examined in 4.2 and 4.6 above. The important point is that in a free market economy there is no *planned* co-ordination of the decision to save and the decision to invest. Since entrepreneurs are repeatedly too pessimistic, investment plans fall short of the savings plans of the consumer and a gap apparently develops which leads to recession. Yet savings must always equal investment. How can this paradox be explained?

Every economic period can be observed from two positions. *Ex ante*, we look to the future and from past experience anticipate an income of say £10; on that basis we *plan* to spend £8 and save £2. Provided that the entrepreneur plans investment of £2, equilibrium national income will remain at £10. If, as repeatedly happens, he underestimates the marginal efficiency of capital, he may plan to invest only £1. In the *ex post* position, we now look back at what in fact happened. The consumption and investment plans were fulfilled but since these amounted to only £8+£1, aggregate demand (C+I) fell to £9, as did national income. With consumption of £8 from an income of £9, savings of only £1 were realized. Thus savings equalled investment, albeit with equilibrium at a lower level of national income and employment. The economy was moving into recession.

Conversely, an inflationary gap implies unusually buoyant investment plans which exceed savings intentions. C+I rises to a new equilibrium to the right of the full employment equilibrium in Figure 42. Consumption plans are fulfilled, but since *money* national income has risen, so have savings – sufficiently to equal the increased investment. Note, however, that *real* national income/output remains unchanged since full employment has been surpassed. Inflation results.

5.5 A GRAPHICAL REPRESENTATION

The reasoning in 5.4 can be shown graphically as in Figure 42.

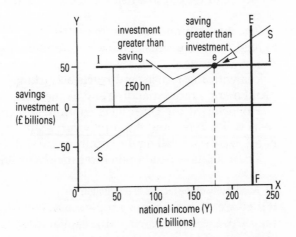

Figure 42. *Determination of equilibrium national income by saving=investment.* Where investment is greater than saving, there is a stimulus to higher income and therefore more saving. Where saving is greater than investment, aggregate demand is insufficient to support that level of income and saving. Both contract.

The condition for equilibrium was discussed in 5.1 as the equation of aggregate demand with national income (C+I=Y). Precisely the same case can be stated in terms of savings equalling investment (S=I).

The savings function SS shows the relation of savings and income and is the reflection of the consumption function in Figure 42. Similarly, investment is assumed to be £50bn., regardless of the size of national income. The investment function is therefore horizontal. As before, equilibrium national income is £175bn., the point of intersection of the saving and investment curves. To the left of *e*, investment is greater than saving and is stimulating further expansion of income, thus making possible more saving. Incomes greater than £175bn. are unsustainable, since saving is greater than investment. Aggregate demand will only support income of £175bn. which produces saving of £50bn., exactly the same as the level of investment.

6. SUPPLY SIDE EQUILIBRIUM

6.1 THE AGGREGATE SUPPLY CURVE

Demand side analysis demonstrated the possibility of deflationary or inflationary gaps between the *actual* equilibrium national income and the *potential full employment* equilibrium. However, since aggregate demand is in part dependent upon the price level (see Figure 41(a) and (b)) it is not possible to determine which type of gap will emerge without reference to the price level. This will be the product of the interaction of aggregate demand and aggregate supply.

Other things remaining constant, in a profit-motivated economy the aggregate supply curve will have a positive slope. Since profit is the difference between selling price and unit cost, it is clear that the response of output to a rising price level depends upon the response of costs.

The first significant feature is that the price of many inputs is agreed for some considerable period ahead, e.g. wage agreements today are normally for a year. The producer now compares selling prices with these costs and reacts accordingly. If they are rising, his profit margins are expanding and he increases output and vice-versa.

However, if the price level continues to rise, in the longer term costs will also rise and the supply curve shifts to the left. On the other hand, if costs are falling the supply curve shifts to the right.

These shifts depend upon three major considerations.

(a) Availability of the factors of production
If they are all in abundant supply, costs will fall and vice-versa, e.g. in the 1970s the slow growth of the capital stock contributed to inflation.

(b) Organization of the factors
Improved technology and organization will increase productivity.

(c) Changes in the cost of inputs

Wages are clearly of major importance and in a period of protracted inflation will react rapidly. In the 1970s, steep increases in the oil price were also of great significance.

6.2 AGGREGATE DEMAND AND AGGREGATE SUPPLY IN EQUILIBRIUM

In Figure 43(b), demand and supply are in equilibrium at E, where price=100. At any price level higher than 100, the quantity supplied would exceed that demanded and there would be downward pressure on prices. At any price level below 100, demand would exceed supply and there would be upward pressure. This particular equilibrium gives a real national income/output of £225bn., the *full employment* equilibrium.

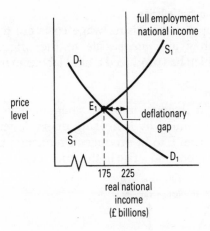

Figure 43(a). *A deflationary gap.* National income is less than the maximum potential.

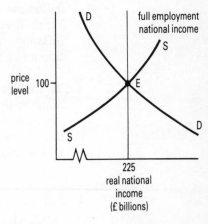

Figure 43(b). *Full employment equilibrium.*

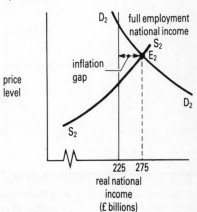

Figure 43(c). *An inflationary gap.* National income cannot be sustained at this level.

There are two other possibilities. Figure 43(a) shows that aggregate demand is weaker and a new equilibrium has been established at E_1 with real national income reduced to £175bn., leaving a deflationary gap of £50bn. In Figure 43(c), aggregate demand has shifted to the right for an equilibrium at E_2, £50bn. higher than the maximum possible full employment income. This is an inflationary gap.

6.3 SELF-ADJUSTMENT OF AN INFLATIONARY GAP

With the major proviso that there are no forces at work which move the aggregate demand curve further to the right, then an inflationary gap contains the seeds of its own destruction. While equilibrium national income is above the full employment level, resources – in particular, labour – are scarce and wage costs rise, moving the aggregate supply curve to the left. Inflation steadily erodes the inflationary gap until equilibrium is restored at the full employment level. We are now led to two major observations:

(a) Demand-induced inflation

While it appears that rising wage costs are the immediate cause of inflation, they are *intermediate* to the original cause – excessive demand which has produced a tight labour market.

(b) Stagflation

Some insight is given into the phenomenon of the 1970s of rising prices accompanied by increasing unemployment. In Figure 44, the movement from E to E_1 produces a reduction in real national income and employment and a rise in the price level.

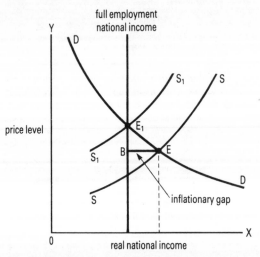

Figure 44. *Self-adjustment of an inflationary gap* The inflationary gap, BE, reflects excessive aggregate demand. Wage costs (and other costs) rise. The entrepreneur responds by shifting his supply curve gradually to the left to the new full employment equilibrium at E_1. As this takes place, prices rise and unemployment increases.

6.4 ADJUSTMENT OF A DEFLATIONARY GAP

It might be thought that by a similar process, a deflationary gap would be self-adjusting. High unemployment leads to reduced wage costs, with firms cutting prices in order to sell their output. The aggregate supply curve moves down until full employment equilibrium is restored.

This process probably took place during the nineteenth century and to a lesser degree during the inter-War depression. It has certainly not occurred since 1945. Keynes was the first to remark upon the downward inflexibility of wages and prices to establish a long-term equilibrium well short of full employment.

6.6 STAGFLATION IN THE MID–1970s

The severe increase in inflation and unemployment of this time was too great to be explained by the self-cancelling process described in 6.3. The explanation lay in the series of supply side shocks as the Organization of Petroleum Exporting Countries (OPEC) raised oil prices and significant world crop failures raised food prices. The result was increased industrial costs – which shifted the aggregate supply curve to the left to an equilibrium at a higher price level – and higher unemployment. *Note:* Such *shocks* have a once-for-all effect upon the price level and are to be distinguished from the continuing inflation which results from repeated movements to the right of the aggregate demand curve.

6.7 CONCLUSION

Inflationary gaps may be closed through the self-adjustment process, provided that the remedy is not offset by continuing increases in aggregate demand. To ensure that this does not happen requires considerable determination by government.

It is pretty clear from modern experience that deflationary gaps do not cure themselves and that there is a role for government policy. It is around the nature of this policy that there is much controversy. 'Keynesians' have always laid emphasis on demand side policies, shifts of the aggregate demand curve to achieve the desired national income equilibrium. 'Monetarists', on the other hand, are associated with supply side policies – attempts to move to a better equilibrium through shifts of the aggregate supply curve.

EXAMINATION PRACTICE 12

MULTIPLE CHOICE　　　One or more of the options may be correct. Code –
(*a*)　　　if 1, 2 and 3 are all correct;
(*b*)　　　if 1 and 2 only are correct;
(*c*)　　　if 2 and 3 only are correct;
(*d*)　　　if 1 only is correct.
The diagram below depicts the savings and investment functions in a two-sector closed economy.

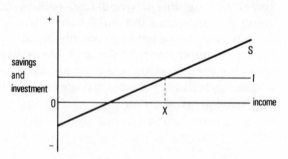

From the diagram we can conclude that
(1)　　　X is the equilibrium level of national income
(2)　　　investment is induced
(3)　　　savings are autonomous　　　　　(*AEB, June 1984*)
Key References 5.4; 5.5 and particularly Figure 42. *Answer* (*d*).

Which one of the following is a necessary condition for the national income of any economy to be in equilibrium?
(*a*)　　　There is full employment;
(*b*)　　　The budget of the central government is planned to balance;
(*c*)　　　Planned savings equal planned investment;
(*d*)　　　There is neither a surplus nor a deficit in the balance of payments;
(*e*)　　　Planned withdrawals from the circular flow are equal to planned injections into it.　　　　　(*O & CSEB, June 1983*)
Key References 3.2; 5.1, but also refer back to Chapter 3.3.1 and Figure 10, *Answer* (*e*).

ESSAYS

Explain carefully what is meant by national income equilibrium in an open economy with a government sector. Describe the factors that might cause a shift in the equilibrium level of national income and indicate how such a shift would be brought about.

(*AEB, June 1985*)

Key References 3.1–2; 4.1; 4.6; 5.1–5; 6.1–4.

Outline the short-term and long-term costs of unemployment to the economy. Discuss, with illustrations, how policies to cure long-term unemployment might differ in emphasis from those to cure short-term unemployment. (*JMB, June 1981*)

Key References 1.2; 2.1–4; 3.2; 4.6; 5.1 for short-term analysis; 6.1–7 for the long-term analysis.

'The main task of economic policy is to reduce inflation; unemployment will cure itself.' Discuss. (*JMB Special, June 1983*)

Key Reference This wide-ranging question which points to the Keynesian/Monetarist controversy requires a full understanding of the whole of Chapter 12.

'Unlike the Keynesian theory of consumption, the permanent and life cycle hypotheses predict that actual consumption is not much affected by temporary changes in income.' Discuss and consider possible implications for the management of the economy of these alternate views of the consumption function. (*JMB Special, June 1982*)

Key Reference Again, a full understanding of the whole of the chapter is required but with particular reference to 4.2–4.

State the conditions for the circular flow of income in an economy to be in equilibrium. Show how this equilibrium is reached.

(*O & CSEB, 9633/2, July 1985*)

Key References Initially, Chapter 3.3.1 and Figure 10. Then, 3.2; 4.1; 4.6; 5.1.

Does the consumption function provide a stable and important link between the levels of national income and expenditure?

(*O & CSEB, 9635/1, June 1983*)

Key References 4.1–4; 5.1.

FISCAL POLICY AND DEMAND MANAGEMENT

CONTENTS

1. FUNCTIONS OF A SYSTEM OF PUBLIC FINANCE

1.1 THE ALLOCATIVE FUNCTION

Certain goods are *social* in character and cannot properly be provided by the market. Collective provision must be made. The distinction between them and *private* goods is that in the former case it is impossible to confine their benefit to selected individuals, while in the case of the latter benefits are restricted to the purchaser, e.g. the law and its enforcement is a benefit enjoyed by all; the benefit of a burglar alarm is limited to the owner.

The consumption of social goods is therefore *externalized*, since their enjoyment by one consumer does not limit their enjoyment by another. The consumption of private goods is *internalized* to one particular individual. Markets cannot function in this context. The price mechanism is rooted in private property, the ability to exclude others from particular benefits in order that exchange may subsequently take place. Since it is impossible for the market to exclude any individual from the benefits of, say, national defence, where social goods are concerned the link between demand and supply breaks down.

The decision on the *quantity* of such goods to be provided becomes a matter for the 'political market'. It is assumed that the electoral system enables the wishes of the majority to be implemented.

Consideration of the State's role in allocating scarce resources requires a distinction between social goods for which collective provision is made – and which may be supplied by privately-owned or publicly-owned enterprise – and private goods marketed by state-owned industries. In other words, it is necessary to define the public sector; it has three characteristics:

(*a*)   No direct relationship exists between the size of tax payment the individual makes and the service he receives.

(*b*)   There is no 'earmarking' of particular taxes for particular services.

(*c*)   In the private but not the public sector, profit is the motive.

Into this framework must be fitted the *public corporation*. There are many, but the most important are those industries which were nationalized after the Second World War. While publicly owned, the Acts of nationalization required them to observe market disciplines and if not actually making profits, at least to break even. In practice this has rarely been the case, therefore we may conclude that to the extent that such industries pursue economic pricing and output policies, they behave in the same way as private enterprise and lie outside the public sector and the scope of public finance. To the extent that social and political considerations take precedence over economic considerations and are subsidized from public revenues, the opposite will be true.

Finally, we note the distinction between *exhaustive* and *transfer* expenditures. Many people are *direct* employees of the State, e.g. police and health service employees. As many again are employed *indirectly*, for example those building police stations and hospitals. Such expenditures are *exhaustive* in the sense that real productive resources are denied to the private sector and reallocated to the public sector. On the other hand, *transfer payments* involve only the transfer of income from taxpayer to beneficiary, who will then spend it in response to market forces.

1.2 THE DISTRIBUTIVE FUNCTION

It is clear from their nature that free enterprise, private capitalist market economies will generate a significantly uneven distribution of income and wealth. For social and political reasons it may seem desirable to make adjustments; what then remains a matter for debate is 'how much?'. *Welfare economics* is of little assistance – it assumes that there is greater economic efficiency if A is better off without B being any worse off, which is helpful in evaluating the way in which markets function, but gives no guidance in setting criteria for optimal distribution. We therefore conclude that such criteria will simply reflect current social and political aspirations. This established, there are two broad fiscal approaches to the reduction of inequalities.

(a) Tax rates and structures
The principle of *progressive direct taxation* of income, profits and wealth implies taxes on a *more than* proportional basis. Rates, reliefs and allowances can be varied to suit the prevailing mood.

(b) Social expenditure
Tax revenues are used to concentrate benefits on low income receivers.

Note: A *direct* tax is one for which *impact* and *incidence* are the same, i.e. the person on whom the tax is levied pays and also bears the burden of that tax. For an indirect tax, impact and incidence are frequently not the same. The person levied and who makes payment transfers the burden to someone else in a higher price. Note also that indirect taxes are *regressive*, i.e. the same tax is paid by all regardless of their *ability to pay*. This is the case, for example, with VAT and excise duties.

1.3 THE STABILIZATION FUNCTION

The question of whether there is a legitimate role for discretionary fiscal policy to stabilize the economy lies at the heart of the Keynesian/ Monetarist debate. Should variations in the volume and structure of taxation and public expenditure be deliberately made to influence aggregate demand? Is it appropriate that large public sector spending deficits should be incurred for the purpose of stimulating aggregate demand? Whatever the answer, it will be immediately appreciated that even if positive stabilization policies are not pursued, it is still necessary to give attention to the effect on aggregate demand of taxation, government spending and the way in which it is financed.

2. THE IMPACT OF GOVERNMENT EXPENDITURES (G)

2.1 THE MULTIPLIER

Like any other form of domestic expenditure, government spending raises aggregate demand and increases national income towards its full employment equilibrium. Figure 45 is a development of Figure 40 in Chapter 12. Without G, equilibrium lies at *e* (£175bn). An injection of £25bn. government spending raises the equilibrium to e_1 (£212.5bn), closer to full employment. In a basic way, this provides the justification for government economic intervention. However, we have yet to consider the effects of taxation and moreover, we must explain why national income has increased by a multiple of G. An injection of £25bn. has raised national income by £37.5bn. The explanation is found through the use of one of the most important tools of economic analysis – *the multiplier*.

The multiplier tells us by how much an increase in spending will raise the equilibrium level of national income, e.g. if an increase of £1 raises national income by £5, the multiplier is 5.

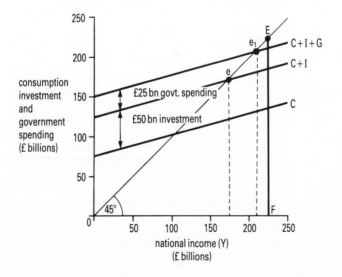

Figure 45. *An injection of government spending.* Aggregate demand is raised by £25bn. but national income by £37.5bn., a multiplier of 1.5.

It should be stressed that the multiplier applies to *all* categories of spending: C, I or G. The effect of an autonomous increase in any of them will be magnified. Thus in Figure 45, the addition of £50bn. *investment* to the consumption function raises national income from an equilibrium of £100bn. to a fresh equilibrium of £175bn. The effect of the injection has been magnified by 1.5. Similarly, the effect of the injection of £25bn. of G has been multiplied by 1.5 to raise national income still further to £212.5bn.

Why do we have, in this illustration, a multiplier of 1.5? We note immediately that the number depends upon the slope of the consumption function, to which the other functions run in parallel. For example, if the consumption function were horizontal, then the addition of £50bn. investment would raise the intersection with the 45° line by only £50bn. and national income by the same amount. The multiplier would be only 1. Conversely, the closer the slope of the consumption function to the 45° line, the greater the multiplier.

More precisely, the multiplier obeys the following formula:

$$m = \frac{1}{1 - \text{MPC}}$$

where MPC is the *marginal propensity to consume*. This is defined as the addition to total consumption from one more unit of income. The proposition is elaborated in Figure 46.

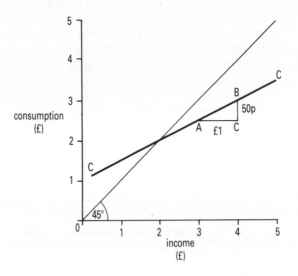

Figure 46. *The marginal propensity to consume.* MPC is equal to the slope of the consumption function, i.e. BC/AC. In this example, MPC=50/100 or 1/2.

An increase in income of £1 leads to an increase in consumption of 50 pence – one-half. The same result is achieved by measuring the distance BC and dividing it by distance AC. Thus BC/AC is the slope of the consumption function, i.e. the marginal propensity to consume.

In our example, the multiplier is calculated as follows:

$$m = \frac{1}{1-MPC} = \frac{1}{1-\dfrac{BC}{AC}} = \frac{1}{1-\dfrac{1}{2}} = 2$$

The same proposition can be stated in terms of the *marginal propensity to save* (MPS), that part of an extra pound which consumers will save. An alternative formula for the multiplier is therefore:

$$m = \frac{1}{MPS}$$

2.2 THE COMMON SENSE OF THE MULTIPLIER

There is nothing mysterious about the operation of the multiplier. An addition to investment of £1 immediately provides income and employment to those associated with the capital goods industries. Assuming MPC of ½, they save half and spend the rest on increased consumption. This provides extra income and employment in the consumer industries, of which half is saved and half spent on still more consumption. The process continues, with the multiplier gradually losing its power due to the erosive effect of saving in every round. It is finally exhausted when saving = investment. Thus in Figure 45, an injection of £25bn. government investment expands national income by £37.5 billion, of which £12.5bn. is spent on increased consumption and £25bn. is saved. *Note:* Contrary to expectations, society does not save first and then invest. Investment occurs first and by expanding national income calls forth the saving necessary to finance it. Saving must equal investment (*c.f.* 15.5.4).

2.3 SOME COMPLICATIONS IN THE CALCULATION OF A MULTIPLIER FOR THE UK

A number of factors dilute the multiplier as we have analysed it so far:

(a) Imports
To the extent that there is increased spending on imports, UK national income does not benefit.

(b) Indirect taxes
With every round of extra spending on domestically produced goods, there is a leakage in indirect taxation.

(c) Transfer payments
Net increases in spending on domestic goods are partially offset by the reductions in transfer payments such as unemployment benefit which occur as income and employment rise.

(d) Income in the form of profits

For every £100 rise in national income, wages will rise by about £80. the whole amount representing a rise in personal incomes. With profits, however, normally only about a third finds its way into personal income as dividends; the remainder is allocated to retained profits or Corporation Tax.

(e) Income tax

Taxation ensures that net disposable income rises by a less than proportionate amount than the increase in gross income with every round of the multiplier.

All these considerations represent leakages from the circular flow of income and consequently reduce the power of the multiplier, which in the UK in 1986 is calculated at about 1.35.

2.4 THE MULTIPLIER IN REVERSE

Just as the effect of an *addition* to aggregate demand will be multiplied, by parallel reasoning so will the effect of a *subtraction* (but see 3.2).

2.5 THE MULTIPLIER AND INFLATION

A major caveat to the power of the multiplier is the erosive effect of inflation. Demand/supply analysis tells us that as demand increases, the supply curve extends *in response to a rising price*. Thus, every round of the multiplier effect produces some increase in real income/output and employment and some rise in the price level. This inflation reduces *real* aggregate demand, since the purchasing power of money is less.

---

3. THE IMPACT OF TAXATION

3.1 GENERAL EFFECTS ON AGGREGATE DEMAND

Different taxes will have significantly different effects. An increase in Value Added Tax (VAT) by immediately raising the price level depresses consumption spending. Changes in Corporation Tax will affect the marginal efficiency of capital and hence the rate of investment. However, the most important single tax is Income Tax and for the purpose of the following analysis we assume that all taxes fall upon the incomes of consumers.

3.2 THE EFFECT OF AN INCOME TAX (T) ON CONSUMPTION

In Figure 47, a tax of £25bn. is introduced. As with an injection of government spending, the effect will be magnified by the operation of the multiplier *but in not quite the same way.* Specifically, the multiplied effect of T is less than the multiplied effect of G. This asymmetry is simply explained: when the first £1 of government spending is added, it immediately increases income by that amount, which is then multiplied. On the other hand, when government taxes £1, income and consumption are reduced but not by the full £1. Had he not been taxed, the consumer would have saved a part of that pound. Still assuming an MPC of ½, consumption is cut by 50 pence. Savings bear the burden of the other 50 pence of the £1 tax. The same multiplier (in our example, 1.5) is employed *but applied to a different starting point.* In the case of an injection of G, it is £25bn.×1.5 to increase national income by £37.5bn. In the case of a leakage through T, it is £12.5bn×1.5 to decrease national income by £18.75bn.

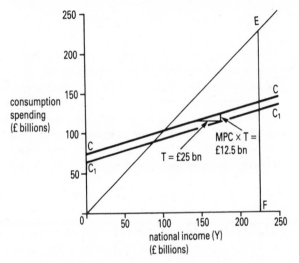

Figure 47. *Effect of taxes on consumption.* The consumption function moves down from CC to C_1C_1, but not by the full extent of the tax. A tax of £25bn. is shown in the *horizontal* movement to the right of CC. However, the effect on national income is determined not by this movement but by the *downward* shift, MPC×T or £12.5bn. when MPC=½.

4. FISCAL POLICY AND MACROECONOMIC STABILITY

4.1 THE BALANCED BUDGET

Traditionally, the first principle of sound public finance was the balanced budget. This sprang from the parallel made with private finance – that you cannot spend more than income without bankruptcy. However, *if* there is a stabilization role for public finance then the picture looks different. When private sector demands (C+I) are weak, a public sector deficit may seem positively desirable. Conversely, a surplus will be desirable when demand is too strong. *In principle*, a balanced budget will only be desirable when C+I+G approximate to full employment. Nevertheless, the previous analysis shows that in practice a balanced budget may still have some expansionary effect.

Combining our observations of the effect on national income of taxation and government spending:

> *Balanced Budget*
> +£25bn.G=+£37.5bn. national income.
> −£25bn.T =−£18.75bn. national income.
> Net   +£18.75bn. national income.

There has been some beneficial effect, but clearly not so great as would have been the case without taxation.

4.2 TAX REDUCTIONS

These may be employed to close a deflationary gap, assuming government spending to remain unchanged. However, the expansionary effect will be less than an equivalent increase in government spending. Some of the increased net disposable income will be saved. More precisely, in our example we observed the asymmetrical effects of G and T. A reduction in taxes of £25bn, will raise national income by £18.75bn., in contrast to the increase of £37.5bn. resulting from £25bn. government spending.

4.3 DEFICIT FINANCE

This policy will be the most expansionary of all. The £25bn. increase in G is financed entirely by an increase in government debt.

This approach has been a particular bone of contention between economists in recent years. Some argue that apart from the expansionary stimulus to income and employment, a greater government participation in the allocation of resources is desirable. Others (with whom the present UK government agrees) believe that it is impossible to reduce unemployment below its 'natural rate' by using fiscal policy and prefer the allocation of resources to be left to a greater extent to market forces. Moreover, they see such policy as the principal source of long-term inflation, establishing links between the scale of public sector borrowing, the money supply and the rate of inflation.

5. THE NATIONAL DEBT

5.1 ORIGIN AND GROWTH

The modern Debt originated in 1693 with a loan by the newly formed Bank of England of £1,200,000 to the government. It continued to grow during the eighteenth century and by 1815 had reached £815 million. During the nineteenth century, there was some repayment and the figure had been reduced to £650 million by 1914. The First World War saw it grow to £8 billion and the Second World War to £25 billion. The significant point is that until that time – an age which increasingly believed in the balanced budget – the only reason for government borrowing was wartime emergency. This part of today's Debt is sometimes called the *deadweight debt*, since it is not backed by any tangible assets. Since that time it has continued to grow, reaching £158bn. in March 1985. Put simply, it grows by the extent of the annual Central Government Borrowing Requirement (CGBR). There are two reasons:

(a) KEYNESIANISM

The general acceptance – at least until the 1970s – that deficit finance of government spending would produce the most expansionary results (see 4.3).

(b) INVESTMENT PROGRAMMES OF PUBLIC CORPORATIONS AND LOCAL AUTHORITIES

Nationalization of many capital intensive industries, together with the expanded responsibilities of local authorities, implied the need for funding. To some extent, these requirements may be met from the capital market, but for the most part they are provided from the National Loans Fund. This is financed from any current account budget surpluses, from interest receipts on past loans and with the balance met by new issues of government debt. This part of the Debt is the *reproductive debt*, since it is backed by income yielding assets.

5.2 MARKET AND OFFICIAL HOLDINGS OF NATIONAL DEBT

Table 10 shows a classification of securities.

The foreign currency debt comprises direct government borrowing in Europe and New York and post-war American reconstruction loans. This amount is normally excluded from conventional debt analysis. Of the remaining sterling debt, official holdings have a different significance from those of the market which can be analysed as follows.

Table 10. Market and official holdings of national debt (£m), March, 1985

Market holdings				% of total
Sterling marketable debt:	Govt. & govt. guaranteed stocks:			
		Index linked	9,482	6.5
		Other	103,714	70.7
		Treasury bills	1,241	.8
Sterling non-marketable debt:	National Savings:			
		Index linked	3,590	2.4
		Other	18,820	12.8
	Interest-free notes due to IMF		3,190	2.2
	Certificates of tax deposit		3,186	2.2
		Other	534	.4
			£143,759	98.0
Foreign currency debt:	North American. govt loans		2,172	
	New York bond issue		285	
	Other foreign currency bonds		452	
			£2,909	2
		Total market holdings	146,668	100
Official holdings			11,583	
		TOTAL	£158,251	

(*Source:* B.E.Q.B., December 1985)

(a) Funded debt
Strictly speaking, this means debt for which no repayment date has been set. More broadly, it includes dated stocks of varying maturities which are publicly quoted. The table shows that at 70% of the total, it is the most important component. (*Note:* Alternative terms are 'bonds', 'gilt-edged securities' or simply 'gilts'.)

(b) Floating debt
Government needs to borrow short term, (for 91 days/3 months) to facilitate the adjustment of irregular tax revenue and regular departmental expenditure. It does so against the issue of Treasury Bills which are of two types: tap and tender. Tap bills represent lending to the Treasury by government departments. These are of much less significance than 'tender bills' which are offered for public tender every Friday on the London Discount Market.

(c) Non-marketable debt
For the first two categories, there are organized markets with daily purchases and sales of maturing securities. The greater part of the

non-marketable debt comprises securities for which there is no set redemption date, although the issuing authority will repay subject to its own conditions. Included are *national savings* – certificates, income bonds, deposit bonds, premium savings bonds, gift tokens, the contractual savings scheme (SAYE) and deposits with the National Savings Bank investment account.

5.3 DISTRIBUTION OF THE STERLING NATIONAL DEBT

Table 11 shows the ownership of the sterling debt.

Table 11. Distribution of the Sterling national debt (£ billions) March 1985

Market holdings

Public corporations & local authorities	1.0
Monetary sector	8.0
Other financial institutions:	
Insurance companies & pension funds	57.5
Other	13.8
Overseas residents	13.2
Individuals and private trusts	34.7
Other	15.6
TOTAL	143.8
Official Holdings	11.6
TOTAL STERLING DEBT	155.4

(*Source*: B.E.Q.B., December 1985)

(a) Public corporations and local authorities
They account for .7% of market holdings and are held for cash management purposes.

(b) Monetary sector
This includes the banks and discount houses, which account for 5.6% of market holdings. They are significant to the rate of monetary growth and this relationship will be examined in the context of the banking system.

(c) Other Financial Institutions
Under this heading are insurance companies, building societies, pension funds, investment and unit trusts. They have 49.5% of market holdings and play a crucial role in the successful funding of public sector borrowing.

(d) Overseas holders
International organizations such as the International Monetary Fund,

central monetary institutions and private sector holdings, which amount to 9.2%.

(e) Other

Public Trustee and various non-corporate bodies such as the Church Commissioners, individuals and private trusts – to which the bulk of national savings are allotted – and industrial and commercial companies. They account for 35% of market holdings.

(f) Official holdings

The holdings of the Bank of England Issue Department (as cover against the note issue) and Banking Department; government departments; the National Debt Commissioners, who invest the funds of the ordinary department of the National Savings Bank.

5.4 THE BURDEN OF THE DEBT

It will be *direct* to the extent that the debtors are deprived of goods and services in consequence of the payment of interest and the repayment of principal. It will be indirect to the extent that the higher levels of taxation necessary to service it depress the economy. Beyond this, a large public sector deficit financed through the monetary sector will lead to an expansion of the money supply with potentially inflationary effects.

Directly, the externally held debt implies the need to make exports for which there are no corresponding imports whenever money payments are made overseas. However, since this portion amounts to only 9.2% of total market holdings, the impact is not great. It also tells us that the term 'national' debt is misleading since it is largely what government owes its own citizens. 'Government' debt would seem more appropriate.

The direct burden of internally held debt depends upon the extent to which income is redistributed from taxpayer to bondholder, from low income groups to high income groups. If debt ownership were evenly distributed throughout the community and taxpayers made an equal contribution to the servicing charge, the burden would be zero. Every tax contribution of £1 would be exactly offset by an interest payment of £1. While it is true that there is a substantial spread of ownership through national savings and the institutional investors, it is likely that there is a net benefit in favour of the higher income groups whose propensity to save is increased. There is a corresponding decrease in the propensity to consume of the lower income groups whose living standards will be adversely affected.

5.5 A MONETARIST VIEW OF A LARGE PUBLIC SECTOR BORROWING REQUIREMENT (PSBR)

(a) 'Crowding out'

In any period there is a limited pool of loanable funds to be divided between private and public sectors. A large PSBR (i.e. CGBR plus other public sector borrowing in the market) competes with the requirements of the private sector and interest rates are bid up. Many private sector firms are crowded out of the market and fail.

(b) Monetary expansion

The pressure on interest rates can be avoided by sales of debt to the banking system. Whenever the banks lend, they 'create' the money to do so (this relationship will be explained in Chapter 15.) In the monetarist view, the subsequent excessive growth of the money supply is the exclusive source of all inflation.

MULTIPLE CHOICE

In an economy in which there are unemployed resources, if the government finances an increase in its expenditure on goods and services by an equivalent increase in income tax this will cause the national income to

(*a*)   remain the same, because the amount of extra government expenditure is exactly offset by the reduction in the disposable incomes of consumers;

(*b*)   fall, because the negative multiplier effect from reducing disposable incomes will outweigh the positive mulitplier effect from the increase in government expenditure;

(*c*)   fall, since the reduction in disposable incomes will lead to a fall in savings and, hence, in investment;

(*d*)   rise, since some of the reduction in disposable incomes would otherwise have been saved and, hence, there is a positive net multiplier effect from increased government spending;

(*e*)   rise, because the increase in government expenditure will lead to an increase in private investment via a rise in interest rates.

(O & CSEB, June 1983)

Key Reference 3.2. *Answer* (*d*).

In a closed economy, with no government sector, the initial equilibrium level of national income is £375 million and the marginal propensity to save is 0.4. Given constant prices, if investment rises from £150 million to £200 million, what is the new equilibrium level of national income?

(*a*)   £395 million;
(*b*)   £435 million;
(*c*)   £445 million;
(*d*)   £455 million;
(*e*)   £500 million.   *(0 & CSEB, June 1985)*

Key Reference 2.1 and in particular Figure 46. *Answer* (*e*).

Which of the following methods of government borrowing is likely to be most inflationary? The sale of

(*a*)   long-term securities to the general public;
(*b*)   long-term securities to the banking sector;
(*c*)   savings certificates to the general public;

(d)   Treasury bills to the banking sector   (*AEB, June 1985*)
Key References 5.2(a) & (b) and Table 10; 5.5. *Answer* (b).

ESSAYS

Distinguish between monetary and fiscal policy. Does monetary policy have any part to play in the Keynesian approach to running the economy and does fiscal policy have any part in the Monetarist approach?   (*JMB, June 1985*)
Key References The link between the two lies in 5.5. Work back to fiscal policy, in particular 4.1 and 4.3 and forward to Chapter 15, in particular 3.2 and 3.3.

What is meant by the 'public sector borrowing requirement'? Discuss why the PSBR has been the focus of so much public debate in recent years.   (*JMB, June 1984*)
Key References 4.1 and 4.3; 5.2(a); 5.3(b); 5.5(a) and 7(b). Chapter 15.3.2–3.

Explain what is meant by the fiscal policy of a government. What are the likely economic and social effects of a change in fiscal policy?
     (*JMB, June 1983*)

Key References 1.1–3

Discuss some of the macroeconomic consequences of a reduction in personal taxation.   (*London, Paper 1, Jan, 1985*)
Key References 4.1; 4.2; 4.3; Chapter 12.4.2.

THE ROLE OF MONEY IN NATIONAL INCOME DETERMINATION

CONTENTS

1. THE ENGLISH CLASSICAL VIEW

1.1 REAL AND NOMINAL INCOME

Following Say's Law of Markets, which claimed that production created its own demand, *real* national income was determined by *real* factors – natural resources and climate, technology, enterprise and innovation, thrift and industriousness etc. Money was simply a medium of exchange which could have no long-run impact on the level of economic activity. However, it had everything to do with the determination of the price level and therefore the nominal national income. This relationship was explained in the quantity theory of money:

1.2 QUANTITY THEORY OF MONEY

This theory is expressed in the formula:

$$M \times V = P \times Q$$

where M is the quantity of money, V the velocity of circulation, P the general price level and Q the real output of goods and services. $P \times Q$ will of course represent the money value of real national income.

By itself, this equation is a truism. Elaborated, the further assertions were made that Q was determined by real factors; velocity was determined by institutional arrangements such as the periodicity of wage payments – money circulates more rapidly if payments are weekly rather than monthly – and current banking practices.

With Q and V as constants, it followed that P would be determined by M. In other words, the price level could be influenced by adjustments to the supply of money.

1.3 CLASSICAL MONETARY POLICY

The primary objective was the stabilization of the price level and the balance of international payments. An unfavourable balance, under the nineteenth-century gold standard, was reflected in a drain on the reserves, a contraction of the cash base and the bank credit built upon it. This monetary restriction was consistent with higher interest rates and therefore a decline in investment, income, output and employment. Deflation continued until the international payments balance was restored and gold flowed back into the country.

The process was now reversed. *An expanded money supply induced lower interest rates, increased investment and therefore economic recovery.* Keynes challenged these conclusions.

2. A KEYNESIAN VIEW OF MONEY

2.1 THE DEMAND FOR MONEY

It has been noted (see Chapter 12,3.2(d)) that Keynes sought to produce a synthesis of the real and monetary economies, giving a pivotal role to money but *not to monetary policy*. By 1931, Bank Rate was down to 2% and the economy showed no signs of recovery. Monetary policy as an *active* instrument remained dormant until 1951. Keynes himself concluded that it was impotent and that the weight of demand management should be borne by fiscal policy.

The reasons for this conclusion rest upon his analysis of the demand for money.

(a) Transactions demand

This is the demand for money in its role as a medium of exchange. The amount which is required depends upon the volume of business transacted, i.e. by national income in money terms. It follows that a monetary expansion which produces lower interest rates, increased investment and higher national income must be sufficient to provide the extra *transactions* money necessary for the increased volume of business. Whether or not this happens depends upon the demand for liquidity money out of a given money stock, at the new lower rates.

(b) Liquidity, precautionary and speculative money

Keynes observed that money has a unique characteristic: liquidity (i.e. instant purchasing power), and for this reason it will be held for its own sake. We desire liquidity not only for the precautionary motive of unforeseen eventualities but also for the speculative motive of taking advantage of some unexpected bargain. However, liquidity has an opportunity cost which is geared to the rate of interest and this cost is high when rates are high. Liquidity preference is correspondingly low and increased cash balances will express themselves in increased holdings of income yielding financial assets. Conversely, when rates are low opportunity costs are low and when coupled with the risk of holding financial assets, liquidity preference will be extremely high. Increased cash balances will simply be held as cash.

2.2 'THE LIQUIDITY TRAP'

This was Keynes's explanation of the impotence of monetary policy in curing depression. When liquidity preference is low, extra cash will be converted into financial assets. For the moment, these are in fixed supply and therefore capital values are forced up and interest rates pushed down.

Note: When the market bids up the price of a 10% £100 bond to £200, the yield falls to £5 per £100, a return of 5%.

If, however, interest rates are already low and liquidity preference correspondingly high, any increase in the money supply will simply express itself as increased cash balances. There is no incentive to purchase financial assets and therefore no change in capital values and interest rates. Without further reductions in rates there is no incentive to greater investment and economic recovery.

2.3 THE DEMAND FOR MONEY AND INTEREST RATE EQUILIBRIUM

In Figure 48, the transactions demand for money and the liquidity demand are shown for a given level of national income Y_o, in the demand curve DD. The transactions element in total demand upon a fixed money stock M_o is shown by the distance T_o. The liquidity demand has then to be satisfied (note that this increases as the rate of interest falls). This is shown by the flattening of the lower part of the demand curve. Ultimately a liquidity trap is reached, where additions to the money supply have little effect on interest rates.

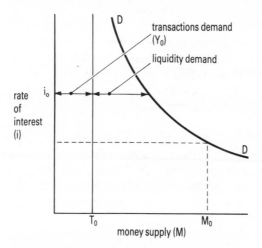

Figure 48. *Equilibrium interest rate for a given national income.* National income of Y_o corresponds to the transactions demand for money of T_o. The curve DD is the total demand for money. Only interest rate i_o balances the transactions demand with the liquidity demand within the fixed money stock, M_o.

Only an interest rate of i_o, will sustain national income at Y_o since it is the only interest rate which balances transactions demand T_o with the liquidity demand, the money stock constant at M_o.

In Figure 49, national income has risen to Y_1 with transactions demand rising to T_1, the amount now necessary to finance the increased volume of business. The increased demand for money is shown by the shift of the demand curve to the right, to D_1D_1. The money supply is still fixed at M_0. It follows that the increased transactions demand can only be satisfied at the expense of the demand for liquidity. Liquidity preference will only be surrendered in exchange for higher interest rates. Rates will rise to a new equilibrium i_1.

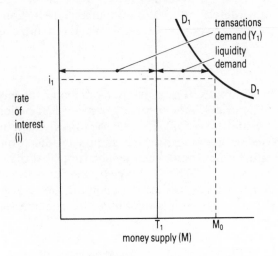

Figure 49. *Equilibrium interest rate for a higher national income.* The demand for money shifts to D_1D_1. The increased transactions demand T_1 corresponds to the higher national income Y_1. The higher interest rate i_1 is necessary to reduce the liquidity demand.

We are led to the conclusion that for any given money stock, the higher the national income the higher the interest rate equilibrium necessary to sustain it. Put another way, higher interest rates are necessary if more liquidity money is to be made available for transactions purposes. The liquidity money (LM) curve therefore slopes up from left to right.

2.4 OVERALL NATIONAL INCOME EQUILIBRIUM

In Figure 50, the X-axis now shows national income. The LM curve reflects the rise in interest rates necessary if liquidity money is to be translated into transactions money consistent with a rising national income.

The investment savings (IS) curve slopes down from left to right. The reasons for this have already been explained in some detail (see Chapter 11,5.2; Chapter 12,4.6 & 5.4). High interest rates reduce investment, which through the multiplier reduces national income. Conversely, lower interest rates encourage investment which, operating through the multiplier, expands national income sufficiently to call forth savings which equate with the original investment. The investment and savings curves are one and the same.

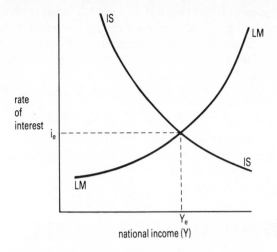

Figure 50. *National income equilibrium.* At interest rate i_e
and national income Y_e, there is overall equilibrium.
Savings=investment, the demand for liquidity money is
in balance with the demand for transactions money and
the funds made available balance the investment
demand.

The equilibrium level of national income lies at Y_e, the intersection
of the IS and LM curves, which point also determines the equilibrium
rate of interest i_e. This equilibrium also reflects the equation of saving
and investment and the balancing of the transactions and liquidity
demands for money within the confines of a fixed money supply.

This analysis has several interesting applications. A study of the
shapes and shifts of both curves produces some useful conclusions,
e.g. an autonomous increase in investment shifts the IS curve to the
right to give a higher national income equilibrium and a higher
interest rate equilibrium; where there exists a liquidity trap, an expansion of the money supply will have little effect on interest rates. The
LM curve will shift only slightly to the right for a slightly higher
national income equilibrium and a slightly lower interest rate equilibrium.

**2.5 SUMMARY OF THE
KEYNESIAN SYSTEM**

So far, we have established that real national income is determined by
C+I+G, with fiscal policy playing a crucial role in manipulating G to
compensate for the deficiencies of C and I. Monetary policy is considered too weak and unpredictable for this purpose. There is certainly a relationship between rates of interest and investment.
Moreover, when interest rates are already low, an expansion of the
money supply encounters the liquidity trap; rates are not reduced
further and there is no recovery of investment. Money has been
introduced into the theory of real national income determination. It is

given a significant role when we observe that it is the interest rate which produces an equilibrium between a given level of national income and saving/investment on the one hand, and the transference of liquidity money to transactions purposes on the other – the money supply being constant.

However, the system pays little attention to the determination of the price level. A criticism levelled at Keynes was that his analysis was static, framed in terms of a fixed price level. We have already noted that variations in prices affect aggregate demand and must therefore be taken into account (see Chapter 12, 5.2).

3. KEYNESIAN ANALYSIS OF PRICE DETERMINATION

3.1 DOWNWARD INFLEXIBILITY OF WAGES AND PRICES

Keynes himself – if not some of his immediate successors – was well aware of the dangers of inflation which would result from monetary expansion once full employment had been reached. In this situation, fiscal policy would be used symmetrically to close an *inflationary* gap. It would also of course be used to close a *deflationary* gap. Unlike the classical economists who believed that the latter would be self-adjusting through a downward movement of prices, he observed that in the twentieth century, prices were downward inflexible (see Chapter 12, 6.4). Since the price mechanism failed to secure equilibrium at full employment, the price level was intrinsically unimportant to the determination of maximum *real* national income. Moreover, since he refuted the quantity theory of money, there existed no systematic method of regulating the price level.

3.2 REFUTATION OF QUANTITY THEORY

This hinges on a rejection of the presumed stability of the velocity of circulation (V). It is accepted that institutional arrangements are factors in determining velocity, but the distinction between transaction demand and liquidity demand for money is also a significant consideration. Quantity theory prevails in respect of transactions demand which corresponds to money national income ($P \times Q$), under given institutional conditions. So far V is stable. However, the demand for liquidity money varies with the rate of interest; the lower the rate, the higher the holdings of cash balances and vice-versa. We conclude that the velocity of circulation of *liquidity money* varies with the rate of interest. What is true for a part of the money supply must have a bearing on the whole. It follows that in the Keynesian analysis, V is dependent not simply upon institutional factors but also upon the interest rate. The causal link between M and P can now be broken. When interest rates are already low, monetary expansion may simply lead to the liquidity trap, increased holdings of cash balances and no further decline in interest rates. In terms of the quantity theory, the increase in M has been offset by the decline in V, leaving P×Q unchanged.

3.3 THE INVERSE L KEYNESIAN AGGREGATE SUPPLY CURVE (KAS)

An approximation of the Keynesian position can be shown in the inverse L aggregate supply curve in Figure 51. At P_e the price level is downward inflexible and supply is elastic at that price to the full employment national income equilibrium Y_e, determined by the aggregate demand curve AD_e. If demand is deficient, equilibrium is short of full employment national income, as at Y_1. There is an assumption that shifts of the AD curve to the right will produce increased income, output and employment up to Y_e with very little effect on the price level. Beyond full employment any further movement, e.g. to AD_2, will be reflected entirely in higher prices, e.g. P_1.

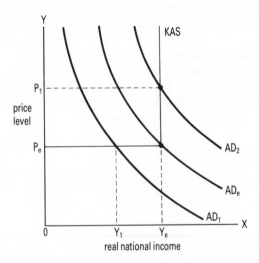

Figure 51. *Inverse L aggregate supply curve.* KAS is elastic at P_e to full employment national income Y_e. It is then inelastic. Further shifts to the right of AD result in higher prices.

4. INFLATION

4.1 COST OF INFLATION

Between the Wars, prices throughout the world were in general stable, with some tendency to fall. Since 1945, varying degrees of inflation have been experienced by all countries. There are significant costs.

(a) Arbitrary redistribution of income
The fiscal and social security systems achieve a *planned* redistribution on a politically agreed basis. Inflation does this in a random way.

Powerfully organized sections of society are able to keep money incomes abreast of inflation, at the expense of those whose money incomes are static or slow to respond.

(b) Redistribution of wealth
Similarly, there is a redistribution from saver to borrower, e.g. nominal deposit rate of 5% with 25% inflation implies a real negative rate of 20%. A nominal lending rate of 5% with 25% inflation implies a cost to the borrower of a negative 20%. There has been a transfer of £20 per £100.

(c) Business confidence
Economists have sometimes argued that a mild upward tilt to prices is conducive to business activity, since expanding profit margins encourage investment. However, there arrives a point where the rate of inflation makes the unit of account so unstable that businessmen can no longer plan the future with any confidence.

(d) Balance of payments
Where a nation's inflation rate exceeds those of its international competitors, it will be priced out of world markets and its exports will decline. Simultaneously, its domestic markets will be increasingly penetrated by cheaper imports.

(e) Political instability
When inflation progresses to hyperinflation, the unit of currency is destroyed and with it the basis of a free contractual society.

4.2 THE NEO-CLASSICAL SYNTHESIS
In the context of post-war inflation, the Keynesian model was modified in the 1950s and 1960s. The result was a synthesis of certain classical and Keynesian propositions. A new theory of price adjustment emerges, based on two observations.

(a) Prices rise when demand exceeds supply
Conversely, they fall when supply exceeds demand.

(b) Asymmetrical adjustment process
The rise in prices resulting from a given percentage excess of demand will be greater than the fall in prices resulting from the same percentage excess of supply.

Figure 52 illustrates both propositions. The vertical axis measures the rate of inflation; the horizontal axis measures excess demand $Y_d - Y_s$. The first proposition is illustrated by the upward slope of the curve; the second proposition by the curvature of the slope. It slopes upward at an increasing rate.

Note: These propositions about price adjustment differ from Keynes's theory, which assumed that prices and wages were completely down-

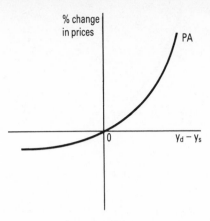

Figure 52. *Neo-classical price adjustment*. The price adjustment curve PA illustrates two propositions. Prices rise when there is excess demand and fall when there is excess supply. Prices rise more quickly for any given percentage of excess demand than they fall for the same percentage excess of supply.

ward inflexible and that beyond full employment, they would move up instantly to clear excess demand. Neo-classical theory asserts that wages and prices *will* fall, but slowly, and that they will rise faster than they will fall.

This theory of price adjustment is often applied specifically to wage adjustment, excess demand being related to the unemployment rate.

4.3 THE PHILLIPS CURVE

In 1958, Professor A. W. Phillips published an essay, 'The Relation Between Unemployment and the Rate of Change of Money Wages in the United Kingdom, 1861–1957' (*Economics*, vol. 25, 1958). He argued that his research revealed a regular inverse relationship between the level of unemployment and the rate at which money wages changed. When there was excess demand in the labour market, i.e. 'too little unemployment', money wages would tend to drift up. Since wages are a major element in total costs, when they moved up profit margins would be squeezed to the point where long-run prices were raised.

This proposition is shown in the Phillips Curve in Figure 53.

At E_O, there is equilibrium. Money wages are stable or rising at the same rate as productivity and there is no inflation. At E_F, there is over-full employment and wages and prices are rising. At E_U, there is excessive unemployment and wages and prices are falling.

There is an assumed 'trade-off' between inflation and unemployment with a clear policy implication. If unemployment is deemed to be too high, it will be reduced by a stimulus to aggregate demand and at the expense of a rather higher rate of inflation. The opposite course

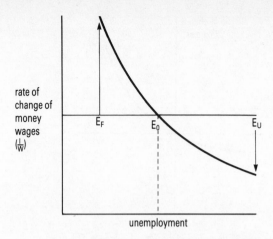

Figure 53. *Phillips curve.* The curve postulates an inverse
relationship between the level of unemployment and the
rate of change of money wages and therefore prices.

will be followed if inflation is thought to be too high. A problem then
arises if, as occurred in the UK in the late 1960s, the 'trade-off'
apparently breaks down and inflation and unemployment increase
together. In this situation, any attempt to check inflation by a
deliberate increase in unemployment is unacceptable and there may
be resort to a prices and incomes policy.

4.4 INCOMES POLICY

Wage controls will be seen variously as a long-term mechanism for
checking inflation at full employment (on the assumption that the
primary cause is wage cost-push); as a means of preventing labour
pricing itself out of the market; and as a way of achieving a more
equitable distribution of income.

Since 1945 there have been six attempts, formal and informal, to
establish incomes policies in the UK.

(a) An appeal for trade union cooperation (1948)

Unions were invited to postpone wage claims so as to assist in dealing
with the prevailing balance of payments crisis. Cooperation lasted
until pressures on the cost of living resulted from the 1949
devaluation.

(b) 'Wage Pause' (1956)

Balance of payments problems which resulted from the Suez crisis
persuaded government to set up a Council on Productivity, Prices
and Incomes as an advisory body and to ask for union cooperation in
a 'wage pause'. The Council proved uninfluential.

(c) National Incomes Commission (1962)

Again an advisory body, with the task of publishing 'guiding lights' for pay claims. The NIC received little trade union cooperation.

(d) National Board for Prices and Incomes (PIB) 1965

This was the first formal attempt at an incomes policy, agreed to by employers and trade unions as a pre-condition for expansionary government policies. The PIB established criteria for wage increases, with 'norms' and exceptions for 'special cases'. It built up a substantial body of case precedents and enjoyed a considerable measure of success on a voluntary basis. In the sterling crisis of 1966, statutory effect was given to a six-month wage freeze. A return was made to a voluntary policy in 1967, but this became increasingly ineffective in the run-up to the 1970 General Election.

(e) Pay Board and Price Commission, (1973)

The 1970 government disbanded the PIB on the view that prices and incomes policies were ineffective. However in 1972 – faced with one million unemployed – it engaged in a substantial reflation while seeking to avoid the impact on prices and wages through a statutory 'pay standstill'. A new Pay Board then introduced three phases of a statutory incomes policy.

(f) 'Social Contract' (1975)

This was the label given to a new voluntary agreement between TUC and government. The policy moved through three phases. The first two limited all pay rises to specific flat rate increases, while the third was a general indication that pay rises should not exceed 10%.

The 1979 government abandoned incomes policy as both ineffective in dealing with inflation and damaging to the structure of a market economy.

4.5 CRITICISMS OF INCOMES POLICY

The UK's experience is not encouraging to those who would see incomes policy – at least in the forms so far attempted – as a permanent feature of the economy. For a variety of reasons they have been relatively short-lived and when they have finally broken down, there has been a determined attempt by labour to make up lost ground.

(a) Percentage increases or flat-rate increases

Formal policies have been divisive, failing to secure general consent. Flat-rate increases reduce differentials and therefore are rejected by skilled labour. Percentage rate increases widen differentials and are disadvantageous to the unskilled.

(b) Voluntary or statutory policies

Since the central function of trade unions is collective bargaining for specific memberships, they will not accept long-term statutory constraints. Voluntary policies may be agreed by trade union leaders, but ultimately rejected by the rank and file if pressures on living standards become too great.

(c) Market distortions

The artificial rigging of relative prices distorts the allocation of labour. If wages cannot rise in one part of the labour market in response to increasing demand, price loses its effectiveness as a signal of shortages.

(d) A check to inflation?

If inflation is not rooted in wage cost-push, then incomes policies will not cure it.

4.6 FRIEDMAN AND THE PHILLIPS CURVE

During the 1960s, the Phillips proposition was widely accepted as a basis for practical policy. At the same time, however, Edmund Phelps and Milton Friedman were independently pointing to a logical flaw in the neo-classical price adjustment theory.

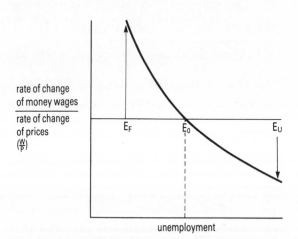

Figure 54. *Friedman's criticism of the Phillips curve.*
The vertical axis now shows real wages W/P. At E_0 there is equilibrium with unemployment and real wages constant. The stability of real wages may be shown as
$$\frac{1W}{1P} = \frac{2W}{2P} = \frac{3W}{3P}.$$ But the rise in these nominal values is the symptom of inflation which has occurred without change in unemployment.

In particular, Friedman criticized the conclusions associated with the Phillips curve, arguing that equilibrium in the labour markets is achieved not through the *money* wage but through the *real* wage, i.e. what the money will buy. The vertical axis of the Phillips curve is therefore incorrectly labelled. When it is correctly designated *real* wages, the curve tells us nothing about the relationship between the level of unemployment and the rate of change of *money* wages and *prices*; i.e. it tells us nothing about the cause of inflation. At E_o, there is equilibrium with neither inflationary nor deflationary pressure on wages and prices. However, real wages will remain stable with money wages and money prices constant at $\dfrac{1W}{1P}$ or doubled to $\dfrac{2W}{2P}$ or trebled to $\dfrac{3W}{3P}$. It is the increase in these nominal quantities which is the symptom of inflation and this can occur without any change in the level of unemployment. What has been overlooked is the role of expectations.

4.7 PRICE EXPECTATIONS AND THE 'NATURAL RATE' OF UNEMPLOYMENT

More precisely, the flaw in this theory of price adjustment is that it fails to take account of the possibility that prices may change because everyone correctly anticipates that they should change in response to changing conditions of demand, and that this can occur without any interim period of excess demand or excess supply. In principle, as firms and unions look to the future, they will desire a change in the price of their output or labour which corresponds to the expected *average* change in prices and wages. In addition, however, firms and unions in expanding sectors of the economy which are experiencing excess demand will look for price and wage rises above the expected average rise. Conversely, in contracting sectors of the economy, price and wage rises *less* than the expected average rise will be sought. We are led to the proposition that: 'the change in prices or wages will equal the expected average change in prices or wages, adjusted for an amount that is positive if there is excess demand and negative if there is excess supply'.

These changes in *relative* prices can now be aggregated to establish the *actual* change in the *absolute* price level, i.e. the rate of inflation. Summarized, a second proposition tells us that: 'the rate of inflation equals the expected rate of inflation of prices and wages, plus an amount which represents the consequences of excess aggregate demand'.

It can be seen that the original Phillips curve expression of the neo-classical theory of price adjustment confused absolute and relative prices. Friedman and Phelps modified it to assert that a change in *relative* prices is a function of excess demand. The remaining element in the change in the *absolute* price is the *expected rate of inflation*.

This modification is illustrated in Figure 55, where SRPC$_o$ is a Phillips curve similar to that shown in Figure 53; it is constructed for an expected inflation rate of zero. With U_n unemployment, there is no excess demand; the two elements combined establish that there is no inflation.

If unemployment now fell to U_a there would be excess demand. As yet there is no expectation of inflation, but inflation of O_a would arise in response to the excess demand.

Once this inflation rate becomes established, firms and unions build it into their own price adjustments. A new Phillips curve $SRPC_a$ is constructed, immediately above U_n and incorporating the expected inflation rate of O_a.

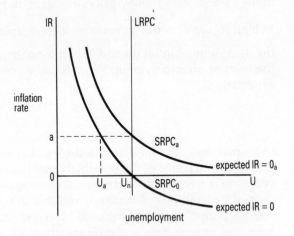

Figure 55. *Expectations augmented Phillips curve.*
A short-run Phillips curve SRPC is constructed for every expected rate of inflation. $SRPC_0$ expects a zero inflation rate. $SRPC_a$ expects an inflation rate of O_a. When inflation is fully anticipated, the long-run Phillips curve LRPC is vertical.

These two curves are known as short-run Phillips curves and imply a trade-off between inflation and unemployment. The long-run Phillips curve (LRPC) assumes that over a long period of time, the inflation rate is fully anticipated. The curve is vertical from U_n and there is no trade-off. Unemployment always reverts to its 'natural rate'. In other words, unemployment only differs from its natural rate when the *actual* rate of inflation differs from the *expected* rate.

Note: The 'natural rate' of unemployment may be defined as that which cannot be reduced by any increase in aggregate demand. Friedman asserts that it is due to imperfections in the labour markets stemming from labour's immobility. Critically, he parodies the phrase and goes on to speak of the 'unnatural rate' of unemployment which he argues results from institutional causes, e.g. trade union restrictive practices, labour legislation which impedes the operation of a free market.

4.8 CONCLUSIONS

The analyses of Phelps and Friedman provide the insights from which recent developments in macroeconomic theory have grown. Keynesian theory was developed in the context of massive under-utilization of capacity and focused upon a sophisticated theory of aggregate demand. It paid little attention to aggregate supply and was unable to explain the post-war phenomenon of pro-cyclical movements of inflation. The 'New Keynesian' and 'New Classical' schools of the past decade have concentrated upon remedying this deficiency, in the terms of theories of rational expectations. These theories suggest in general that firms and households form rational expectations about the price level and what they will supply to the market at those prices. These expectations, although rational, are based upon imperfect information which it is too costly to update and react to on a short-term basis.

On the demand side, there is a government and a central bank which generate a certain volume of money and expenditures. If the aggregate demand which results determines a price level which is the same as the expected price level, the economy settles at full employment equilibrium. If it exceeds that expectation, the economy moves to a higher level of prices, output and employment – and vice-versa.

MULTIPLE CHOICE
In Keynesian monetary theory, an increase in the supply of money will *not* cause a fall in interest rates if
(*a*)   bond prices are expected to rise;
(*b*)   investment demand is interest inelastic;
(*c*)   the velocity of circulation of money increases;
(*d*)   the liquidity preference schedule is perfectly elastic;
(*e*)   the liquidity preference schedule is perfectly inelastic.
(*O & CSEB, June 1983*)
Key References 2.1–3. *Answer* (*d*).

In Keynesian theory, which one of the following is a determinant of the demand for money?
(a)   the central bank;
(b)   special deposits;
(c)   the commercial banks;
(d)   the ratio of cash to total bank assets;
(e)   the rate of interest.   (*O & CSEB, June –1984*)
Key References 2.1–3. *Answer* (*e*).

On the assumption of a constant income-velocity of circulation of money, if real output grows by 5% and the rate of growth of the money supply is 8%, what will be the approximate change in the price level?
(*a*)   −3%;
(*b*)   +3%;
(*c*)   +5%'
(*d*)   +8%;
(*e*)   +13%.
Key References 1.2. *Answer* (*b*).

One or more of the options may be correct. Code –
(*a*)   1, 2, 3 all correct;
(*b*)   1, 2 only correct;
(*c*)   2, 3 only correct;
(*d*)   1 only correct.
Individuals and companies will demand money to hold
1   as a form of highly liquid asset;

2 for the purpose of normal transactions and as a safeguard against unforeseen circumstances;

3 when the opportunity cost of holding money is negligible
(AEB, November 1983)

Key References 2.1(a) & (b). *Answer (a).*

ESSAYS

Compare the relative costs of unemployment and inflation to the economy. Can policy-makers choose the level of unemployment and inflation for an economy? *(JMB, June 1985)*
Key References Chapter 12, section 1; Chapter 14, 4.2 and particularly 4.3. Then 4.6–8.

What is meant by the 'natural rate of unemployment'? To what extent can actual unemployment diverge from the natural rate?
(JMB Special, June 1984)
Key References 4.2; 4.3; 4.7; 4.8.

Why is inflation generally regarded as undesirable? Do you regard inflation as the cause of Britain's problems or the result of them?
(JMB, June 1984)
Key References 4.1; 2.5; 4.2; 4.3; 4.7; 4.8.

What is meant by the term 'natural rate of unemployment'? Explain how government policies aimed at reducing unemployment below the natural rate may only serve to cause an accelerating rate of inflation. *(AEB, November 1984)*
Key References 4.6; 4.7; 4.8.

Examine the effects of changes in the value of money on the level of economic activity. *(O & CSEB, 9635/1, July 1985)*
Key References 2.5; 3.1–3, but particularly 4.2.

THE MONETARY SYSTEM

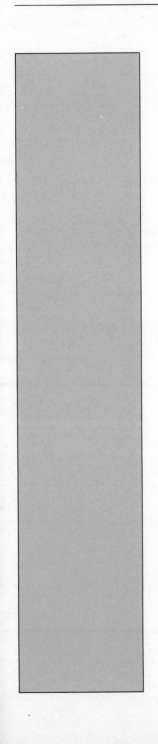

MONEY AND THE COMMERCIAL BANKS

1. WHAT IS MONEY?

1.1 'MONEY IS WHAT MONEY DOES'

The question 'What is money?' can be answered by the simple assertion that 'money is what money does'. In other words, if we first determine the functions of money, then whatever is capable of performing those functions *is* money. These functions are:

(a) Medium of exchange
This is the central function in an exchange economy. Without money, reliance would have to be placed upon barter, which has the disadvantage that 'rather than there being a coincidence of wants, there is a want of coincidence'. In other words, the periodicity of the wants of the shoemaker for bread will not coincide with that of the baker for shoes. In an advanced economy, money is the essential lubricant which makes possible a high degree of specialization.

(b) Standard unit of account
On a barter system, it would be necessary to operate multiple exchange ratios, each item entering into trade being paired with every other item. Money provides a common denominator against which all exchange values can be measured.

(c) Store of value
While it would be possible to save a portion of some physical goods for future use, it would not be true for services 'which are consumed in the instant of their creation'. Recognizing that in times of inflation money is an imperfect store, it is the best mechanism we have for conserving purchasing power for future use.

(d) Standard of deferred payment
Money permits the granting of credit. Present purchasing power is advanced against the assurance of restoring that purchasing power at some future date.

(e) Extension of individual choice
Even in command economies where production is fully planned, money is necessary to give the consumer some freedom of choice when the end product is distributed. Rationing would be the only alternative.

1.2 THE CHARACTERISTICS OF THAT WHICH WILL PERFORM MONEY'S FUNCTIONS

The earliest forms of money were commodities which different societies prized, e.g. olive oil in classical times, cowrie shells in the Pacific islands, cattle in Africa – but most significantly in Western Europe gold and silver. This observation might lead to the erroneous conclusion that the primary characteristic of money is some intrinsic value.

However, any such illusion is dispelled when we observe the emergence of paper money, although this paper at first circulated merely for convenience and was simply the title to the 'real' money – the gold which it represented – held in the vaults of banks. During the eighteenth century an increasing number of private banks issued their own bank-notes. In 1844, the Bank Charter Act vested the monopoly right of note issue for England and Wales in the Bank of England. At the same time, the Act established a gold standard. Save for a small fiduciary issue, the Bank was required to back all its notes with gold of a fixed weight to which they were convertible on demand. This standard remained in effective operation until 1913 and theoretically so until 1931, when it was formally abandoned.

Subsequently, paper of no intrinsic value has continued to circulate in performance of money's functions. Why should this be so? The paradoxical answer is that anything can serve as money, provided that everyone accepts it for that purpose. Universal acceptability is the key. The important proviso is that to be acceptable, whatever is used must have some limitation on its supply. The Bank of England note issue is subject to certain statutory constraints. However, this is not of any great importance, since today notes and coin represent only the 'small change' of the economy. By far the greater part of the money supply, on any definition, comprises nothing more tangible than a figure on a bank computer (sometimes described as *bank deposit money*), which can be transferred from one account to another by some instrument, usually the cheque.

Note: It is the figure transferred in making payment which is money, *not* the cheque.

1.3 WHICH DEPOSITS SHOULD BE INCLUDED IN A DEFINITION OF MONEY?

In 1959, the Radcliffe Report on the working of the British monetary system offered the broad definition of money as being 'notes, coin and bank deposits'. At this time, there was little interest in a more precise definition. Of greater importance to Radcliffe than the money stock was the general liquidity of the economy, i.e. the ability to get out of financial assets into cash. Only under the influence of monetarism during the 1960s did the Bank come to express a greater interest in a statistical definition. This became necessary when in 1971 it introduced a new statistical series for the money supply; it had then to confront the problem of which types of deposit – and with which institutions – to include.

On a narrow view of money as a medium of exchange, only those deposits which can be used in association with a cheque should be included. In practice, the distinction between sight and time deposits is blurred, as is indeed the distinction today between bank and building society deposits.

The Bank concluded that there was no single satisfactory definition. Subsequently, a range of aggregates has been developed and continues to evolve in response to a rapidly changing financial environment, in which new assets may be considered to have a monetary function. Different aggregates are thought to be useful indicators for different purposes.

1.4 MONETARY AND LIQUIDITY AGGREGATES, 1986

Table 12 shows current definitions, but it should be stressed that these are subject to change.

Table 12. Monetary and liquidity aggregates

Notes and coin in circulation with the public

+	Private sector non-interest-bearing sterling sight bank deposits	+	Banks' till money
		+	Banks' operational balances with Bank of England
=	Non-interest-bearing component of M1		
		=	**Wide monetary base M0**
+	Private sector interest-bearing sterling bank deposits	+	Private sector interest-bearing retail sterling bank deposits
=	**M1**	+	Private sector holdings of retail building society deposits and National Savings Bank ordinary accounts
+	Private sector sterling time bank deposits (original maturity up to two years)	=	**M2**
+	Private sector holdings of sterling bank CDs		
+	Private sector sterling time bank deposits (original maturity over two years)	+	Private sector holdings of money market instruments (bank bills, treasury bills, local authority deposits) and certificates of tax deposit
+	Private sector foreign currency bank deposits		
=	**M3**	=	**PSL1**
		+	Private sector holdings of building society deposits (excluding term shares and SAYE) and National Savings instruments (excluding certificates, SAYE and other longer-term deposits)
		=	**PSL2**

Of these definitions, the two most important indicators are MO – the wide monetary base or 'narrow money' – and £M3, 'broad money'. Target figures are set for their rates of growth.

In addition to the monetary aggregates (M), figures are published for 'Private Sector Liquidity 1' and 'Private Sector Liquidity 2'. These take the wider view of *quasi-money*: financial assets which can very quickly be converted to cash.

It should now be recognized that even if monetarists are correct in their assertion that excessive monetary growth is the sole source of inflation, the central bank is left with the practical problem of deciding which monetary aggregate is the appropriate one to regulate. Even if the most suitable one is selected, it is still probable that in a sophisticated and rapidly evolving financial system, banks, firms and individuals will seek to frustrate controls. *These are the problems to which monetary policy must respond.*

2. THE STRUCTURE OF BRITISH BANKING

2.1 THE BANK OF ENGLAND

The focal point of the system, over three centuries it has evolved functions which are unique to a *central bank*.

2.2 COMMERCIAL BANKS

These are joint stock companies whose commercial aim is to produce a profit for their shareholders. They include:

(a)   *Retail banks* This is the term the Bank now uses to designate the 'high street' banks and includes the London and Scottish clearing banks and the Northern Ireland banks.

(b)   *British overseas banks* with London offices.

(c)   *Foreign banks*, in particular American and Japanese, with London offices.

(d)   *Consortium banks* Formed for specific purposes by two or more other banks.

2.3 DISCOUNT HOUSES

Unique to the UK financial system, they are specialist intermediaries in the provision of short-term finance.

2.4 MERCHANT BANKS

These have specific roles in the provision of finance for trade and industry.

2.5 NATIONAL SAVINGS BANK	Caters for the nation's small savings, which provide a useful source of funds for the finance of government debt.

2.6 NATIONAL GIRO	Established in 1969, primarily for the purpose of providing current account payment facilities for those without clearing bank accounts.

3. THE PRIMARY BANKING SYSTEM

3.1 A DEFINITION	The primary banks are distinguishable by their central role, which is the operation of the country's money transmission service. They include the London, Scottish and Northern Ireland banks, the banking department of the Bank of England, the discount houses and the National Giro

3.2 THE CLEARING BANKS AND THE CREATION OF 'BANK DEPOSIT MONEY'	The retail banks provide a wide and increasing range of financial services. These may be seen as an aspect of the increasing degree of 'service competition' which has developed, particularly since 1971. However, from the economist's point of view their chief interest lies in examining their principal activity, which is moneylending. Whenever they make a loan, there is a corresponding expansion of 'bank deposit money'. In this way, they create for the economy a medium of exchange, i.e. they expand the money supply.

At Stage 1, a new deposit liability of £10 is balanced by a £10 asset, but this is an asset of a particular kind: it is liquid, i.e. it represents instant purchasing power. The banker is now confronted with a dilemma. He wishes to maximize his profitability and this he can only do by

Table 13. A notional clearing bank balance sheet

Deposit liabilities		Assets	
		Liquid	'Earning'
			Advances & investments
Stage 1.	£10	£10	
Stage 2. ('underlent')	£40		£40
Stage 3. ('fully lent')	£50		£50
	£100		£100

maximizing his loans. On the other hand, he must maintain sufficient liquidity in his asset structure to enable him to meet all possible demands for cash on a day-by-day basis. The dilemma is resolved by adopting an appropriate liquidity rule, in the illustration a 10% rule. He will not permit the ratio of his liquid assets to his deposit liabilities to fall below 10%. He now creates 'earning assets', i.e. makes loans, but NOT as might be supposed by lending a proportion of the first £10 deposit. He parts with no cash over the counter, but continues to hold the whole amount. Instead he makes (in our illustration) an advance of £40 to his first borrower, i.e. he creates an overdraft facility. When this is used, *a cheque is drawn*, which when cleared results in two entries on the balance sheet. At Stage 2, a new 'earning asset' of £40 has been created and when the cheque is paid into the payee's account, a new deposit liability of £40 appears. This is new money in the fullest sense. At this stage, liquid assets bear a 20% ratio to deposit liabilities and the bank is substantially 'underlent'.

At Stage 3, the process is repeated with a further advance of £50. Once more there are two entries on the balance sheet; liabilities of £100 are balanced by assets of £100, of which £10 are in liquid form. The ratio of liquid assets to deposit liabilities has been reduced to the minimum permitted 10% and the bank is 'fully lent'.

Banking systems which function in this way are said to operate *a fractional reserve system.* In the UK, the rule has varied. From 1948 to 1971, a 'liquidity ratio' of 28% was observed. From 1971 to 1981, a 'reserve ratio' of 12½% was imposed. Since 1981, bankers have been required to establish independently their individual *'prudential requirements'*, which have then to be approved by the Bank.

3.3 THE MONEY SUPPLY AND THE PSBR

The principle established above holds good whether the bank creates an advance or an investment. Traditionally, the banks have considered their major role to be the provision of advances to industry, agriculture and commerce – the working capital of the economy. This is the riskiest and most illiquid bank asset and therefore the most profitable; banks will seek to maximize it. In broad principle, the balance of a bank's lending capacity will go into *investments*. In the banking sense, this specifically means holdings of gilt-edged securities, i.e. government debt. It follows therefore that the money supply will expand in consequence of an increase in bank lending to the private sector, *or because of increased public debt sales to the banking sector*.

This observation explains, in economic terms, the anxiety of the 1979 and 1983 governments to hold down public spending in order to keep tight control of the PSBR. The money supply would then be easier to regulate and, on a monetarist view, inflation would be squeezed out of the economy.

3.4 THE NATURE OF CLEARING BANK LIQUID ASSETS

So far we have spoken of liquid assets as if they were simply cash but this is far from the truth. The greater part of bank liquidity is expressed in financial assets which can quickly be converted to cash and these are structured in the following way.

(a) Notes and coin

Sometimes described as 'till money', it is required for the everyday purposes of the general public. In October 1985, it amounted to only £2 billion, relative to total sterling liabilities of £107 billion.

(b) Operational balances with the Bank of England

The clearers need these accounts to facilitate the operation of the clearing. They are also the source of new notes and coin. However, in October 1985 they stood at only £84 million. The remaining assets are *quasi-money*.

(c) Market loans

These represent highly liquid funds which have been lent in the short-term money market.

(i) Secured money with the LDMA Since 1981, as a condition of 'eligible bank' status the banks have been required to maintain a minimum average level of advances to the members of the London Discount Market Association. Advances are made against security and earn a return which fluctuates but which relates to the rate at which the Bank will provide funds to the market. To the extent that the banks are *obliged* to maintain this position, there is a constraint upon the liquidity of this asset.

(ii) Other UK monetary sector This includes money advanced to the LDMA on an unsecured basis, as well as funds lent to other banks and financial institutions. It largely comprises what is described as the *'inter-bank market'* in which banks make short-term unsecured loans directly to each other.

(iii) UK monetary sector certificates of deposit (CDs) Banks accept, in large denominations, fixed term deposits at fixed interest rates, against which they issue certificates which are negotiable in the London Discount Market. Amongst the holders of CDs are other banks who acquire them to satisfy their need for liquidity.

(iv) UK local authorities They have substantial short-term borrowing needs and funds are channelled to borrowers through specialist brokers in this local authority market. Maturities range from two days to two years.

(v) Overseas There exists a fairly substantial market in short-term loans to overseas borrowers.

(d) Bills

These are also highly liquid, since they are easily marketed, and are of minimal risk since they represent borrowing by government, other banks and financial and commercial institutions of the highest standing. Characteristically, they have a maturity of 91 days. They include:

(i) Treasury bills (see Chapter 13,5.2(b)). Short-term (usually 3-month) borrowing by central government.

(ii) Local authority bills They represent short-term borrowing by local government, and with the decline in recent years in the volume of Treasury bills, are now as important as the latter in bank balance sheets.

(iii) Eligible bank bills These are by far the most important component of bill holdings. They are 'bank' bills because they have been accepted by banks of the highest creditworthiness and they are 'eligible' because the bank will re-discount them through the discount houses.

(iv) Other bills The banks also hold a very small number of bills which are not eligible for re-discount at the Bank of England.

It is upon this foundation of liquid assets that the banks can create their 'earning assets', thereby expanding the money supply. The liquidity of these assets is *ultimately* dependent upon the unique relationship which exists between the London discount houses and the Bank of England.

3.5 THE DISCOUNT HOUSES AND THE BANK OF ENGLAND

Since 1829 when the modern discount market began to emerge, the houses have enjoyed the unique privilege of re-discounting and borrowing against security at the Bank of England. However, for this facility they have been obliged to pay a rate of interest determined by the Bank, known until 1972 as Bank Rate. They would be reluctant to use this facility, since normally Bank Rate would be substantially in excess of market rates. They therefore depend upon an adequate flow of advances from the commercial banks.

These advances are for the most part *'call money'*, i.e. having been made on one day, they can if necessary be recalled the next day, which provides an extremely useful asset for supporting bank cash balances. If these are under pressure, then the practice is to call in money in the morning and – if later in the day the banks have a surplus – it will be re-lent to the houses. The rates on these advances are determined by demand and supply. The houses use these funds to discount precisely those items which the banks view as liquid assets, i.e. Treasury bills, local authority bills, commercial bills and CDs, short-dated central and local government stocks, as well as a variety of market loans.

The market can therefore be seen as a financial intermediary in the provision of short-term finance for government, industry and trade. It stands between:

(a) Original lender and ultimate borrower
The commercial banks are the source of funds which are then on-lent.

(b) Banks with cash shortages and banks with cash surpluses
A bank with pressure on its operational balances can easily recall money from the market, which will immediately seek to replace this money with further advances from a bank with a surplus.

Note: this equalizing function has now been largely superseded by direct lending in the inter-bank market (see 3.4(c) (ii) above and 5.2 below).

(c) Commercial banks and the Bank of England
When the *whole* banking system is short of cash, it is entirely dependent upon its ability to realize liquid assets in the discount market. This is guaranteed by the access which the market has to new money at the Bank of England.

Note: Since it is only through this route that fresh money can be injected into the economy, it is the focal point of monetary policy.

4. THE SECONDARY BANKING SYSTEM

4.1 A DEFINITION

This includes the merchant banks, British overseas banks, foreign banks and consortium banks. While it is true that they also play a minor role in the domestic money transmission system, they are distinguishable by the structure of their liabilities. For the most part, they are term deposits in very large amounts, made by relatively few depositors. These banks therefore have no need for a 'high street' branch network. Further, the bulk of these deposits are denominated in foreign currencies and therefore are not a part of the UK payments mechanism.

4.2 MERCHANT BANKS

In origin, they were *accepting houses* and *acceptances* still represent a substantial part of their business. When a bank accepts a commercial bill of exchange on behalf of a trade customer, the acceptance is known as a bank bill, a first-class security which can be easily marketed.

Note: A commercial bill is a method of providing trade credit. It is drawn up by the supplier and 'accepted' by the buyer (or a bank on his behalf) that the bill will be redeemed on maturity (normally 3 months) at its face value. Meanwhile, whoever *discounts* it pays less than face value. Such instruments are traded regularly in the discount market.

Since the 1960s, the interests of the accepting houses have diversified and they have played a major role in the development of the 'parallel sterling money markets' and the Eurocurrency markets.

4.3 BRITISH OVERSEAS BANKS

Banks such as Standard Chartered, Grindlays Bank Group and Lloyds Bank International were primarily concerned with catering for British residents and business interests across the world. Like the accepting houses, however, since the 1960s they have provided a major source of funds to the parallel markets and the Eurocurrency markets.

4.4 FOREIGN BANKS

Prior to the Second World War, a number of banks – in particular, American – had London offices. Like the British overseas banks, their chief function was to cater for the needs of their own nationals.

The rise of the Euromarkets in the 1960s attracted them to London, the city in which this new development in banking originated. Today, no major international bank could afford *not* to have a London office.

4.5 CONSORTIUM BANKS

In order to participate in the Euromarkets, some foreign banks with inadequate resources or insufficient expertise joined with others to finance specific projects, using Eurocurrencies. Some London clearing banks participated in these consortia, e.g. European Banking Corporation (Midland) and Orion (Natwest).

5. THE PARALLEL STERLING MONEY MARKETS

5.1 A DEFINITION

The markets in short-term finance are sometimes described as 'parallel', since they operate alongside the primary or traditional London Discount Market. They developed from the 1960s in response to the growth of specific borrowing requirements, at the same time as new and expanding sources of loanable funds were being made available from the secondary banking system.

5.2 THE INTER-BANK MARKET

This is a market in unsecured loans between banks. The term ranges from overnight to one year and the interest rate is the London Interbank Offered Rate (LIBOR) – highly volatile, since it is determined entirely by short-term market forces.

The market enables banks with temporary cash shortages to borrow from banks with temporary cash surpluses, bypassing the equalizing function of the London Discount Market (see 3.5(b) above).

5.3 THE LOCAL AUTHORITY MARKET

This is the market in which local authorities satisfy their short-term borrowing needs against bills, short-dated bonds (often of one year) or temporary deposit receipts. These securities are taken up by banks, other financial and commercial institutions and individuals.

5.4 THE FINANCE HOUSE MARKET

In this market finance houses, i.e. instalment credit companies, secure funds for periods of one month to one year. Banks are major depositors.

5.5 THE MARKET IN CERTIFICATES OF DEPOSIT

The major advantage to a depositor of a CD over a normal time deposit is that the former is negotiable in this market.

5.6 THE INTER-COMPANY MARKET

Companies with surplus funds lend them through a broker to other companies, thus cutting out the banks as financial intermediaries. This market is very small in comparison with the others.

6. THE EUROMARKETS

6.1 A DEFINITION

There are Euromarkets in most of the world's major currencies, e.g. Eurodollars, Eurosterling, Euromarks, Euroyen. Note that the only significance of the designation 'Euro' is that the markets originated in Europe, specifically London. The common feature of all Eurocurrencies is that they are deposited outside the currency's country of origin. They are then on-lent to borrowers world-wide – in particular the governments of developing countries, but again to borrowers outside the country of origin.

This is largely an inter-bank market in which banks obtain deposits of foreign currencies and then re-lend them to other banks, or borrow Eurocurrencies from other banks and re-lend them. The location of the market has no significance for a country's money supply, unless a loan is converted across the exchanges into that country's currency. London is still the paramount centre, but for tax and regulatory reasons there are today centres in Singapore, Hong Kong, Bahrein, Nassau and Cayman as well as Paris, Frankfurt and Luxembourg.

6.2 GROWTH OF THE EUROCURRENCY MARKETS

During 1984, the rate of growth slowed down due to massive capital borrowing in the USA and the 'repatriation' of large quantities of dollars, the major Eurocurrency. Several factors led to the foundation of the markets in the 1960s and their subsequent expansion.

(a) Origin
In the 1960s, the international payments of the USA moved into deficit. Nevertheless, the world retained its confidence in the dollar as an 'international' currency and the London secondary banks seized the opportunity to secure these 'surplus' 'expatriated' dollars to lend to their world-wide customers. These developments were at a time when the world economy was booming and the demand for finance increasing, while exchange controls were being rapidly dismantled.

(b) Extension to other currencies
The market extended from the original Eurodollar to other internationally acceptable currencies, largely due to the practice of bank customers (such as international companies) depositing their foreign currency earnings in their home banks.

(c) The impact of the oil crises in the 1970s
The massive dollar earnings of the oil exporting countries were frequently deposited outside the USA. These Eurodollars were then recycled through the market to finance the trade deficits of many oil-consuming countries.

(d) Profitability
Attracted by the profitability of foreign currency lending, banks have offered competitive rates of interest on foreign currency deposits.

(e) Countries in deficit disequilibrium
Many underdeveloped nations have been led to finance their continuing payments deficits by borrowing from the Euromarkets, where the conditions of a loan have been less stringent than those imposed by the International Monetary Fund.
Note: The escalation of these loans in recent years has been a cause of major concern to the international banking community. The continuing prospect of default by a national debtor could threaten major banks; the failure of one of them would then jeopardize the stability of the world's banking system due to the interlocking of deposits.

(f) Lack of regulation
Banks have not been restricted in respect of the amount of foreign currency which they can hold, or the amount of foreign currency lending they can undertake. Unregulated markets flourish more rapidly and this again is a cause for concern. The possibility of the 'pyramiding' of credit on credit suggests the danger of inflation.
    The dangers indicated in (e) and (f) above have led banks in the

1980s to adopt more cautious lending policies and this has contributed to a slower rate of market growth. Of particular significance have been the debt rescheduling problems of Latin America.

6.3 TERM OF DEPOSITS AND INTEREST RATES

Deposits are made by industrial corporations and central banks, but most importantly by other commercial banks. They range from 'overnight' to five years, but are usually for one year. These inter-bank deposits yield current interest rates determined by the market, the six-month rate providing the basis for the London Interbank Offered Rate (LIBOR). The interest rate paid on *Euroloans* is then geared to LIBOR, allowing for the term and the risk of the loan.

6.4 EUROBONDS

These should be distinguished from Euroloans in Eurocurrencies. They represent a resumption of an earlier practice, when foreign governments raised funds in European and American financial markets against the issue of 'foreign bonds'. Characteristically they are fixed-term loans, usually for 5–15 years at fixed interest rates. The bond issue will be managed by one bank, but underwritten by many and marketed to investors world-wide.

EXAMINATION PRACTICE 15

MULTIPLE CHOICE

Which definition of the money supply specifies money as notes, coins and current account deposits?

(a)   M1;

(b)   M2;

(c)   M3;

(d)   Sterling M3.   (*AEB, November 1984*)

Key References 1.3; 1.4 and particularly Table 12. *Answer* (*a*).

One or more options may be correct. Code –

(a)1, 2, 3 all correct;

(b)1, 2 only correct;

(c)2, 3 only correct;

(d)1 only correct.

The functions of money include

1   acting as a store of wealth;

2   providing a standard for credit transactions;

3   avoiding the need for a double coincidence of wants.

                               (*AEB, June 1984*)

Key Reference 1.1. *Answer* (*a*).

Which one of the following is included in money supply as measured by M3 but not by M1?

(a)   building society deposits;

(b)   current accounts;

(c)   deposit accounts;

(d)   notes in circulation;

(e)   Treasury Bills.   (*O & CSEB, June 1983*)

Key References 1.3; 1.4; Table 12. *Answer* (*c*).

'The less liquid the asset the more profitable it is.' Which one of the following assets of a commercial bank represents an exception to this general rule?

(a)   Money at call and short notice;

(b)   Bills discounted;

(c)   Advances;

(d)   Special deposits.   (*AEB, November 1985*)

Key References 3.4; Chapter 16.2.7. *Answer* (*d*).

ESSAYS

Explain what is meant by the discount market of the City of London and discuss its functions and importance.   *(AEB, June 1984)*
Key References 3.5; 3.2; 3.4.

What is money? Explain what acts as money in the UK at present?
(JMB, June 1982)
Key References 1.1–4, but refer also to 3.2.

What is the main function of commercial banks? Why might they need to be supervised and, if necessary, controlled?
(O & CSEB, 9635/1, June 1981)
Key References 3.2; 3.3; Chapter 14.1; Chapter 16.2.1; 2.3.

What is meant by the money market? How does it determine *either* the price of money *or* the quantity demanded?
(O & CSEB, 9635/1, July 1984)
Key References 3.5; 5.1–6; 2.3; 2.10.

Some economists place great emphasis on controlling the money supply as a means of dealing with inflation. What problems are involved in the pursuit of such a policy?
(London, Paper 1, June 1985)
Key References Section 1; Chapter 16, section 2, in particular 2.3.

THE BANK OF ENGLAND

CONTENTS

1.FUNCTIONS

1.1 NATURE OF CENTRAL BANKING

The primary function of *any* central bank is the regulation of money and credit. Typically, there will be other functions such as responsibility for the note issue, although this could be carried out by private institutions, as for example in Hong Kong or the UK from 1914–1918 when the Treasury also issued notes.

An important question is the relationship of the central bank to government. Often, as in the USA and West Germany, there may exist a considerable degree of independence and indeed there may be constitutional provision to ensure this.

The position of the Bank of England is rather ambivalent. It was founded in 1694 as a privately owned institution, by an Act of Parliament which gave it the sole right of joint stock banking. At the same time, it made a loan of £1,200,000 to government, the origin of the modern National Debt. From the outset there was therefore a special relationship with government, which developed as the Bank acquired special functions unique in the UK banking system.

At the end of the Second World War, there remained the anomaly that a bank with these functions remained in private ownership. This was resolved by the Bank of England Act 1946, the first Act of nationalization, which established very clearly a formal relationship with the Bank subordinate to the Treasury. In the final analysis, therefore, the Bank must carry out the policies of the government. However, such is the position of the Bank that it is able to express its own views very forcibly to government and in a way which it would be damaging to ignore. In practice, much depends upon the strength of personality of the Governor.

The Bank is managed by a Court of Directors, comprising the Governor, the Deputy Governor, four full-time executive directors and twelve part-time directors. They are all appointed by the Crown, i.e. the government.

1.2 BANK OF ENGLAND BALANCE SHEETS

The functions of the Bank can be observed by reference to its two balance sheets.

Table 14. Issue department: November, 1985

Liabilities	£ millions	Assets	£ millions
Notes in circulation	12,041	Government securities	1,350
Notes in banking dept.	9	Other securities	10,700

The twofold division of the balance sheet is for accounting purposes only and has no operational significance. Apart from a small issue by Scottish and Northern Ireland banks, the Bank of England is the sole note-issuing authority. Issue Department liabilities are the notes in circulation and currently held in the Banking Department.

Balancing assets comprise government securities – i.e. National Debt – but overwhelmingly since 1979 other securities which are for the most part commercial bills which the Bank has acquired in the course of its money market operations.

Table 15. Banking department: November, 1985

Liabilities	£ millions	Assets	£ millions
Public deposits	1,415	Government securities	612
Special deposits	–	Advances and other accounts	910
Bankers deposits	830	Premises, equipment and other securities	2,173
Reserves and other accounts	1,447	Notes and coin	11

Public deposits

This item demonstrates the Bank's role as banker to government and into this Exchequer Account are paid all revenues from both taxation and borrowing. The money is known as the Consolidated Fund, from which all expenditures are met. The Bank also maintains the account of the National Loans Fund, from which government makes loans to nationalized industries and local authorities.

Special deposits

These are an aspect of monetary policy and will be explained later. There have been no calls outstanding since 1979.

Bankers' deposits

The Bank is the bankers' bank. Various banking institutions maintain operational balances which are of particular importance to the clearing banks. They are used to settle inter-bank indebtedness at the clearing and are also the source of notes and coins. In addition, since 1981 all recognized banks and licensed deposit takers have been obliged to maintain non-operational balances, the *cash ratio deposits* of ½% of a bank's deposit liabilities. These deposits are for the purpose of 'securing the Bank's resources and income'.

Reserves and other accounts

These comprise unallocated profits, the accounts of overseas central banks maintained for the purpose of assisting in settling international trade indebtedness, accounts of overseas governments and a few remaining private accounts from the days when the Bank engaged in commercial banking.

Not immediately revealed by the balance sheet are certain other functions:

Manager of the National Debt
Perhaps the most important operational department is the National Debt department which is responsible for new issues of stocks, the weekly Treasury bill tender, maintenance of stock registers, interest payments and redemptions.

Manager of the Exchange Equalization Account
This is a Treasury account, but is operated by the bank when it chooses to intervene in the foreign exchange markets to stabilize the sterling exchange rate.

Banking supervision
The Banking Act (1979) places a statutory duty upon the Bank to supervise the sound operation of the whole banking system.

Lender of last resort (see 15.3.5(c))
Through its relationship with the discount market, the Bank must ensure that the banking system has adequate cash to function effectively.

Monetary policy
It is the Bank's duty to apply policies which secure the desired level of interest rates and/or the appropriate rate of monetary growth.

2. THE BANK AND MONETARY POLICY

2.1 POLICY OBJECTIVES

The ultimate objectives are the control of inflation and the establishment of balance of payments equilibrium in a way which is consistent with real economic growth and high employment. In other words, like fiscal policy monetary policy seeks to operate on the demand side of the economy.

The possible *intermediate* targets of monetary policy are control of the money supply, of interest rates, of credit creation, of exchange rate or of the total volume of spending. As a matter of practical policy, whichever targets are selected they must be quantified and given a time-scale, e.g. in the UK the Medium Term Financial Strategy (MTFS) has set annual targets for the rate of growth of MO and £M3 over a medium-term planning period.

2.2 EFFECTIVENESS OF MONETARY POLICY

It was the alleged weakness of monetary policy in achieving its objectives, particularly in respect of stimulating the economy, which led Keynes to conclude that fiscal policy should be the primary instrument. For twenty years, 1931–1951, monetary policy remained inactive. It was revived in 1951, but only as a complement to fiscal policy. The growing influence of 'monetarism' in the 1960s and 1970s culminated in the 1979 government view that only through stringent monetary control could inflation be remedied. This did not imply any belief in the power of monetary policy to 'fine tune' the economy, but rather expressed the view that only through the monetary control of inflation would it be possible to create a sufficiently stable economic environment in which real growth could occur.

2.3 THE DILEMMA OF MONETARY POLICY

In attempting to influence aggregate demand, the Bank is faced with the choice which confronts all monopolists. (The Bank, at least in principle, has monopoly control of the money supply.) They would like to control price and quantity in the market, but must settle for one or the other. Similarly, the Bank must choose between determining the interest rate – in which case it loses direct control over the quantity of money – or regulating quantity directly – in which case the interest rate will be determined by the market.

Traditional monetary policy rested upon the control of the interest rate.

2.4 TRADITIONAL MONETARY POLICY INSTRUMENTS

There were two:

(a) A moving Bank Rate
Until 1972 Bank Rate – the rate at which the Bank would re-discount eligible securities for the discount market – was determined every Thursday by the Bank. It was an administered rate which might remain unchanged for long periods and when it did move, there was an immediate reaction in the money market. It was deliberately a 'penal rate', i.e. in excess of market rates. The discount houses could not afford to allow the gap to widen excessively, since there always remained the possibility of being 'forced into the Bank' to satisfy their marginal borrowing requirements at a rate above that at which they had already discounted. Moreover, until 1971 the commercial banks treated Bank Rate as the *base rate* to which their deposit and lending rates were directly geared.

In due course, rates in long-term lending in the capital market would have to rise competitively if it was to retain its share of funds.

The belief was that a policy of 'dear money' would discourage borrowing and therefore the creation of bank deposit money; inflationary tendencies would then be controlled. The opposite would be true with a policy of 'cheap money'. (It was this view which Keynes contested.)

(b) Open market operations in gilt-edged securities

A disinflationary rise in Bank Rate could be 'made effective' by sales of government stocks to the *non-bank sector*. (Remember that a sale to the banks results in the creation of a new 'earning asset' and a corresponding expansion of bank deposit money – see 15.3.3.) When the general public made purchases, they paid with cheques drawn on their banks in favour of the Bank of England. At the clearing, their cash balances were reduced; these were easily made good by recalling money from the discount houses, who were now forced into the Bank – 'the lender of last resort' – where they were obliged to pay the newly raised Bank Rate. Money was now both scarce and dear.

Conversely, a cheap money policy implied a lower Bank Rate and *purchases* of stock from the non-bank sector.

While the instruments of monetary policy have seen much experimentation and development since 1951, these two traditional instruments are still important to an understanding of certain fundamental relationships.

2.5 OVERFUNDING

This is a monetary control technique which has been much used in the 1980s as a means of influencing the *monetary base*. The effects are the same as those described in 2.4(b) above. The Bank sells to the non-bank sector more government debt than is necessary to finance the current PSBR. Bank liquidity is reduced and therefore also the capacity to create 'earning assets' and expand the money supply.

Note: This technique has in practice produced a perverse effect. The resulting shortages in the money market have repeatedly produced upward movements of short-term rates which the Bank did not always wish to see. It has therefore relieved these shortages by purchases of commercial bills – '*the bill mountain*' – which explains the large item 'Other Securities' in the Issue Department balance sheet. In October 1985, the Chancellor indicated the suspension of this technique.

2.6 TREASURY DIRECTIVES

As a supplement to the traditional instruments of monetary control, in the 1950s and 1960s the Bank experimented with 'Treasury directive' which were of two types:

(a) Qualitative directives or moral suasion

Banks were invited to concentrate their lending in those areas which were in the national interest, e.g. export manufacturers rather than personal lending.

(b) Quantitative directives

Banks were *instructed* to limit the growth of *all* lending to a given percentage over a set period.

In the event, these directives proved both ineffective and distortional. Faced with the alternative of compliance or observing good customers go into liquidation, the banks increasingly ignored the directives and government lacked the political will to insist.

A stimulus was also given to lending by institutions which did not fall within the remit of Treasury directives.

2.7 SPECIAL DEPOSITS

This scheme was introduced in 1960, retained in the 1971 *Competition and Credit Control* arrangements and again in the 1981 changes in monetary control technique. As observed in the Banking Department balance sheet (1.2 above), this is at present a nil item.

The Bank has the power to call upon all banking institutions to deposit in cash a given percentage of deposit liabilities. This special deposit cannot be treated as a liquid asset although it earns interest, normally the current Treasury bill rate. The effect is similar to sales of gilts to the non-bank sector, only more precise and immediate. The liquidity base of the banking system is reduced and hence its power to create earning assets and expand the money supply.

2.8 'COMPETITION AND CREDIT CONTROL', 1971

This Bank of England discussion paper reflected the disposition of government to a more market-orientated economy. Banks would be encouraged to compete with each other and the Bank would no longer dictate interest rates. In 1972, Bank Rate was abolished and replaced by *minimum lending rate* (MLR). This was still the minimum rate at which the Bank would re-discount eligible securities for the discount market, but was now market *determined* rather than market *determining* as had been the case with Bank Rate. The formula for MLR was the market determined current Treasury bill rate + ½%, rounded up to the nearest ¼ point. It therefore remained a 'penal rate', in excess of market rates, and the Bank was still 'the lender of last resort'. The new approach was reinforced with new constraints upon bank liquidity, a 12½% reserve ratio of strictly defined eligible reserve assets to eligible deposit liabilities and applicable to all banks.

In practice, during the 1970s market forces produced changes in MLR which conflicted with the interest rate that the Bank wished to see. On several occasions the formula was suspended and in 1978, the Bank announced that in future MLR would be administered: i.e. Bank Rate was resurrected under another name.

2.9 SUPPLEMENTARY SPECIAL DEPOSITS

The apparent lack of potency of the 1971 arrangements led to further experimentation with the so-called 'corset'. This differed from those techniques of monetary control which focused on the assets side of bank balance sheets. Banks were instructed to restrict the rate of growth of their interest-bearing eligible liabilities (IBELS) to given percentages over fixed periods. A proportion of any excess growth would obligatorily be deposited in a supplementary special deposit with the Bank and *would yield no interest*. When a bank creates 'earning assets', there is a corresponding expansion of deposits which may be non-interest-bearing sight deposits or interest-bearing time deposits. The implication was that any excessive creation of 'earning assets' would – at least in part – express itself in an excessive expansion of time deposits. Since the banker paid interest on these and would now be obliged to deposit a proportion with the Bank at zero interest, he would be under penalty.

Like quantitative directives, this scheme proved largely ineffective and distortional. Bankers were able to persuade customers away from conventional bank time deposits into money market holdings. Their ability to create credit was hardly affected.

2.10 MONETARY CONTROL TECHNIQUES, 1981

In March 1980 a government Green Paper, *Monetary Control*, recognized three major problems in devising appropriate instruments of monetary policy. Is the correct approach through control of the interest rate or some method of directly controlling the money supply? If the latter, what technique should be employed? If a technique can be developed, which particular monetary aggregate/ aggregates should be controlled?

The changes which were put into effect in 1981 implied that the 'dilemma of monetary policy' had been resolved in favour of an attempt at the direct control of the money supply, while leaving the market relatively free to determine interest rates. Major changes were envisaged in three areas:

(a) Monetary base control

As a concept, this is very simple. Banks keep a known proportion of their deposits in *base money*; this is defined as bankers' deposits at the central bank and may also include notes and coin held by either or both the banks and the general public. The proportion is maintained either because there is a mandatory requirement or for reasons of prudent banking. The central bank then either:

(i)   controls the amount of base money and therefore the total money supply which is limited to multiples of the base; *or*

(ii)   uses any divergence of base money from the required trend to initiate interest rate changes which will correct the divergence.

In the first case, if the money supply is growing too fast, banks compete for the limited supply of base money which they need to match their expanding deposit liabilities. Interest rates rise until the monetary growth rate is brought back to the desired trend.

In the second case, the intention is to provide for more rapid and automatic adjustments in the interest rate than occurs with a discretionary Bank Rate. The timing of changes is dictated by changes in the base.

In the event, it has been a variant of the second approach which has been developed. The Bank has had an eye to the rate of growth of M0, 'the wide monetary base', and has reacted through they way in which it operates in the bill markets.

(b) Operations in the bill markets

In August 1981 an administered MLR was again suspended. Nevertheless, the Bank indicated that it would still take a view of the interest rate that it desired to see, and would achieve this through the terms on which it did business with the discount market. It would not announce these terms, however. There would be four bands of bill maturities:

> Band 1 – 1–14 days
> Band 2 – 15–33 days
> Band 3 – 34–63 days
> Band 4 – 64–91 days

If there was a shortage of funds in the market, the Bank would offer to buy bills from the discount houses in some or all of the four bands. The houses would then offer bills to the Bank, specifying the discount rate, and the Bank would decide which offers to accept, rejecting those which were too low.

The implementation of this technique has given the market more freedom in the determination of rates, while the Bank has retained the ultimate power to influence them. Since the ability to do this depends on the presence of a sufficiently wide bill market and since the volume of Treasury bills has declined, the Bank invited applications from all commercial banks to have their acceptances treated as 'eligible' for re-discount. The list of 'eligible banks' has now grown to more than a hundred.

This privilege carries a parallel responsibility. To ensure that the discount houses receive adequate funds to maintain their role as market-makers, eligible banks are required to hold – on a secured basis – a minimum average 5% of eligible liabilities in the form of advances to the discount market. On a day-to-day basis, this secured money must not fall below 2½%.

(c) Liquidity requirements

The 12½% 'reserve ratio' was abandoned in 1981. The Bank recognized that there was variation in the structure of balance sheets between different banks; e.g. merchant banks have a high proportion of term deposits and, in principle, have a lower need for liquidity than clearing banks with a high proportion of sight deposits. Prudence required the matching of the maturity of assets to the maturity of liabilities. Therefore, subject to consultation with the Bank of England, bankers have determined their own 'prudential requirements'.

EXAMINATION PRACTICE 16

MULTIPLE CHOICE

If the Bank of England calls for more special deposits from the commercial banks
(*a*)　　their liquid assets will be reduced;
(*b*)　　their capacity to create credit will expand;
(*c*)　　they will have less incentive to attract deposits from the public;
(*d*)　　their loans to the money market will increase;
(*e*)　　they will be forced to lower their base rates.

(*O & CSEB, June 1985*)

Key Reference 2.7. *Answer* (*a*).

If the Bank of England decides to pursue a restrictionist policy, it will
(*a*)　　buy Treasury bills;
(*b*)　　encourage lower interest rates;
(*c*)　　sell securities;
(*d*)　　reduce special deposits;
(*e*)　　borrow from foreign central banks.

(*O & CSEB, June 1984*)

Key References 2.4(b); 2.5. *Answer* (*c*).

A fall in the money supply could be produced by the government acting to
(*a*)　　reduce short-term interest rates;
(*b*)　　release special deposits;
(*c*)　　increase funding operations;
(*d*)　　buy securities in the open market.　　(*AEB, June 1985*)

Key References 2.4(b); 2.5. *Answer* (*c*).

ESSAYS

Discuss how the Bank of England seeks to control the money supply and consider why recently there have been problems in meeting monetary targets.　　(*JMB Special, June 1982*)

Key References 2.3; 2.5; 2.10.

How does government influence the supply of money in the UK? Explain how monetary policy can be used to reduce the level of aggregate demand (*JMB, June 1980*)
Key References 2.1–5; 2.7; 2.10.

What methods are used to control the money supply? How successful have they been? (O & CSEB, 9633/3, 9635/2, July 1985)
Key References 2.1–10.

Direct controls, interest rates and monetary base control are all methods of regulating the money supply. Describe these three methods and discuss the advantages and disadvantages of each.
(*AEB, June 1985*)

Key References 2.3; 2.4; 2.6; 2.8; 2.10.

INTERNATIONAL TRADE AND PAYMENTS

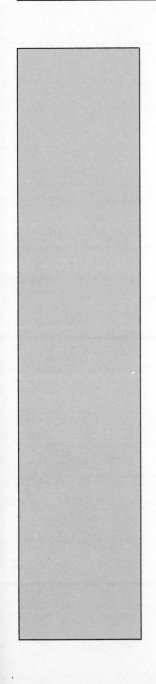

THEORY AND PRACTICE OF INTERNATIONAL TRADE

CONTENTS

1. COMPARATIVE COSTS

1.1 FREE TRADE AND EFFICIENCY

One of the major contributions of English classical economics was the proposition that if all restrictions on trade were removed, all would benefit. Earlier *mercantilist* theory had postulated that in international trade, if one nation gained another must lose (see 1.1.2) National self-sufficiency was therefore desirable.

1.2 DAVID RICARDO 'ON FOREIGN TRADE'

One of the first theoretical protagonists of free trade was David Ricardo, who illustrated his argument with reference to trade in wine and cloth between Portugal and England. For England to produce the cloth required might take the labour of 100 men for one year, while to produce the wine might take 120 men. To produce the wine in Portugal might take the labour of only 80 men, with cloth requiring 90 men. Even though Portugal had an absolute cost advantage in the production of both commodities, it would still be of benefit to produce only wine and exchange for cloth. Equally, it would profit England to concentrate solely upon the production of cloth.

In the terminology of modern analysis, this proposition can be presented in the form of *production-possibility curves*.

1.3 PRODUCTION POSSIBILITY CURVES FOR THE RICARDIAN ILLUSTRATION

In Figure 56(a) and (b) are two production-possibility curves for two commodities for England and Portugal. They are drawn as straight lines since Ricardo is speaking of only one factor of production – labour – which does not vary with output. No account is taken of the laws of increasing and decreasing returns. While this hypothesis is reflected in curves of constant slope, the degree of slope differs between England and Portugal.

The curve for England is steeper, since less labour is employed in cloth than in wine production. The opposite is the case for Portugal. This information is transferred to the production-possibility curves RS and QT in Figure 57. Without trade, England lies at some point on RS – say E_1 – while Portugal lies at P_1. Complete specialization and trade take place. England produces OR units of cloth, Portugal OT units of wine. Y units of cloth are exchanged for X units of wine. England is now positioned at E_2 with more wine and more cloth. The

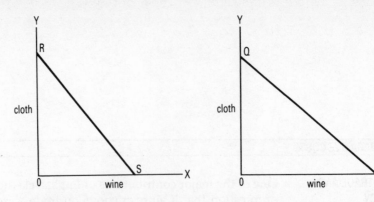

Figure 56(a). *Production-possibility curve for England.*

Figure 56(b). *Production-possibility curve for Portugal.*

same is true for Portugal, which has moved to P_2. Both countries are better off.

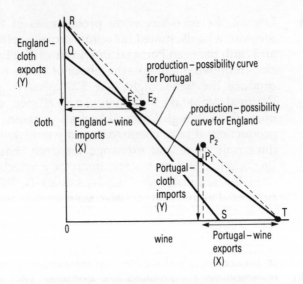

Figure 57. *International specialization increases total output.* Before trade, English production is located at E_1 and Portuguese production at P_1. In the Ricardian illustration, with complete specialization, the position of both countries are improved to E_2 and P_2.

1.4 DOCTRINE OF COMPARATIVE ADVANTAGE

This asserts that trade between two countries in two commodities can take place to their mutual advantage, even when one country has an *absolute* cost advantage in both activities, provided that it has a *comparative* cost advantage in one activity relative to the other, while the trading partner has a *comparative* advantage in the alternative activity.

In Ricardo's example, Portuguese labour costs are lower for both wine and cloth production, yet it still pays to trade with England.

The proposition therefore focuses upon the dissimilarity of cost ratios and this is often shown arithmetically.

1.5 DISSIMILAR COST RATIOS

In the following examples, trade in wheat and cloth is assumed between the UK and USA.

(a) A comparative advantage for the UK in cloth; for the USA in wheat

It is assumed that in the USA, 10 resource units – i.e. land, labour and capital – produce either 20 tonnes of wheat or 10 metres of cloth. In the UK, 10 resource units produce either 20 metres of cloth or 10 tonnes of wheat. The USA has a total of 300 resource units, the UK has 200 and both divide them equally between the two activities.

Table 16. Production of wheat and cloth before trade

	Resource units	Metres of cloth	Tonnes of wheat
USA	300	150	300
UK	200	200	100
Total	500	350	400

The UK now specializes in cloth and the USA in wheat.

Table 17. Production of wheat and cloth after specialization

	Resource units	Metres of cloth	Tonnes of wheat
USA	300	–	600
UK	200	400	–
Total	500	400	600

Specialization has led to the maximization of total output, and trade will take place to the benefit of both countries at any exchange rate within the parameters of their respective cost ratios. For the USA this is 20 tonnes of wheat: ten metres of cloth, for the UK, 20 metres of cloth: ten tonnes of wheat.

Note: In Figure 57, the exchange rate is shown by the *slope* of the dotted lines, RE_2 or P_2T. An exchange rate of 1 would mean that $x/y=1$ or that $x=y$. Such an exchange rate is not of course necessary to mutually beneficial trade. What *is* necessary is that the *slope* of RE_2 and P_2T should lie between the *slopes* of the two production possibility curves.

(b) An absolute advantage for the USA in both wheat and cloth

This is the Ricardian example and shows that trade will still be mutually advantageous, even when the USA has an *absolute* cost advantage in both activities.

Table 18. Production before trade, the USA with an absolute advantage in wheat and cloth

	Resource units	Metres of cloth	Tonnes of wheat
USA	300	270	300
UK	200	160	80
Total	500	430	380

It is now assumed that with 10 resource units, the USA can produce 20 tonnes of wheat or 18 metres of cloth, while in the UK the same resources will produce only 16 metres of cloth or 8 tonnes of wheat. Production figures before specialization are shown in Table 18.

Still assuming the same cost ratios, trade takes place with the results shown in Table 19.

Table 19. Production after specialization in the activity with a comparative advantage

	Resource units	Metres of cloth	Tonnes of wheat
USA	300	–	600
UK	200	320	–
Total	500	320	600

1.6 INCOMPLETE SPECIALIZATION

So far we have assumed complete specialization, but this in fact is unlikely. Tables 18 and 19 show that while specialization substantially increases the total output of wheat, the output of cloth declines and in this respect both countries are worse off. The USA will therefore continue to devote some resources to cloth production. Suppose that this amounts to 30%, 90 resource units being used for cloth production? The results are shown in Table 20.

Output of *both* commodities is greater than was the case either before specialization or with complete specialization. Trade will take place to the benefit of both countries, again at any exchange rate within the limits of their respective cost ratios – cloth: wheat. The benefit of the increased total output will not however be equally divided between the trading partners; it will depend upon their relative trading strengths, i.e. *the terms of trade*.

Table 20. Production with incomplete specialization

	Resource units	Metres of cloth	Tonnes of wheat
USA	300	162	420
UK	200	320	–
Total	500	482	420

1.7 TERMS OF TRADE

These are determined by the elasticity of demand for imports in each country, relative to the elasticity of supply of the other country's exports.

In Table 20, if demand for cloth in the USA is stronger than the demand for wheat in the UK, the terms of trade will move in favour of the UK. The exchange ratio of wheat to cloth will settle closer to the US production cost ratio of 20:10. In general terms, wheat will be cheap relative to cloth. The opposite will be the case when the terms of trade move against the UK and the exchange ratio moves towards 20 units of cloth: 10 units of wheat.

1.8 FREE TRADE

There is a general unanimity amongst economists that, for the reasons explained, free trade is a desirable objective.

The UK's historical experience supports this theoretical conclusion. The gradual removal of all protective customs duties in Britain between the 1820s and 1870 is associated with an enormous expansion of trade and industry. By 1900, Britain stood at the pinnacle of her industrial, military and political power. This was based upon intensive specialization in a relatively small number of products – coal, iron, shipbuilding and marine engineering, steam-engines, cotton, wool and chemicals.

International specialization was disrupted by the First World War and after 1920, world depression led to one country after another adopting protective policies as a means of alleviating unemployment. In 1932, Britain followed suit. Protection and bilateral trade agreements were accompanied by a massive contraction of world trade.

In short, both theory and experience would seem to support the advocacy of free trade. Nevertheless, the free trade *v* protection debate continues in particular contexts.

2. ARGUMENTS FOR PROTECTION

2.1 RELIEF OF UNEMPLOYMENT

Arguments for some form of protection are frequently heard in industrialized countries which are suffering from high levels of unemployment. In the UK at present, the Cambridge Economic Policy Group advocates selective import controls of a kind which would limit the growth of specified imports rather than cutting back the existing volume. This they believe to be an answer to critics who maintain that such a policy would only invite from countries to which unemployment was 'exported' the kind of retaliation seen in the 1930s. Whatever that reaction might be, it would still be the case that in the long term, the cost advantages of free trade would be lost. Moreover, it can be argued that protection simply postpones the structural changes in the economy which must be made if the country is to compete in international markets.

2.2 STRATEGIC CONSIDERATIONS

These may be military/political or purely economic. In the first case, the need is asserted to ensure national security by denying – as far as possible – equipment and technology to a potential adversary. Further, it would be undesirable to be excessively reliant upon uncertain sources of supply for vital imports. An example might be the West's heavy dependence upon OPEC for its energy during the 1970s.

2.3 DEVELOPING INDUSTRIES

This argument is particularly applicable to developing countries. It may also be relevant in advanced countries, where a secure home market base is necessary to enable the 'infant industry' to develop sufficiently to enjoy the economies of scale which will permit it to compete effectively in world markets.

The difficulty is that once an industry has enjoyed protection, it will not easily relinquish it.

2.4 IMPROVING THE TERMS OF TRADE

As the volume of a particular import into a country increases, the price is likely to rise, with a resulting deterioration in that country's terms of trade. It may seek to pre-empt this by restricting that import. Again, the problem is that retaliation is likely, with both parties worse off.

2.5 DECLINING INDUSTRIES

This is the reverse side of the 'infant industries' argument. It is seen that when major industries with heavy investment in physical capital and human skills go into decline, there will be severe hardship. This will be accentuated when such industries are concentrated in particular regions. Protection should therefore be employed to spread the burden of adjustment over a longer period. It may be that such socio-political arguments will take precedence over the purely economic. However, the economist will observe that, as with 'infant industries', once protection is granted there will be a reluctance to abandon it. Moreover, rather than forego the benefits of free trade, it might be preferable to allocate resources directly to the relief of social hardship.

2.6 DUMPING

It may arise that a foreign producer is able to practice *discriminating monopoly*. He segregates his home market from his overseas market and restricts domestic supply in order to secure a high price. Output is increased to achieve economies of scale and the surplus is 'dumped' overseas at any price which covers variable costs (see 10.3.5).

Protective action may now seem wholly legitimate. However, it will be remembered that the importing country is enjoying the benefit of very low prices.

2.7 'UNFAIR' COMPETITION

It is sometimes asserted that competition from low-wage countries is 'unfair'. However, such countries are simply specializing in products where low wage costs give them a comparative advantage. They might equally argue that imports from advanced countries with low cost and high technology outputs are 'unfair'.

2.8 PROTECTIONIST METHODS

Several devices may be employed:

(a) Tariffs
A duty may be *specific* in the way that it is applied to particular imports, or *ad valorem*: representing a given percentage of their landed value. Effectiveness depends upon the price elasticity of demand for imports.

(b) Quotas
Imposed unilaterally or by agreement – e.g. the present Multi-Fibre Agreement – a system of licensing restricts the quantities imported.

(c) Subsidies
These may be aimed at import substitution with home produced goods. Often they are covert – e.g. the facilities of the Export Credit Guarantee Department – in the sense that overt subsidization of

exports may be in contravention of the General Agreement on Tariffs and Trade (GATT).

(d) Exchange controls
Foreign currencies are 'rationed' between importers, effectively establishing a system of selective import controls.

(e) Administrative procedures
Complex bureaucratic regulations may be used as another covert way of avoiding outright breaches of GATT, while still impeding the free flow of trade.

3. GENERAL AGREEMENT ON TARIFFS AND TRADE (GATT)

3.1 ORIGIN

During the 1940s, attention was being given to ways in which – after the war – international co-operation in trade and payments could be achieved and the nationalistic, 'beggar-my-neighbour' policies of the inter-war period avoided. The ultimate objective was the liberalization of world trade and the promotion of an effective system of multi-lateral payments. The latter manifested itself in the foundation of the International Monetary Fund (IMF) in 1944. The parallel organization was to have been an International Trade Organization, but the charter for the ITO was never ratified and in its place emerged GATT. This was a treaty signed in 1947 by a number of industrial countries including the UK, USA, Canada, France and Benelux. Today it includes all the major industrialized countries, many developing nations and some Eastern bloc countries such as Czechoslovakia and Poland.

3.2 OBJECTIVES

The Agreement comprises 38 Articles, with many schedules and annexes in respect of the many thousands of trade concessions which have subsequently been made. There are four basic principles:
(a)   *Non-discrimination* The 'most favoured nation' (mfn) clause requires any concession made to one signatory to be extended to all.
(b)   *No quotas* A general prohibition of quantitative restrictions.
(c)   *Developing countries* They enjoy special provisions and exemptions.
(d)   *Regularly negotiated tariff reductions* While it is a treaty rather than an organization, GATT has a permanent secretariat based in Geneva. Progress was to be achieved through regular 'rounds' of tariff conferences.

3.3 EXCEPTIONS TO THE MFN RULE

The rule applies except in the cases of:
(a)   *An existing and established tariff preference*
(b)   *A full customs union (e.g. EEC) or free trade area (e.g. European Free Trade Area (EFTA)).*

3.4 THE RECORD

During the 1950s and 1960s, GATT achieved considerable success in removing quotas and reducing tariffs, culminating in the Kennedy round which was completed in 1967 and which cut tariffs by about one-third. By the early 1970s, the average duty on manufactures stood at about 10%. Subsequently, the problems caused by world recession have made further progress more difficult and the major achievement has been in preventing countries from re-introducing protectionist measures.

3.5 UNITED NATIONS CONFERENCE ON TRADE, AID AND DEVELOPMENT (UNCTAD)

A criticism of GATT has been that it is of benefit chiefly to the advanced nations. The first UN Conference on Trade, Aid and Development was convened in 1964, with the primary purpose of enlarging the new industrial nations' share of world trade. It also seeks to increase the level of aid to these nations.

The Conference meets every four years, but developments have been limited due to the diversity of the problems of developing countries.

4. REGIONAL TRADING BLOCS

4.1 ORGANIZATION FOR EUROPEAN ECONOMIC CO-OPERATION (OEEC)

This organization, set up in 1948, originally comprised sixteen nations and had the purpose of administering American aid in the Joint European Recovery Programme. It then developed as an instrument of general economic co-operation.

4.2 ORGANIZATION FOR ECONOMIC CO-OPERATION AND DEVELOPMENT (OECD)

By the late 1950s the European recovery had been achieved and there was a growing awareness of the interdependence of Europe and America. In 1961, this was recognized with the substitution of OECD for OEEC. To the existing membership of OEEC were added Canada, USA and Spain and – in 1965 – Japan.

4.3 EUROPEAN COAL AND STEEL COMMUNITY (ECSC)

During the early 1950s, arguments were being pressed in Europe for closer economic integration than was possible under the auspices of OEEC. A major rationalization of the European economy was thought necessary if it was to compete successfully with the continental economies of the USA and the Soviet Union. ECSC was the product of this thinking and the next step towards the foundation of EEC; it was established in 1952 to remove all trade restriction on coal, iron ore and steel between France, Germany, Italy and the Benelux countries.

4.4 EUROPEAN ECONOMIC COMMUNITY (EEC)

The members of ECSC widened their agreement to cover the whole of their economies in the Treaty of Rome (1957) implemented on 1 January 1958. The original 'Six' became 'Nine' in 1973 with the accession of the UK, Eire and Denmark, and subsequently 'Ten' in 1981 with the entry of Greece. Spain was added in 1985, while in 1986 there is the prospect of the further addition of Portugal.

The main objectives of the treaty can be summarized as follows:

(a)   *A customs union* This means a free trade area but with a *common external tariff.*

(b)   *Free Movement of labour, capital and enterprise* This was seen as the next step in the rationalization of the European economy.

(c)   *Fusion of national economies* This is clearly a long-term objective since it implies, for example, the full harmonization of taxation, social security, industrial and competition policy and the creation of a common currency with a single central bank.

(d)   *Political union* Whatever form this might take, it is seen as the ultimate objective.

4.5 COMMON AGRICULTURAL POLICY (CAP)

With agriculture occupying a significant role in the economies of many continental European countries (in 1957 one in five workers in the original 'Six' were so employed), it is not surprising that the CAP has received so much attention. The objectives were to create a single market for agricultural produce and to protect it from imports, thus ensuring the stability of supplies and employment.

The European Agricultural Guarantee and Guidance Fund (EAGGF – or in French, FEOGA) has the twin roles of guaranteeing farm incomes and guiding farm production.

To achieve the former, a *target price* is set based upon the price necessary to cover costs and a profit mark-up. An *intervention* or guaranteed price is then set, about 7% to 10% below the target price. This establishes a 'floor' below which market prices will not fall, since once it has been reached the Commission intervenes to buy in the surplus. To make this system effective, levies are imposed upon agricultural imports to ensure that they are no cheaper than the target price less transport and other importation costs, i.e. *the threshold price*.

In respect of guidance, the 'Common Structural Policy' of 1972 sought to use CAP funds to persuade farmers to leave marginal land and to promote larger-scale farming. In this area, the CAP has not had much success in recent years. The result has been the survival of many small, high-cost producers with correspondingly high target prices. This in turn has led to excessive production, much intervention and the accumulation of 'butter mountains' and 'wine lakes' etc.
Note: The encouragement of high-cost EEC producers at the expense of low-cost producers elsewhere indicates the distortion of comparative advantage.

4.6 EUROPEAN FREE TRADE AREA (EFTA)

In the 1950s Britain – with her global trading connections – was more interested in a free trade area than a customs union. She took the lead in negotiating the Stockholm Convention in 1960, which set up EFTA; it comprised seven countries, including the UK. Subsequently, the UK and Denmark transferred to EEC and were replaced by Finland and Iceland who joined the remaining members: Sweden, Austria, Switzerland, Norway and (for the moment) Portugal.

4.7 ORGANIZATION OF PETROLEUM EXPORTING COUNTRIES (OPEC)

For most of the twentieth century, the terms of trade have moved against the primary producers. OPEC is an international cartel which has attempted to redress the balance by restricting oil output and providing a countervailing power to the industrial countries in the market.

EXAMINATION PRACTICE 17

MULTIPLE CHOICE

The principle of comparative costs refers to
(*a*)   factor costs;
(*b*)   fixed costs;
(*c*)   money costs;
(*d*)   opportunity costs;
(*e*)   variable costs.   (*O & CSEB, June 1985*)
Key Reference 1.1–5. Answer (d).

The following table shows the terms of trade for a particular country
(1970=100):
1969 97.3; 1970 100; 1971 100.8; 1972 101.3; 1973 90.2; 1974 74.9.
Which one of the following explanations could account for the post-
1972 figures?
(*a*)   Export prices rose faster than export volumes.
(*b*)   Import volumes rose more slowly than before.
(*c*)   Import prices rose more rapidly than before, and export
prices did not change.
(*d*)   Export prices rose more slowly than before, and import prices
fell.
(*e*)   Export prices did not change and import prices fell.
           (*O & CSEB, June 1983*)
Key Reference 1.7. Answer (c).

One or more options may be correct. Code –
(a)   1, 2, 3 all correct;
(b)   1, 2 only correct;
(c)   2, 3 only correct;
(d)   1 only correct;
(e)   3 only correct.
A country's terms of trade are said to be moving adversely if its
1   export and import prices both rise but export prices rise faster;
2   export prices fall and import prices rise;
3   export and import prices both fall but export prices fall faster.
           (*London, Paper 2, June 1985*)
Key References 1.5–7. Answer (c).

ESSAYS

'Free trade promotes a mutually profitable regional division of labour and greatly enhances the potential real national product of all nations.' (P.A. Samuelson.) Discuss this view and consider whether protectionism has any role to play in the UK at the present time.

(JMB Special, June 1984)

Key References 1.1–6; 2.1–8; 3.1–4; 4.4.

Discuss the economic arguments for and against customs unions.

(AEB, November 1983)

Key References 4.1–5; 1.1–5; 2.1–7.

Evaluate the economic arguments for and against import controls.

(AEB, November 1984)

Key References 1.1–5; 2.1–7.

BALANCE OF PAYMENTS

CONTENTS

1. UK BALANCE OF PAYMENTS ACCOUNTS

1.1 PRESENTATION

They include all transactions between UK residents and non-residents, the transactions being recorded at the time when the goods or assets changed hands or when the services were performed. The accounts are in sterling, conversions from foreign currencies being made at current exchange rates.

In the spring of each year, a Government White Paper gives estimates for the preceding year. These are revised and finalized in a 'Pink Book', *United Kingdom Balance of Payments Accounts*, published in the autumn.

1.2 COMPOSITION

Reference to Table 21 demonstrates a basic proposition that, by definition, the accounts must balance. The table summarizes the main items and shows trends over the past ten years.

(a) Current account
This comprises two headings:

(i) **Visibles** The balance of all tangible imports and exports.

(ii) **Invisibles** They include the balance of government expenditures, not appropriate to visible trade or other invisibles; transport – shipping and civil aviation; the balance of personal expenditure on travel; interest, profit and dividends; miscellaneous services, including financial and educational; private transfers of migrants' funds.

(b) Investment and other capital flows
To the current account balance must be added the capital account which comprises:

(i) **Overseas investment in the UK** Investment by non-residents in UK company shares or government securities (portfolio investment), or the acquisition of real capital assets, e.g. a factory.

(ii) **UK private investment overseas** Similarly, portfolio and direct investment by UK residents overseas.

Table 21. Summary UK
balance of payment
accounts, 1975–1984

	1975	1976
Exports	19463	25424
Imports	22699	29013
Visible balance	−3236	−3589
Total invisibles (net)	1885	2452
Current balance	−1381	−1137
Total investment & other capital flows	278	−2896
Balancing item	112	404
Allocation of SDRs	—	—
Total currency flow	−1465	−3629
Total official financing	1465	3629

Source: United Kingdom Balance of Payments Accounts

Note: An inflow of investment funds appears as a credit item in the accounts. In due course, a debit item will appear under 'invisibles' when profits, interest and dividends are paid overseas. The opposite will be the case with an outflow of funds.

(iii) Official long-term capital Inter-government loans – in particular, aid to underdeveloped countries – together with the UK's subscriptions to international bodies such as the International Development Association (IDA).

The short-term capital flows include:

(iv) Trade credits An export will be recorded under 'visibles' as a credit. However, if payment is not made simultaneously, then this trade credit is the equivalent of a capital outflow and will be registered as a debit. The reverse will be the case with an import credit.

(v) Foreign currency borrowing and lending abroad by UK banks Borrowing from and lending by UK banks to non-residents in currencies other than sterling, as part of the banks' Eurocurrency market operations. An overseas loan in foreign currency is an outflow of funds and is shown by a minus sign. Increased borrowing is an inflow of funds and appears as a plus sign.

(vi) Exchange reserves held in sterling Reserves of overseas countries and international organizations. They may be invested in Treasury bills, UK government stocks or deposits with banks or local authorities.

(vii) Other external banking and money market liabilities in sterling This item represents *'hot money'* or speculative flows which are extremely volatile and sensitive to interest rate differentials in the world's financial centres; they contribute to the instability of exchange rates under a floating exchange rate regime.

They arise in various ways. Non-residents may increase or de-

1977	1978	1979	1980	1981	1982	1983	1984
32182	35063	40687	47422	50977	55565	60776	70409
33891	36605	44136	46061	47617	53234	61611	74510
−1709	−1542	−3449	1361	3360	2331	−835	−4101
2115	2514	2713	1739	3168	2332	4003	5036
406	972	−736	3100	6528	4663	3168	935
4416	−4137	1865	−1503	−6972	−3199	−4865	−3291
2539	2039	581	−405	−401	−2748	877	1040
—	—	195	180	158	—	—	—
7361	−1126	1710	1192	−845	−1284	−820	−1316
−7361	1126	−1710	−1192	845	1284	820	1316

crease their holdings of deposits with UK banks or of money markets assets. UK banks may increase or decrease overseas sterling lending, including loans to banks. The latter includes the acceptance and discounting of sterling bills of exchange other than those connected with UK export credit. Finally, individuals and corporate bodies resident in the UK may also be involved in borrowing and lending abroad in sterling.

When current and capital accounts are totalled we arrive at what is frequently described as a balance of payments 'surplus' or 'deficit'. More correctly, it is the *balance for official financing*. The construction of the accounts is such that necessarily they must balance. For any surplus, there must be a corresponding adjustment under the heading *official financing* and shown by a *minus* sign. Any deficit will be reflected in a *plus* sign for official financing.

(c) Balancing item

It is important to remember that it is *not* this item which achieves overall balance in the accounts, but as stated above the adjustment under official financing. The balancing item provides for the *errors and omissions* in recording the vast number of international payments which are made each year. It is recognized that, for practical reasons, the *balance for official financing* may be inaccurate. What is known with certainty is the *actual* figure for *official financing* which the Bank of England is able to observe directly because of the effect on the reserves and overseas borrowing. The balancing item is the difference between the two and may be positive or negative.

Reference to Table 21 shows that on occasion, it may be extremely large and would seem to put in question the validity of the accounts. Indeed, there have been instances when after revision an apparently favourable situation has turned out to be adverse. This has to be accepted as one of the problems of producing any set of national accounts.

(d) Allocation of SDRs

The figures for 1979–81 show the most recent distributions of 'paper gold' to members of IMF (see Ch. 19, 7.6). They must be added in order to discover the net figure for official financing.

(e) Official financing

If a deficit is to be financed (shown in the accounts as a minus), then there will be a reduction in the nation's central monetary reserves of gold and foreign currencies and/or an increase in borrowing from overseas monetary authorities, e.g. IMF and overseas central banks; this will be shown as a *plus* in the accounts. The opposite occurs with the financing of a surplus.

2. EQUILIBRIUM IN THE BALANCE OF PAYMENTS

2.1 DEFINITION

We have demonstrated that, by definition, international payments must balance. However, in the long term they need not necessarily be in equilibrium. This can be defined as a situation in which – at any given rate of exchange – current account surpluses over a period of years are sufficient to finance all net external capital transactions, including a sufficient expansion of central reserves to cover any net increase in capital account liabilities.

For example, it may be the case that for a protracted period, current account deficits are financed by repeated capital account surpluses. This may seem desirable if such investment leads to a real increase in economic activity, bearing in mind that profits, interests and divi-dends may be 'repatriated' and become a debit in the accounts. Moreover, if the capital is relatively short-term *financial* investment, it may move back across the exchanges as quickly as it arrived. Whether a deficit is a good or bad thing is difficult to determine without reference to a particular economy in a specific situation.

Problems are usually associated with a deficit disequilibrium, but difficulties can also arise when a country experiences repeated balance of payments surpluses, i.e. a surplus disequilibrium (see 2.4 below).

2.2 REASONS FOR PAYMENTS DISEQUILIBRIA

There may be the failure of some important crop or a rise in the world price of a major export commodity. In the case of industrialized countries with diversified economies, the two most likely reasons are:

(a) Price competitiveness

While it is true that product design, after-sales service, quality and reliability and delivery dates all exert influence, they are relative to price; e.g. if a product is thought to be particularly cheap, the custo-mer may not mind a delayed delivery.

(b) Domestic demand

If this is excessive, potential exports are diverted to the home market.

2.3 REMEDIES FOR A DEFICIT DISEQUILIBRIUM

A number of policies may be adopted, singly or in combination.

(a) Exchange controls and other trade protection devices (see 17.2.8)

It was argued in Chapter 17 that, as a long-term policy, protection denies the benefits of comparative advantage and perpetuates inefficiency in the domestic economy. It cannot therefore be seen as a long-term cure for disequilibrium. Moreover, if an advanced country were unilaterally to adopt such measures, it would probably be in breach of international agreements such as GATT and IMF.

(b) Deflation of domestic demand

Excessive aggregate demand may produce a domestic rate of inflation higher than that of a country's competitors. Exports become less competitive in world markets and imports more competitive in home markets. The current account thus moves into deficit. However, this situation may take some time to develop. More immediately, domestic output is unable to respond to the increased demand and even before prices rise the volume of imports increases. This was the recurrent experience of the UK with every attempt to reflate the economy out of recession.

Deflationary measures may include restrictive monetary and fiscal policies and cuts in public expenditure. They should have the short-term effect of closing the gap between domestic demand and supply and the longer-term effect of reducing the rate of inflation.

(c) Devaluation/depreciation

Devaluation describes a change from one *fixed* exchange rate to a lower *fixed* rate. Depreciation under a floating exchange rates regime means a continuing movement from higher rates to lower rates. In both cases, the implication is that exports become more price-competitive in world markets and imports less so in the home market. It should then follow that the *volume* of exports will increase while the volume of imports diminishes. Whether this in fact occurs depends upon the elasticity of demand for exports and imports and the elasticity of supply of exports.

If demand for exports is price inelastic, then the same volume is sold at a lower price to produce a smaller revenue and the country is worse off. It should be recognized that in the short term demand *will* be inelastic, since markets will require time to adjust to the new conditions. In the long run, it must be sufficiently elastic to restore and then surpass the original sales revenue.

The experience of the 1967 devaluation and the depreciation of the 1970s suggests a fairly high degree of elasticity for UK exports.

There must also be elasticity of supply, i.e. industry must be capable of responding to improved market conditions. Equally, it is hoped for a price-elastic demand for imports. Higher prices in home markets should produce a contraction of demand.

In this respect, the British experience has not been encouraging. An inelastic demand for primary products and certain foodstuffs may be expected, but what has been disappointing is the continuing resilience of demand for imported manufactures.

2.4 CORRECTING A SURPLUS DISEQUILIBRIUM

Why should countries like Germany and Japan – which in the post-war period have experienced repeated surpluses in their payments – wish to change a situation which is an indicator of the strength and dynamism of their economies? Instinctively, they will *not* wish to do so. However, it must be remembered that for every creditor nation there are corresponding debtor nations, and it is normally on the latter that the burden of adjustment falls. If this burden becomes intolerable, there exists the danger of unilateral action counter to the cooperative spirit which the international community has attempted to develop since 1945, e.g. trade protection or debt default.

If a surplus nation is so persuaded, its most likely policy will be *revaluation* (under a fixed exchange rate regime), or *appreciation* of its currency (under a floating rate system). By implication, its exports become more expensive and the volume decreases, while its imports are cheaper and increase. Again, the result depends upon the elasticity of demand and supply of imports and of demand for its exports.

2.5 INCREASING SIGNIFICANCE OF THE CAPITAL ACCOUNT

The policies for correcting disequilibria which have been considered so far relate specifically to the current account where the problem is likely to be rooted. However, for some countries like the UK, capital account movements are of increasing significance. It is possible that a healthy current account surplus could be repeatedly nullified by capital account deficits. Equally, a current account deficit may be made worse by an accompanying capital account deficit. In this situation, a country may be tempted to resort to some restrictions on capital movements.

By the same rule, a surplus country may seek to avoid revaluation/appreciation by encouraging overseas investment and expanding its capital account deficit.

2.6 CORRECTIVE POLICIES IN SPECIFIC CONTEXTS

The policy selected will depend upon the underlying cause of disequilibrium.

(a) Excess demand + external deficit
Excess demand expresses itself in rising wages and prices, and shor-

tages. For devaluation to be the appropriate method of achieving current account balance, there must be increased exports and import substitution. Both of these consequences would impose further demands upon an economy which is already suffering from excess demand. *Disinflation* would be more suitable, since it would reduce the domestic demand for imports and at the same time release capacity for exports.

(b) Excess demand + external surplus
Disinflation in this instance – by reducing domestic demand – would simultaneously decrease imports and *increase* the *surplus* disequilibrium. *Revaluation*, on the other hand, will decrease exports and increase imports. Domestic demand is satisified at the same time as the current account surplus is eliminated.

(c) Deficient demand + external deficit
Where demand is apparently deficient, Keynesian thinking may suggest *reflation*, to stimulate the economy and 'accelerate out of' recession and payments deficit. (Such a policy was pursued in the UK in 1962–66.) In practice, while there may be some temporary alleviation of unemployment, increased demand results in more imports, exports diverted to the home market and a greater deficit. *Devaluation* is the appropriate solution, as was concluded in 1967.

(d) Deficient demand + external surplus
Devaluation would clearly be an inappropriate method of achieving both internal and external equilibrium, since the external surplus would be *increased*. Keynesians would argue for *reflation* to stimulate the domestic economy. At the same time imports would rise, exports decline and payments would be brought into equilibrium.

3. TRENDS IN UK TRADE

3.1 CURRENT ACCOUNT With the exception of the Second World War, the UK's current account has been in deficit on only twenty-eight occasions between 1816 and 1984. This gives a first impression of consistent performance by both the visible and invisible accounts. However, during that period there have been only six surpluses on the visible account and two deficits on the invisible account. It is clear that, historically, Britain has always been highly dependent upon its invisible trade. Table 22 indicates that this situation continues, but in the 1980s the picture has been complicated by Britain's arrival as a net oil exporter.

3.2 VISIBLE TRADE

The fear of 'the destruction of Britain's manufacturing base' and 'an excessive reliance upon oil' receives some substantiation from an examination of the figures in Table 22.

Table 22. Visible Balance,
1974–1983 (£m)

	Oil	Non-oil	Total
1974	−3357	−1994	−5351
1975	−3057	−276	−3333
1976	−3947	+20	−3927
1977	−2771	+493	−2278
1978	−1999	+426	−1573
1979	−774	−2723	−3497
1980	+273	+904	+1177
1981	+3112	−104	+3008
1982	+4605	−2486	+2119
1983	+6924	−7878	−954

Source: United Kingdom Balance of Payments Accounts

The total figures for visibles reflect the historical trend. The overall improvement in the non-oil account from 1976 to 1980 was primarily the response to stringent economic management at the behest of IMF. Since 1981 there has been a massive deterioration of this position, not entirely offset by the continuing expansion of the oil account.

The collapse of world oil prices in 1986 has in some quarters accentuated the fear that this reliance upon oil will be exposed sooner rather than later. The opposite view is that lower energy costs will improve industrial profit margins sufficiently to provide both the motivation and the cash to trigger an investment-led recovery of manufacturing while simultaneously improving Britain's competitiveness.

3.3 WEAKNESS OF THE NON-OIL ACCOUNT

This could be attributed to three factors:

(a) Inappropriate trade structure
If the composition of exports – both in terms of commodities and geographical areas – was biased towards low-growth markets, this might be an explanation. The evidence does not support this view, however. Since the 1960s, there has been a shift in UK trade *from* low-growth areas in the developing world towards the rapidly expanding industrial economies, particularly in Europe. Moreover, the commodity structure of UK exports is similar to that of her major competitors such as Germany.

(b) Price competitiveness
When considering the price elasticity of demand for UK exports, it is important to remember that the UK cannot be seen in isolation from its competitors. It is not simply a matter of *absolute* prices, but also of

relative prices in competitive markets. One way of looking at relative price competitiveness is to examine the underlying comparative costs. It may be the case that, for the moment, the selling prices of two competing nations are comparable but that in one of them unit labour costs are rising more rapidly. (In 1986, this is the case in the UK *vis-à-vis* European competitors.) This implies the reduction of profit margins, future investment and sales.

There is a further technical problem in measuring the price elasticity of demand for exports. Measures are often calculated over different time periods which lead to different results. Estimates of *short-run* demand elasticity for UK exports suggest a figure between .26 and .46, i.e. inelastic. In the longer run of up to two years, the figure for visibles rises to between 1.5 and 2.6, i.e. elastic. Similar studies in respect of visible imports indicate a figure of less than unity, i.e. inelastic.

It must then be re-emphasized that we are concerned not simply with the *volume* of trade flows but the *revenues* which accrue to that trade. In this respect, price elasticities for UK exports and imports appear to meet the Marshall-Lerner prescription, i.e. a fall in export prices and a rise in import prices (e.g. by devaluation) must raise the value of exports relative to the value of imports, thus improving the visible balance. (Technically, the sum of price elasticities of demand for exports and imports must exceed 1.)

In the longer run, this total is nearer to 2 than to 1 and is therefore encouraging. In the shorter run, a *J-curve effect* may be observed, i.e. devaluation and improved price competitiveness worsens the visible balance.

(c) Non-price competitiveness

Surveys indicate that the *income* elasticity of demand for UK exports is low relative to that for the exports of her competitors, i.e. when world incomes are rising, UK exports are not so favoured. On the other hand, in similar circumstances the UK demand for imports is *income elastic*, particularly in respect of manufactures which display a 'ratchet' effect. Increased demand in the upswing of the business cycle is not matched by a corresponding decrease in the downswing.

The less-than-average response of exports to a rise in world incomes, paralleled by a more-than-average sensitivity to import penetration, may be explained firstly by the instinctive disposition of industry to prefer the 'softer' home market. Contrary to the erstwhile assertion of the Department of Trade that 'exporting is fun', it involves more risk and effort. Second, it is a question of the *elasticity of supply* of UK industry. This is not only a matter of the ability to create new productive capacity but, more importantly, of fully utilizing existing capacity, i.e. *a question of productivity*. This in turn raises a complex of issues, not least those relating to institutional structures such as the tax and social security systems, trade union and employer relationships.

Finally, it should be repeated that price and income are not the only factors which affect the demand for UK exports. Indirectly, account must also be taken of the aggressiveness of overseas marketing; the willingness not only to employ overseas agents but also to send well-briefed representatives abroad; designs appropriate to specific overseas markets (not everyone necessarily likes British tastes); efficient after-sales service and reliable delivery dates.

EXAMINATION PRACTICE 18

MULTIPLE CHOICE
Which one of the following policies would be *least* likely to be effective in rectifying a deficit on a country's balance of payments?
(a)   devaluing the currency;
(b)   raising tariff barriers;
(c)   imposing exchange controls;
(d)   encouraging the export of capital;
(e)   permitting the currency to float;
(O & CSEB, June 1982)
Key Reference 2.3. Answer (d).

Which one of the following would appear as a debit item on the invisible trade account of the UK balance of payments?
(a)   the sale to foreigners of shares in UK oil companies;
(b)   the payment of dividends to foreigners on shares they already hold in UK oil companies;
(c)   the purchase of oil rigs from foreigners by UK oil companies;
(d)   the payment of dividends by foreigners to UK citizens on shares held abroad;
(e)   the purchase of oil from foreigners for re-export from the UK?
(O & CSEB, June 1983)
Key Reference 1.2(a) (ii). Answer (b).

One can say with certainty that, other things being equal, the revaluation of sterling must lead to an improvement in the United Kingdom
(a)   balance of visible trade;
(b)   balance of payments on current account;
(c).   balance for official financing;
(d)   terms of trade.   *(AEB, June 1984)*
Key References 1.2(a); 1.2(b); Chapter 17, 1.7. Answer (d).

ESSAYS
Outline and comment on the effects of a currency devaluation upon the activity of the devaluing country.   *(O & CSEB, July 1982)*
Key References 2.2; 2.3(c).

Why must the balance of payments account always balance?
(O & CSEB, July 1985)

Key References 1.2 and particularly Table 21; 2.1.

What information can be gained about the state of an economy by looking at its balance of payments accounts over a number of years?
(O & CSEB, June 1981)

Key References 1.2; 2.1; 3.1–3.

INTERNATIONAL MONETARY RELATIONS

CONTENTS

1. EXCHANGE RATE SYSTEMS

1.1 SETTLING INTERNATIONAL INDEBTEDNESS

Internationally as domestically, without money there would necessarily be dependence upon barter. In practice, even today barter deals are not infrequently concluded, particularly between the USSR and the West. For the most part, however, international indebtedness is settled through a monetary transaction, which implies that a satisfactory international monetary system has two central functions:

(a) International liquidity

Money is a medium of exchange. When the domestic economy expands, there must be an appropriate increase in the money supply to finance the increased volume of transactions. The same is true for the world economy. The nineteenth-century gold standard restricted the extent to which the world money stock could expand, and since 1945 attempts have been made through international cooperation to achieve a balanced expansion of international liquidity.

(b) An exchange rate mechanism

Since national currencies are acceptable only within a country's boundaries, a suitable system of currency conversion is necessary. Whatever system is adopted, it will reflect a two-way linkage between the exchange rate and the balance of payments. The balance of payments affects the exchange rate, which in turn changes export and import prices and affects the balance of payments.

1.2 MARKET SYSTEMS

Setting on one side the possibility of an exchange control system, there are several market possibilities, each with certain advantages and disadvantages. The range of possibilities is shown in Table 23.

Table 23

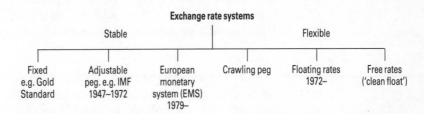

	Exchange rate systems				
	Stable			Flexible	
Fixed e.g. Gold Standard	Adjustable peg. e.g. IMF 1947–1972	European monetary system (EMS) 1979–	Crawling peg	Floating rates 1972–	Free rates ('clean float')

1.3 THE GOLD STANDARD

This was a fixed exchange rate system which was adopted by Britain in the Bank Charter Act, 1844, observed fully until 1913 and partially until 1931 when it was abandoned. With the nineteenth-century expansion of world trade, the use of gold as a means of international payment increased to include most of the major trading nations. Each currency was convertible to a fixed weight of gold, e.g. the £ was defined as 113 grains and the $ as 23.22 grains. Since the £ represented 4.8665 times as much gold as the $, the *mint parity* rate of exchange was £1:$4.8665. This rate could only vary within the narrow limits set by the gold export and import points.

Supposing a balance of payments with the USA which is unfavourable to the UK, there would be a tendency for the rate to fall below mint parity. This would be checked at the point where the UK importer – having allowed for freight and insurance costs – would find it worthwhile to convert £s to gold, ship it to the USA and reconvert to $s. This was the *gold export point*.

By parallel reasoning, the American importer would not accept a $ exchange rate below the UK *gold import point*.

In the former case, as gold flowed out from the Bank of England's reserves, its ability to issue notes was constrained. More significantly, the 'bank deposit money' created on this cash base was put under pressure. The Bank would seek to protect the reserves by raising Bank Rate, in the hope of persuading overseas depositors to hold sterling. Money was now both scarce and dear.

Monetary contraction in due course deflated the price level; exports increased, imports declined and the balance of payments rectified itself.

1.4 ADVANTAGES OF FIXED RATES

Protagonists of the Gold Standard would claim for it several important advantages.

(a) A self-righting mechanism

As explained above, long-run balance of payments equilibrium was guaranteed without any need for corrective action by governments.

(b) An external discipline on government domestic policies

In the modern context, some monetarists would argue that the domestic money supply is far too important a matter to be left to the whim of government. Instead there should be some fixed rule such as that imposed by the Gold Standard which prevents government from 'printing money' to finance expenditure policies which result in inflation.

Note: Under any stable rate regime, a payments deficit brings a run on the reserves. Since these are finite, government is then *obliged* to pursue remedial policies to check the inflation which caused the deficit, as was the case in the UK during the 1950s and 1960s when every upswing of the business cycle terminated in a 'sterling crisis'. This external discipline was removed when sterling was floated in 1972.

(c) Reduces trading risks

Widely fluctuating exchange rates increase risk for both importers and exporters and have been considered incompatible with the expansion of world trade. This was the major fear in 1971, when the IMF stable rate system disintegrated. While it is true that world trade did not subsequently collapse, there remains a good deal of disquiet with the volatility of rates under the present floating rate system.

1.5 FREE RATES OR A CLEAN FLOAT

In this situation, rates are determined in the foreign exchange markets entirely in response to demand and supply: e.g. if during a day's trading an excessive amount of sterling is seeking conversion to too few dollars, the price of sterling in terms of dollars will fall.

1.6 ADVANTAGES OF A FREE RATE SYSTEM

They are equally the disadvantages of a wholly fixed rate system.

(a) No requirement for reserves

In the extreme case of a completely clean float, central monetary reserves become unnecessary and an adverse balance of payments is simply reflected in a depreciation of the exchange rate. Government is no longer inhibited in its domestic economic policies by the need to safeguard the reserves.

While Keynes did not subscribe to the concept of completely free exchange rates, he was an opponent of the gold standard, which he viewed as barbaric. Adverse payments inevitably meant adjustment through deflation, with accompanying unemployment and social hardship. He considered that governments ought to be capable of devising a more flexible system which avoided these problems and was, indeed, the principal architect of such a system for IMF.

(b) An automatic mechanism for adjusting payments imbalance

Paradoxically, some monetarists also favour free exchange rates, for much the same reasons that they favour all free markets as the most efficient allocators of resources. The major proviso is that there should be some form of constitutional constraint which prevents governments from expanding the domestic money supply at will, thus causing inflation. Payments deficits are then reflected in a depreciation of the exchange rate, which continues until such time as imports become impossibly dear and exports irresistibly cheap. Balance is restored at an exchange rate which reflects true relative trading strengths and this is accompanied by appropriate structural changes within the domestic economy. The market has prevailed.

2. INTERNATIONAL MONETARY FUND (IMF)

2.1 OBJECTIVES

Like GATT, IMF was conceived in the spirit of international co-operation with the ultimate objective of promoting the expansion of world trade. For this to occur, there would need to be adequate international liquidity coupled with an exchange rate mechanism which facilitated the free convertibility of currencies.

2.2 FOUNDATION AND ORGANIZATION

IMF was the product of a conference at Bretton Woods, New Hampshire. The Agreement was implemented in 1947, with membership rising to its present level of 143. Members from the Communist bloc include China, Yugoslavia, Hungary and Rumania. Located in Washington, it has a board of governors comprising one governor from each member nation. Operationally, an executive board of 22 members makes day-to-day decisions.

2.3 THE FUND'S RESOURCES

The Fund comprised a pool of currencies. Initially each member was assigned a *quota*, related to the size of its GNP and calculated in dollars. The quota was subscribed 25% in gold (the gold tranche), and 75% in the member's currency. The size of the quota is important in determining the voting power of each executive director and the extent of a country's *drawing rights*.

The rules permitted the drawing of foreign currencies against a country's own currency to a maximum of 125% of its quota. Normally, borrowing was restricted to 25% of quota in any one year. The first 25% was an automatic right. The remaining 100%, the *credit tranche*, might be subject to conditions.

The Fund provided a first step to the expansion of world liquidity by creating a credit facility for nations with *temporary* payments deficits. This was believed to be to every nation's advantage, since debtors could remain good customers in world markets while having a breathing space to adopt remedial economic policies.

2.4 THE ADJUSTABLE PEG EXCHANGE RATE SYSTEM

IMF looked for a system which would provide the degree of stability lacking in the 1930s with the disintegration of the gold standard, while at the same time avoiding the latter's rigidity. In short, what was desired was short-term stability together with long-term flexibility. The advantages of fixed and free rate systems would be combined while eliminating their disadvantages. A degree of stability was desirable to encourage confidence in international trading, but it was recognized that in the long run nations would experience varying changes in their domestic price levels and the terms of trade would also vary. Periodically there would need to be a realignment of exchange rates.

At the centre of the system stood a dollar, convertible to gold at the pre-war price of $35 per fine ounce. On joining IMF, a member country declared a parity rate of exchange with the dollar and was then committed to using its central reserves to stay within 1% of parity.

In any one year, a country was permitted to vary its exchange rate parity unilaterally by a maximum of 10%. Any variation in excess of this required consultation with and approval by IMF. Such permission would be given only when a country could demonstrate a *fundamental disequilibrium* in its payments.

In this way, it was expected that there would be regular adjustments of 'pegs' or parities to give the system the necessary flexibility. In practice, this rarely happened.

2.5 THE COLLAPSE OF THE IMF EXCHANGE RATE SYSTEM

For a variety of reasons, there was a reluctance to devalue or revalue from original parities except under great pressure.

(a) Preference for the status quo
There was a general disposition to avoid any changes which disturbed existing trade patterns.

(b) Resistance to revaluation
Surplus countries such as Germany and Japan were reluctant voluntarily to weaken their international trading competitiveness.

(c) Resistance to devaluation
After a first post-war devaluation in 1949, Britain was committed to a parity of $2.80 with *dealing margins* of $2.78 and $2.82. With the abandonment of exchange controls on current account transactions in 1958, it quickly became apparent that sterling was over-valued. Even during the exchange crisis of 1966–7, there was resistance to devaluation as a solution, attention being directed to the effect upon import costs and upon Britain's reputation as a world banker. A devaluation was seen as the equivalent of telling an overseas depositor that he had less on account than he had deposited. Only with the greatest reluctance did Britain devalue by 15% in 1967.

The result was that by the late 1960s, the pattern of exchange rates simply failed to reflect the true relative purchasing power of different currencies. The seeds of the collapse of the system were there and it survived only for as long as the world retained confidence in the key currency, the $US.

2.6 THE DOLLAR CRISIS OF 1971

In 1958 – for the first time since 1945 – US international payments moved into deficit. With any other currency there would have been pressure on the exchange rate, but such was international confidence in the power of the US economy that 'surplus' dollars were readily held overseas and deposited in the newly developing eurocurrency markets (see Ch.15.6). This confidence was, however, underwritten by the willingness of the USA to convert dollars to gold at $35 per fine ounce. Periodically during the 1960s there were in fact a number of large-scale conversions, and in 1968 convertibility was limited. The run on the reserves continued, as did the US deficit, and in 1971 convertibility was totally suspended.

Since the key currency was no longer related to a fixed weight of gold, the dollar was now simply a paper currency like any other and therefore there was no confidence that existing parities with the dollar were appropriate. It followed that there could be no confidence that *cross-parities* between all other currencies were correct. Foreign exchanges across the world suspended dealing and when the markets reopened it was in large measure to a free exchange rate system, with new rates gradually emerging in response to demand and supply.

2.7 THE 'SMITHSONIAN AGREEMENT' 1971

The new uncertainties in the foreign exchanges brought fears of a collapse of world trade, and in December 1971 the 'Group of Ten' major central bankers concluded an agreement at the Smithsonian Institute in Washington.

The dollar remained inconvertible, but remained the currency in which new parities were calculated. To give the system greater flexibility, dealing margins were widened to 2¼% either side of parity, which for the UK meant a parity of $2.60 with margins of $2.54 and $2.66.

The attempt to reinstate the adjustable peg system was short-lived and in 1972, one country after another floated its exchange rate. This was far from the system which IMF had considered necessary for stable and orderly monetary relations, but nevertheless it worked and in 1976 was legalized by an amendment to the Articles of Agreement at the IMF Jamaica Conference.

3. FLOATING EXCHANGE RATES

3.1 A 'CLEAN' FLOAT OR A 'DIRTY' /MANAGED FLOAT

The merits of a clean float were assessed in 1.4 and 1.6 above. In practice, governments have been disposed to permit exchange rates to float cleanly for extended periods but ultimately, for reasons of domestic policy, have felt obliged to manage the float; e.g. in January 1985, the UK government professed its willingness to let the market determine the sterling rate, but as it fell towards £1:$1 finally intervened to check the slide.

3.2 TECHNIQUES FOR MANAGING THE FLOAT

There are three approaches:

(a)   *Dealing in the 'spot' market* The central bank uses its monetary reserves (in the UK, the Exchange Equalization Account) to make purchases or sales at the present or spot rate in order to influence that rate.

(b)   *Dealing in the forward market* Similarly, the reserves are used to influence forward rates, deterring speculation and assisting in stabilizing present rates.

(c)   *Domestic interest rate policy* This may be used to influence the flows of short-term capital (hot money) across the exchanges.

The traditional method has been the use of the reserves, but such is the volume of today's hot money flows that it is doubtful if any country has sufficient independent reserves to check a determined run on its currency. Bank of England intervention in January 1985 relied upon the reintroduction for one day of an administered MLR, in order to produce an immediate upward movement of interest rates. A suggested solution has been the *'concert party'*, in which central banks act jointly in the exchange markets.

4. EUROPEAN MONETARY UNION

4.1 OBJECTIVES

The Werner Report in 1970 advocated closer monetary co-operation as a means of speeding the economic and political objectives of EEC. This would be achieved through the progressive narrowing and ultimate elimination of the margins within which EEC currencies fluctuated against each other. In due course, this would lead to a common European currency and a single central bank.

4.2 THE 'SNAKE IN THE TUNNEL'

These proposals ran counter to the Smithsonian Agreement, which established *wider* dealing margins. As an interim measure, therefore, 'the snake in the tunnel' system was adopted, whereby members were committed to restricting exchange rate movements between themselves to a narrow band of 2¼%, 'the snake'. These currencies would then move as a bloc within the wider band of 4½% permitted by the Smithsonian arrangements – 'the tunnel'.

The breakdown of the Smithsonian Agreement in 1972 removed 'the tunnel', leaving 'the snake' to float freely against the currencies of the rest of the world.

The system began in 1972 with the original six EEC members, Eire, Denmark and – briefly – the UK.

The oil crisis of 1973 and world recession produced international payments problems and volatile exchange rates which made it difficult for some members to hold within the narrow margins permitted by 'the snake'. Consequently the UK left after a few months, followed by France in 1974. The system continued without France, the UK and Eire but including four EEC non-members; Norway, Sweden, Switzerland and Austria.

A fresh impetus was given by a conference at Bremen in 1978, which led to a more formally planned and sophisticated system.

4.3 EUROPEAN MONETARY SYSTEM (EMS)

The scheme was implemented in March 1979, and included all EEC members with the exception of the UK. In 1986, UK membership continues to be considered imminent.

There are three elements in the system:

(a) European currency unit (ECU)

This is valued in relation to a weighted basket of EEC currencies, including sterling but excluding Greece and Spain. Since it is a weighted average, it is more stable than any single currency. In addition to its function as a *'numeraire'*, it serves as a European reserve currency. Members 'invest' 20% of their gold and dollar reserves in ECUs, which are then held by the European Monetary Co-operation Fund (FECOM in French). Central banks draw on these holdings to purchase each other's currencies.

(b) Exchange rate mechanism (ERM)

This is a refinement of 'the snake' and is based upon two principles:

(i) A parity grid

Like 'the snake', a maximum divergence of 2¼% is permitted.

(ii) The ECU divergence indicator

Unlike 'the snake', the permitted divergence is calculated against the ECU (the weighted basket), rather than against other *individual* currencies. The difference is that the burden of adjustment is shared between surplus and deficit countries instead of being carried solely by the latter. When weaker currencies depreciate, so does the value of the ECU. Surplus countries are then obliged to take action to prevent their currencies appreciating above their permitted deviation.

(c) European Monetary Co-operation Fund

This is Europe's embryonic 'central bank'. It holds 20% of members' monetary reserves and is empowered to make loans to members of up to 25bn. ECUs. In due course, it is intended that it should operate to support the ECU against external currencies.

5. CRAWLING PEG

5.1 AN ACADEMIC VARIANT

Conceptually, there are many possible variants on exchange rate systems, but they all involve some compromise between the two contrasting principles of fixed and free rate systems. One such is the crawling peg.

The large and infrequent devaluations/revaluations of the adjustable peg system are replaced by smaller and more frequent changes. If the long-run trend is for a currency to depreciate, then it does so in an orderly way through a stable series of steps. A fundamental payments disequilibrium which is resolved belatedly by a substantial devaluation is thus avoided.

6. THEORY OF PURCHASING POWER PARITY

6.1 WHAT IS THE 'RIGHT' EXCHANGE RATE?

Gustav Cassell attempted to answer this question in the 1920s with the argument that the equilibrium rate of exchange between two currencies ought to reflect the ratio between their domestic purchasing powers. If, for example, £1 buys the same basket of goods in the UK as can be purchased with $1.50 in the USA, then there is exchange rate equilibrium at £1:$1.50.

While this is a useful concept, as a practical policy guide it is beset with difficulties.

(a) Incomplete coverage
The 'basket' includes only visibles and takes no account of invisibles and capital account transactions which have a major influence on the exchange rate.

(b) Comparison difficulties
It is clearly easier to compare 'the UK shopping basket' with that of the USA than that of, say, Indonesia.

(c) 'Irrational' influences on the exchange rate
Political uncertainty and ill-founded economic speculation may lead to a flight from a currency and pressure on its exchange rate.

7. INTERNATIONAL LIQUIDITY

7.1 DEFINITION

Long-run equilibrium in international payments may exist, but in the short term inevitably some countries will experience surpluses and others deficits. Surpluses will be adjusted by an increase in reserves or a decrease in overseas debt. *International liquidity* – that is, an acceptable form of international payment – is necessary for the latter to be possible. If these facilities are inadequate, then the country may be forced into short-term corrective action which is not appropriate to the situation.

In the narrowest sense, international liquidity may be considered as internationally acceptable assets held by central banks, for the purpose of *official financing* or for influencing the exchange rate.

In the broadest sense, it will include internationally acceptable assets which can be acquired through borrowing from international organizations, foreign central banks and governments and from the overseas commercial banking system.

7.2 COMPOSITION OF RESERVES

About 40% of world official reserves are in gold and about 53% in foreign currencies. Some 60% of the latter is denominated in dollars. For the UK, France, West Germany, Japan and Switzerland, this rises to 90%. IMF credits and SDRs provide about 3% each.

7.3 GOLD

Historically, gold is the oldest form of payment in international trade. The reason has been its general acceptability as a store of value, and it was this which gave rise to the nineteenth-century gold standard. However, gold displays a number of deficiencies:

(*a*)   *Wasteful of resources* It is dug out of the ground, only to be returned to bank vaults.

(*b*)   *Favours rich nations* The richer industrial nations with large gold stocks are benefited at the expense of the poorer nations: those most likely to require liquidity.

(*c*)   *Political reasons* The two principal gold producers are the USSR and South Africa. For political reasons, there may be distaste for the advantage which this position confers.

(*d*)   *Doubtful store of value* In recent years the market price of gold has shown considerable volatility, making it a less than stable store of value.

Note: (*e*)   *Inelastic supply* The chief objection to gold is that its supply cannot be increased in line with the needs for greater world liquidity. During the 1970s world trade was increasing by 5% p.a., but world gold stocks by only 2% p.a.

For these reasons, there has been a general disposition to demonetize gold and in 1978, the second amendment to the Articles of Agreement of IMF was implemented. This had the objective of substituting SDRs for gold as the world's principal reserve asset.

7.4 FOREIGN CURRENCIES

These comprise balances in convertible currencies such as the $US, the £sterling, Swiss francs and Deutschmarks etc.

The dollar is no longer so dominant. From a peak of about 85% of official world reserves in 1976 (including Eurodollars), it has now declined to about 60%.

In 1979, the European Currency Unit (ECU) appeared as a new international reserve, held by European central banks.

Foreign currencies as an international reserve also pose a problem, because their availability depends largely upon those countries which provide the currencies experiencing a balance of payments deficit. If the deficit continues, the resulting paradox is that the world loses confidence in the ability of the currency to hold its value. The dollar predominated in the 1940s and 1950s when it was in short supply and commanded total confidence. In the 1960s, as the supply increased so confidence diminished.

7.5 BORROWING FROM THE INTERNATIONAL MONETARY FUND

Strictly speaking, the exercise of drawing rights at IMF does not increase *total* world liquidity, although these facilities form part of official world reserves. The reason is that such borrowing is usually financed with the borrower's own currency, i.e. as foreign currencies are drawn, the Fund's holdings of the borrowing country's currency increase. However, to the extent that a *less* negotiable domestic currency is exchanged for a *more* negotiable international currency, international liquidity *is* increased.

(a) Reserve tranche
The original 25% gold tranche is now described as the reserve tranche and is made up of the 25% of quota subscribed in foreign currencies and SDRs. Since it may be drawn automatically without IMF conditions, it is considered as part of a country's reserves.

(b) Credit tranches
There are four, each of 25% of a country's quota, which with the reserve tranche give a total facility of 125% of quota. Since the terms which IMF imposes for credit tranches become progressively tougher, they are *conditional reserves*.

(c) Borrowing facilities
IMF offers other borrowing facilities subject to conditions:

(i) Compensatory financing facility (CFF)
Introduced in 1963, its purpose is to assist countries with problems resulting from a temporary fall in exports, as for example, consequence of a crop failure.

(ii) Supplementary financing facility (SFF)
This was introduced in 1979, with a subscription from the oil-producing countries of SDR 7.5bn. Given the difficulties of non-oil producers, particularly amongst the developing countries, the purpose was to extend the credit tranche so as to permit borrowing above quota.

(iii) Extended credit facility (ECF) With normal drawings from IMF, the expectation is that they will be reconstituted in about three years. ECF extended the period, initially to eight.

(iv) Oil facility This was a response to the oil price crisis of 1973–4. Countries which consequently experienced severe payments difficulties were given facilities of between 450% and 800% of quota. In 1979 this facility was replaced by SSF.

(v) Trust fund facility As an aspect of the attempt to demonetize gold, in 1976 IMF made gold sales at market prices. Over $4bn. of the proceeds were used to finance a trust fund to assist developing countries, but the funds were exhausted in 1981.

(vi) Enlarged access facility This was set up in 1981 to assist those countries with large payments deficits relative to their quotas. They are permitted to borrow up to 150% of quota in any one year, and up to 450% over three years.

(d) Standby credits
Periodically IMF has arranged a provisional credit available for immediate use but often not taken up. However, its existence has bolstered world confidence in a currency under pressure, thus relieving that pressure.

7.6 SPECIAL DRAWING RIGHTS (SDRs)

The IMF introduced this scheme in 1969. The simplest way to see SDRs is as 'international bookkeeping money' which all countries will accept in payment of debt. More precisely, they take the form of an automatic right to receive foreign currency by transferring SDRs to another member chosen by the Fund. Each member is under the obligation to provide IMF – on request – with up to three times its allocation of SDRs.

The SDRs which IMF has created are today valued in terms of a weighted basket of currencies: $US–42%; DM–19%; Sterling, French franc and Yen – 13% each. In terms of the dollar, an SDR is worth approximately $1.1. Since 1970 there have been two series of annual allocations, totalling SDR21bn. A country's allocation is related to its quota, an arrangement which has produced the criticism that it is the richest countries which benefit most.

7.7 'SWAP ARRANGEMENTS'

Central banks agree to make balances available to each other for specified periods of time.

7.8 GENERAL ARRANGEMENTS TO BORROW (GAB)

Since 1962, IMF resources have been supported by a fund contributed to by the 'Group of Ten' major central banks.

7.8 EUROCURRENCIES (see p.281)

The chief Eurocurrency is the Eurodollar. Since it is banked outside the USA and therefore not subject to US exchange and reserve regulations, it can be borrowed more cheaply than the 'domestic' dollar. There is thus an incentive for governments to support their official reserves by borrowing in this market.

Beyond such government borrowing, it has already been noted that since the 1960s there has been an enormous expansion of these markets as a means of financing trade and industry. It therefore follows that total world liquidity has been expanded by a far greater amount than is revealed in the figures for the *official* world reserves.

7.9 THE LINK BETWEEN AN EXCHANGE RATE SYSTEM AND THE NEED FOR INTERNATIONAL LIQUIDITY

IMF used the reserve/import ratio (R/M ratio) as a measure of the adequacy of international liquidity. A decline in the ratio, it is thought, would suggest insufficient world reserves. However, it may be argued that the need for liquidity is not related to the *volume of world trade*, but to the *scale of deficits* which must be financed. If payments deficits are rapidly adjusted through an effective exchange rate mechanism, there is a correspondingly reduced need for world reserves.

On the other hand, managed floats have meant that exchange rates have been prevented from moving easily to levels at which deficits and surpluses would be eradicated. High levels of exchange rate intervention imply high levels of demand for reserves.

7.10 THE DANGER OF LIQUIDITY PROVIDED THROUGH THE COMMERCIAL BANKING SYSTEM

Many countries, in particular the non-oil developing countries, have experienced persistent balance of payments disequilibrium. Their deficits have frequently been relieved not through strictly regulated IMF loans, but through the easier access to commercial bank funds across the world. In the 1980s, there is ample evidence that some banks have become over-extended. Debts have been rescheduled and, on occasion, there has been the threat of default. Consequently there is pressure for a return to a more centralized and regulated system for exchange rates and the provision of international liquidity.

EXAMINATION PRACTICE 19

MULTIPLE CHOICE

The monetary authorities of a country, whose currency is floating freely, raise the market rates of interest. Other things being equal, the exchange rate of the currency is likely to

(*a*)   fall, as domestic fixed capital formation declines in response to higher rates of interest;

(*b*)   fall, because the quantity of money must be reduced to cause rates of interest to rise;

(*c*)   remain unchanged, because the supply and demand for the currency in world markets will be unchanged;

(*d*)   rise, as foreigners buy the domestic currency in order to acquire assets with a higher yield;

(*e*)   rise, as exporters increase the volume of exports to acquire foreign currency.   (*O & CSEB, June 1983*)

Key Reference 3.2(c). *Answer* (*d*).

One or more options may be correct. Code –

(*a*)   1, 2, 3 all correct;

(*b*)   1, 2 only correct;

(*c*)   2, 3 only correct;

(*d*)   1 only correct.

An increase in international liquidity could arise from an increase in

1   special drawing rights;

2   the price of gold;

3   the supply of gold.   (*AEB, June 1984*)

Key References 7.1–8. *Answer* (*a*).

The diagram opposite shows the determination of the sterling exchange rate with a two-country model (United Kingdom and United States of America).

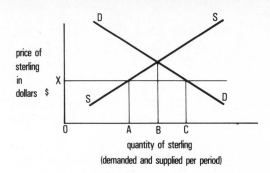

quantity of sterling
(demanded and supplied per period)

If the Bank of England wishes to intervene to maintain an exchange rate of OX it should
(a)   sell AB sterling;
(b)   sell AC sterling;
(c)   buy AB sterling;
(d)   buy AC sterling.   (AEB, November 1985)
Key Reference 3.2(a). Answer (b).

ESSAYS

Explain what is meant by saying that the Pound is 'weak' against the Dollar. Under a flexible exchange rate system, should the Government be concerned about the value of the Pound against other currencies?

JMB, June 1985)
Key References 3.1; Chapter 18, 2.3(c); 1.5; 1.6; Section 2.

'Both fixed and floating exchange rates provide automatic adjustments to balance of payments disequilibria.' Discuss.

(AEB, June 1985)
Key References Chapter 18, 2.1; 2.2; 2.3(c); Chapter 19, 1.3; 1.4(a); 1.5; 1.6(b).

What, if any, are the merits of a system of fixed exchange rates?

(O & CSEB, 9635/1, June 1981)
Key References 1.3; 1.4; 2.1–7.

What constitutes international liquidity? How can the amount of international liquidity be increased?

(O & CSEB, 9633/2, July 1984)
Key References 7.1–9.

INDEX